Dead Fathers

Dead Fathers

The Logic of Transference in Modern Narrative

Nina Schwartz

Ann Arbor

THE UNIVERSITY OF MICHIGAN PRESS

Published in the United States of America by
The University of Michigan Press
Manufactured in the United States of America
∞ Printed on acid-free paper

1997 1996 1995 1994 4 3 2 1

A CIP catalogue record for this book is available from the British Library.

Library of Congress Cataloging-in-Publication Data

Schwartz, Nina, 1954–
Dead fathers : the logic of transference in modern narrative / Nina Schwartz.
p. cm.
Includes bibliographical references and index.
ISBN 0-472-10523-X (alk. paper)
1. English fiction—20th century—History and criticism.
2. American fiction—20th century—History and criticism.
3. Transference (Psychology) in literature. 4. Psychoanalysis and literature. 5. Emotions in literature. 6. Modernism (Literature)
7. Fathers in literature. 8. Narration (Rhetoric) I. Title.
PR888.P75S38 1994
823′.91209353—dc20 94-5117
CIP

For my parents,
Ann Siena-Schwartz and Donald Alan Schwartz

Contents

Acknowledgments

It is a pleasure to be able to acknowledge here the many colleagues and friends who have contributed to the production of this book. John Carlos Rowe was among the earliest supporters of the project; I am grateful for the brilliance of his professional example, and even more for the warmth of his friendship.

Patricia Donahue gave me my title and continues to provide me with much more. Robert Gregory, Philip Kuberski, and Jean McGarry made up my first informal committee of readers, and I thank them for the generosity with which they allowed me to borrow from their work so much that would improve my own.

My colleagues in the English department at SMU have also provided me with a stimulating intellectual community, particularly the members of the Psychoanalytic Reading Group. John Paul Riquelme and Martha Satz read early versions of the manuscript and made many helpful suggestions. I am also grateful to Willard Spiegelman for his support in difficult times and to Brenda Silver for her astute counsel. I especially wish to thank Eric Cheyfitz, who sometimes seemed to believe in this project more powerfully than I did and whose help has meant a great deal to me. Steven V. Daniels and Marie-Luise Gättens have been tremendously careful, constructive readers; I learn from them at each encounter.

I am grateful to LeAnn Fields and Eve Trager of the University of Michigan Press for both their efficiency and their humanity.

I thank my family, Ann and Don Schwartz, Julia Schwartz, and Tony Schwartz for their unfailing support and their constant contributions, direct and indirect, to this project.

Finally, most, always, I thank Dennis Foster, for everything.

Earlier versions of chapters 2 and 4 appeared, respectively, in *New Orleans Review* 12 (1986) and *Criticism* 26 (1984); a portion of chapter 3 appeared in the *Henry James Review* 12 (1991). Grateful acknowledgment is made to Marie-Luise Gättens for permission to cite from *Reconstructing Histories: Language, Gender, and Fascism,* forthcoming from University Press of Florida in 1994.

Chapter 1

The Real Problem with Fathers

Dead, but still with us, still with us, but dead.

—Donald Barthelme, *The Dead Father*

In the Freudian field, repetition does not preclude surprise, but breeds it. The unconscious repeats, but is nevertheless unforeseeable in its manifestations.

—Jacques-Alain Miller

In Western cultures, fathers tend to be objects of some ambivalence. Admired and revered as our origins, gratefully loved as protectors, they nevertheless inevitably seem to become oppressive, suffocating. The subject of this book is the way ambivalence toward fathers—figures of respected and yet not always trusted authority—manifests itself in modern narrative. Specifically, my interest is in delineating how passions and passionate conflicts over authority are reproduced both in individual behavior and in the literary representations of such behavior. In readings of four exemplary modernist texts—*Heart of Darkness, The Wings of the Dove, The Sun Also Rises,* and *A Room of One's Own*—I examine structures of repetition in narrative and its criticism. My argument is that such repetition frequently occurs on the oedipal model, in which those with less power, resisting authority, end up forming their *own* authority on the model of the simultaneously hated and loved parental precursor.

More generally, I am interested in how the *representations* of resistance to social power structures demonstrate and reproduce those structures in the form of the representation itself. What I am describing here is first of all a repetition compulsion occurring at the level of character: these books tell stories about people who are locked into self-destructive patterns of behavior. Despite their best efforts to escape from or transform the structures or habits that injure them, people like Marlow, Jake Barnes, Kate Croy, and Milly Theale end up doing to themselves or soliciting others to do what, previously, others had done to them against their will.

But another kind of repetition compulsion may be at work in these narratives beyond the plots that sympathetically render the blindnesses of characters. These depictions of entrapment may themselves enact the very double binds they represent. That is, insofar as these narratives offer up coherent visions of the doomed nature of rebellion, they embody something like an oedipal dynamic themselves: they receive *their* authority to tell this truth from their commitment to the parental pattern (or original), and thereby demonstrate the extent to which the pattern itself is the source of cultural authority, the extent to which their own authority is derivative.[1] The realistic depiction of Milly Theale's and Kate Croy's tragic failure to make anything productive of their lives is, after all, the novel's (and James's) triumph. Similarly, we may admire Hemingway's masterly account of his impotent characters, even if we are not taken in by their transparent romanticism. Such a pattern in modernist narrative may suggest how writers compensate for their own fury at being determined and caught up by preexisting cultural and psychological forces. The failure of characters who struggle futilely to rebel both validates the writers' superior knowledge *and* makes that knowledge the ground of his or her refusal to rebel. This metonymically displaced revenge becomes, I argue, the means to the writers' power over others—characters and readers—as well as a strategy for displacing and coping with their own desire for freedom.

The final form of repetition I consider is alluded to above; it occurs in the literary criticism of these texts. Fredric Jameson's claims about the importance of criticism to our reception of texts are relevant here: "we never really confront a text immediately, . . . as a thing-in-itself," Jameson says. Rather, we understand it "through sedimented layers of previous interpretations, or . . . through the sedimented reading habits and categories developed by those inherited interpretive traditions."[2] For Jameson, interpretation must be construed "as an essentially allegorical act": we interpret literature almost by "translating" it into the familiar terms of a "master code" (10). These master codes, or "master narratives" as Jameson also refers to them, are difficult to escape because, as manifestations of the "political unconscious," they reflect "our collective thinking and our collective fantasies about history and reality" (34). Jameson's theory here accounts for a certain kind of repetition—from literary text to literary text, from one critical account to another, all the effect of certain master stories or themes that constitute us as members of a given reading and writing community.

What Jameson's Marxist model leaves out, however, is an important element of the repetition I am interested in: despite its apparent concern with a psychoanalytic notion of the unconscious, this description does not account for the question of desire in repetition, of the will to power manifested as much in the will to interpret as in various other enterprises. This will is of particular importance to me as it informs both the literary and critical—that is, writerly—endeavors.

Different from Jameson's notion of the master narrative is Shoshana Felman's "reading effect," a phenomenon in which readers themselves often reproduce, formally or thematically, the structures, language, or concerns of the writers they write about. Felman considers this effect in her discussion of the critical reception of Henry James's "The Turn of the Screw." Much of the tale's criticism, Felman claims, not only employs the story's vocabulary of possession and salvation; it actually *embodies* the thematic concerns of the story it analyzes: "The scene of the critical debate," Felman argues, "is . . . a *repetition* of the scene dramatized in the text. The critical interpretation, in other words, not only elucidates the text but also reproduces it dramatically, unwittingly *participates in it*."[3] In the same way that the governess grapples (according to her understanding of the situation) with the ghosts of Bly for possession of the childrens' souls, so do critics often see themselves as struggling against other readers to save the story from bad or crazy interpretations.

However, this appropriation by critics of the story's language and themes does not derive primarily from the importance in our culture of the master narrative of salvation. It has to do with something more specific to the dynamic of reading. The theory of the reading effect, that is, acknowledges the power of literature to determine the forms of readers' understanding; but it also says something about the relation between reading and the desire for authority that it either provokes or sublimates in particular ways. Felman implies that texts solicit readings that reproduce themselves—their images, language, ambivalences, and anxieties. Reading, then, becomes a reader's means to authority, but only as it is mediated by the authoritative structures of the text and the author. As a model of the relation between readers and writers, the theory of the reading effect thus extends our understanding of how the oedipal model works to inform the struggle for and manifestations of intellectual as well as other kinds of cultural authority.[4]

The structures of relatively unconscious repetition I describe here entail, I believe, examples of the psychological phenomenon of transference, in both its positive and negative manifestations. In pursuing how the "logic of transference" manifests itself in modern narrative and its criticism, this study makes no pretense of a "cure" for criticism. However, insofar as the texts I read make transference both a subject (among others) and a method of their representations, they may offer insight into powerful psychological and ideological forces in our culture.

The multileveled analysis I seek to engage in here—of the complex status of agency and authority in authors, texts, and critics—requires attention to both the individual experiences and the social determinations of desire and subjectivity. The recent work of Slavoj Žižek, a commentator on Lacan and a prolific writer on both high culture and theory and popular cultural forms, has been particularly important to me in this consideration. The linkage of psychoanalysis and ideological criticism that Žižek's work undertakes suggests a more complex way than either Marxism or psychoanalysis alone offers to understand how subjects are produced and take up their identities within specific cultural circumstances and signifying practices. This association also makes possible a reading of cultural practices that initially seem to resist the knowledge of such historical determinism, as modernism is so often purported to do. Indeed, Žižek's construction of the subject as actually *constituted* by the trauma that Freud mythologizes in *Totem and Taboo*—the murder of the father that I will analyze later—enables us to consider the questions of agency, authority, and repetition so as to acknowledge Marx's contributions to an analysis of the culture of capitalism without falling into the reductionism of Marxism's bracketing of the unconscious. In *The Sublime Object of Ideology*, for example, the title of which provocatively performs the connection I mentioned above, Žižek links ideology to what is understood in psychoanalysis as "fantasy," a structure that artificially and symptomatically produces a sense of wholeness, order, and coherence.[5] Žižek's work interprets cultural fantasies of power and control to account for both their psychological seductiveness and their ideological function in perpetuating social modes. His readings of Lacan, Hegel, and Freud will thus appear here with frequency as I try to negotiate the roles of desire for and anxiety about authority in the literature of modernism.

The Logic of Transference

I am certainly not the first critic to locate in literary history a version of the ambivalence manifested familially as the oedipal complex. Paul de Man, for one, characterizes this ambivalence in his argument about modernity and defines it as a writer's powerful desire for originality coupled with his or her knowledge that such originality is impossible.[6] Modernity is a "desire to wipe out whatever came earlier," a fairly parricidal-sounding impulse, "in the hope of reaching at last a point that could be called a true present, a point of origin that marks a new departure" (148). The problem is that this drive toward originality leads to a troubling discovery of the enterprise's impossibility. The essential ambivalence of literary writing, de Man says, involves its simultaneous "fluctuation . . . away from and toward its own mode of being" (163), this mode being precisely "a form of language that knows itself to be mere repetition, mere fiction and allegory, forever unable to participate in the spontaneity of action or modernity" (161).[7] What characterizes literary writing is its consciousness of itself as a logical impossibility: a desire for self-generation coupled with the troubled knowledge that even the desire is evidence of derivativeness.

Modernity, then, is the name de Man gives to the double bind of originality in the West: the only way to be an original, a figure of some power and authority (a father, say)—something to which we are taught to aspire—is to appropriate culture's means for achieving originality: "Only through history is history conquered" (150). One conquers the past/history by writing/history. Authoring, the begetting of words, implies authority, the legitimate right to choose the words begotten; and these word-progeny draw their legitimacy from that authority. But if writing is the means to the writer's assertion of *authority*, then the struggle can occur only in forms determined by tradition, forms that necessarily thwart their ostensible purpose.[8] As usual, ambivalence leads to repression, in this case the repression of that paradox.

The double bind de Man describes here seems clearly oedipal in nature (though he does not refer to Freud in the essay) and therefore similar to the phenomenon Harold Bloom describes in *The Anxiety of Influence*. Indeed, Bloom's account of strong poets who "wrestle with their strong precursors, even to the death" hearkens back to Freud's theory of the origin of the oedipal complex in the primal horde (about which I will say more later).[9] But Bloom's argument about poetic misprision is, in his words, "The study of the life cycle of the poet-as-poet" (7), a study, therefore, that preserves a faith in the individuality that his theory so powerfully calls in question. Bloom manages to suggest that rebellion, in the form of misprision, can be momentarily successful even as it leads inevitably to "the death of poetry" (10), its ultimate exhaustion from the endless "[battling] between strong equals" (11). De Man, then, never speaks of individuals, displacing the life-and-death struggle of modernity so deeply into language that his theory's debt to Freud is completely obscured; Bloom, on the other hand, speaks *only* of individual strong poets, thus tempering the bleakness of his vision of repetition to produce a romance of tragic poetic heroes.

I want to shift the terms somewhat in my own analysis of literary and critical repetition and suggest a way to consider both the personal struggles of people (writers and others) toward originality and the impersonal structures of language and cultural convention in which those struggles occur. To do so, I will employ the psychoanalytic notion of transference, one of the unconscious dynamics that organize our relations to authority. I find this model to be particularly useful because it enables us to understand repetition as a structural matter with no particular necessary *content*. As such, this dynamic is equally effective in accounting for characters' relations to each other, authors' connections to their texts, and readers' interests in their reading.

In psychoanalysis, transference is the phenomenon in which the analysand experiences for the analyst feelings of affection or hostility more proper to other figures in his or her life. Though initially an obstacle to treatment, this displacement of passion is nevertheless essential to a cure. Freud tells us,

> We overcome the transference by pointing out to the patient that his feelings do not arise from the present situation and do not apply to the person of the doctor, but that they are repeating something that happened to him earlier. In this way we oblige him to transform his repetition into a memory. By that means the transference, which, whether affectionate or hostile, seemed in every case to constitute the greatest threat to the treatment, becomes its best tool, by whose help the most secret compartments of mental life can be opened.[10]

The experience of so-called inappropriate feelings in the analytic setting functions as both an impediment to—that is, *avoidance* of—the analytic work *and* as a representation of the analysand's "habits of loving," which makes those habits visible. The very impropriety of the feelings makes them evidence of *something else*, of another force at work in the patient's life, which, when recognized, may be subjected to conscious memory and understanding.[11]

Although there are limits to the curative power of transference, its ubiquity makes it an important concept outside the analytic field. All love, Freud is clear, is transference love: "There is no such state which does not reproduce infantile prototypes."[12] He might well have added that there is no passion of any sort that does not reproduce infantile prototypes, though there are important distinctions among the ways these prototypes reproduce themselves. The object of transference is precisely one to whom one does not feel indifferent, a fact that makes transference a dynamic relevant to all situations of power.[13] What is important to remember here is that transference is a repetition that constitutes the *resistance* of something to conscious understanding; it is thus a way of preserving that something, either a fantasy about the "original," or one's unconsciousness of the centrality of repetition itself in one's life. In Miller's formulation, it is the choice of love *instead of* knowledge.[14] The question is, what exactly does transference repeat, and why is it so difficult to know?

The Real, the Symbolic, and the Subject

In *Totem and Taboo,* Freud describes the fate of the father murdered by the primal horde he had ruled so brutally and effectively for so long. The description is provocative, so I quote it here at some length. "One day," Freud speculates,

> the brothers who had been driven out came together, killed and devoured their father and so made an end of the patriarchal horde. . . . The violent primal father had doubtless been the feared and envied model of each one of the company of brothers: and in the act of devouring him they accomplished their identification with him, and each one of them acquired a portion of his strength. The totem meal . . . would thus be a repetition and a commemoration of the memorable and criminal deed, which was the beginning of so many things—of social organization, of moral restrictions and of religion.[15]

Indeed, the murder of the primal father was also the beginning of the human subject, the "split subject," insofar as it instituted the need for repression, divided the subject between the conscious and unconscious mental operations, and produced the superego that derives from another, more metaphorical internalization of the father and his prohibitions. Following the murder, Freud posits, the sons experienced the guilt that derived from their originally ambivalent feelings for the father. The effect of this guilt was to make the dead father even more powerful than the living one. Ironically, that is, the sons themselves began to prohibit precisely those acts that had previously been forbidden by the threat of the father's punishment.

In Freud's explanation, the authority of the dead father emerged from real and terrifying material circumstances. Even if he is only imagining the events here, he does so in terms that suggest a founding trauma, a disruption in the physical world involving loss and a consequent transformation of meaning. Indeed, these circumstances and the violence they involve are so traumatic as to be unsymbolizable except through the screen memory implicit in both totems and taboos. As Freud wrote later in *Moses and Monotheism*, the two taboos of culture—against incest and parricide—"operate on the side of the father who has been got rid of: they carry on his will, as it were."[16] The dead father assumes his greatest power in the authority of cultural traditions, a repetition-with-a-difference that ensures the father's continued authority in disguised form.[17]

The need to disguise the father's will suggests the enormous repression at the root of the Law itself. Its founding cause is a "lost cause" in Lacan's punning terms (*Four Fundamental Concepts* 128), an event that cannot be remembered, but that insistently recalls itself in the form of superegoic *negations* of the event: *don't* eat the totem, *don't* sleep with the women you want, revoke the deed, renounce the fruits of victory, resign the object of desire.[18]

Žižek is particularly helpful in clarifying the Law's relation to violence. In emerging from the murder—or in the case of the individual subject, from the primal violence of separation—the superego is inevitably experienced as traumatic, a logical as well as a physical violation. The Law cannot quite present itself in the form of reason, because if it did, it would have to undo its own repression and acknowledge its genealogy, its origin in the violent transgression of a previous order. The trauma that initiates the cultural superego is an example of what, in the later Lacan, is defined as the "Real." According to Žižek, "The paradox of the Lacanian Real . . . is that it is an entity which, although it does not exist . . . exercises a certain structural causality . . . in the symbolic reality of subjects" (*Sublime Object* 163). The Real, apparently, is *not;* it *is* absence or lack, as in the lack of a good-enough reason for the Law. According to this interpretation, the symbolic arises from the Real precisely as an effort to manage and to disguise the traumatic perception of the absence of true authority, the arbitrariness of power: "Belief [in the Law] is an affair of obedience to the dead, uncomprehended letter" Žižek says, and, we might add, to the dead uncomprehended father (43).

The fact that the missing father's Law was itself unlawful, absolutely arbitrary, leaves a residual guilt and fear that sustains the Law. We choose to live with the dead father rather than understand, lest a recognition of the father's lack of authority return us to his rule, to the horror of the Real.[19] This is why Žižek can claim that the Real is that which does not exist but which nevertheless produces effects; it is the *lack,* the need for whose disguise produces the symbolic. The idea of the Real is retroactively fabricated, theorized after the fact, in order to account for certain otherwise inexplicable "distortions" in our cultural-symbolic structure.

Freud's myth of the primal patricide, like Hegel's construction of the primal fight that gives rise to the Master and the Servant, are both such distortions, symptomatic fictions that give evidence of a Real and/but therefore literally unrepresentable trauma.[20] These two myths presume a primal experience of violence at the heart of human consciousness, but they further explain how that violence constitutes the origin of culture in some version of the master/servant relationship. Indeed, Freud's theories of the primal horde and of the oedipal complex seem in themselves to be disguised tributes to Hegel's founding theory of the trauma that initiates human consciousness. They may thus also be evidence of Freud's unconscious debt to his unacknowledged predecessor, Hegel, something else I will talk more about later.

Psychoanalysis and Ideology

The Real/traumatic foundation of the Law/symbolic suggests that there is a kind of repetition compulsion inherent in the symbolic itself insofar as the kernel of the symbolic is the traumatic (non)knowledge of its arbitrariness: consciousness for Lacan is always a consciousness of loss rather than of some object. To live in the symbolic is thus to be perpetually caught up in the simultaneous approach to/escape from such recognition. The Law as "return of the repressed" is thus perhaps the first occurrence of transference, the relation of the superego and the ego (two parts of the split subject), in Freud's words, "a *return,* distorted by a wish, of the real relationships between the ego, as yet undivided, and an external object."[21] Except within the analytic setting, then, where this transference can be used therapeutically, "read through," this "encounter with the real" (Lacan's *tuché*) is always frustrated, always a missed encounter.[22]

The "missing" of this encounter is thus both represented in and compelled by the symbolic order. In his reading of the dream of the burning child, for example, Lacan argues that, far from awakening from the pleasurable illusion that his son is still alive into the horrible truth of his son's death, the dreaming father actually awakens to *escape* from the knowledge that his dream gave him. What he experienced in the dream-child's reproachful question, "Father, can't you see I'm burning?" is the "knowledge" of his own inability to have protected his son. The reality of the boy's death was for the father preferable to a consciousness of his own impotence, a violation of the cultural fantasy of what it means to be a father (*Four Fundamental Concepts* 57–59). Žižek sums up the implication of this reading by noting that, for Lacan, reality is the ideological fantasy whose very function is to disguise "the Real of our desire" (45). In dreams, we encounter the Real, from which we escape by waking into reality. Reality (the symbolic) and its Real/traumatic kernel exist in something like a dialectical relation to one another; there is, however, no *Aufhebung* that would synthesize these mutually constitutive terms, only the continually repeated missed encounter.[23]

The fact that the missed encounter occurs within the order of social law and language makes this a theory of more than just individual subjectivation or the mythical origins of culture. This is a theory about contemporary culture as well, since it is always in the "externality of the symbolic" that "our internal, most 'sincere' and 'intimate' beliefs [are] in advance staged and decided" (Žižek 43). It is in culture, that is, that we encounter our most personal and intimate experiences; it is the symbolic that makes possible our certainty that such experiences are indeed personal and unique to us. As subjects, we are products of the dialectic of symbolic and Real.

Žižek explains the form of this relation between the Real and human culture. The death drive, another name for the traumatic kernel that motivates and founds the Law, "cannot be reduced to an expression of alienated social conditions . . . : there is no solution, no escape from it; the thing to do is not to 'overcome,' to 'abolish' it, but to come to terms with it" (5). In this reading, Žižek very importantly rejects the Marxist notion that particular cultural practices produce human alienation, that we would otherwise be able to live in some harmonious accord with nature and one another. He also rejects the notion that *any* cultural form could permanently overcome this traumatic kernel of humanness, the antagonism that is essential to our being. Rather, he says, we *are* this traumatic kernel, in addition to the systems we produce to enable us to live with our traumatically split selves.

In addition to dismissing the telos of much progressive social and literary theory, this passage may appear to embody the essentialist view of the subject that Marxists and others have frequently objected to in psychoanalysis. But Žižek is quick to socialize these observations and to point to their potential usefulness for ideological criticism when he characterizes culture itself as a "reaction-formation." Laplanche and Pontalis define this psychic phenomenon as an "attitude or habitus diametrically opposed to a repressed wish, and constituted as a reaction against it," an example of *negation* manifested in both feeling and action.[24] To define culture as such a negation is to see human symbolic forms as efforts to deny, rather than to manage, the antagonism that constitutes the subject. In fact, Žižek says, provocatively, "The aspiration to abolish [this drive antagonism] is precisely the source of totalitarian temptation: the greatest mass murders and holocausts have always been perpetrated in the name of man as harmonious being, of a New Man without antagonistic tension" (5; Žižek's emphasis). In 1993, it is hard not to read these words as fairly accurately describing the consequences of the Marxist experiment in Eastern Europe and the Soviet Union, whose conscious intentions might have been far from any totalitarianism, but whose drive toward the harmonious being of socialism had unforeseen repercussions. The very striving toward an "outside" of such tension, then, is itself the reaction-formation that attempts to belie the truth of its own motive.

The reaction-formation is also perhaps an apt description of the symbolic itself, the response to the lack revealed by a violent trauma, whether embodied in the primal murder or in the infant's experience of separation. If culture and the symbolic are to be understood as modeled on the reaction-formation, then ideology is the illusion that structures them both. Not a false consciousness, ideology is rather a fantasy that supports reality itself; it is the illusion that enables reality to obscure the insupportable Real: "The function of ideology is not to offer us a point of escape from our reality but to offer us the social reality itself as an escape from some traumatic, real kernel . . ." (Žižek 45). Here, of course, we see the similarity between the reality into which the dreaming Father awoke in order to sustain another dream and the ideological reality in which we all dream.

What ideology obscures, however, is not some particular truth about the origin of the Law—the murder of the father, say—but something even more disturbing: "the very fact that the Law is not to be accepted as true, only as necessary—the fact that *its authority is without truth*" (38; Žižek's emphasis). What makes the ideological disguise of this fact possible is transference, which Žižek describes as the "supposition of a Truth, of a Meaning behind the stupid, traumatic inconsistent fact of the Law" (38). The oedipal model of authority as properly *derived from* imitation and repetition helps to obscure the Law's stupid inconsistency. And the only way to escape the ideological dream sustained by the mechanism of transference is to acknowledge the Real that is disguised and yet present in this dream, to read it and take responsibility for its revelations. Such a task is far more difficult to do than to describe (I will defer further consideration of its meaning until chap. 6), but whatever possibility exists depends, I am arguing, on a thorough understanding of how and why transference works.

If ideological belief is an effect of transference, then it depends on the Lacanian "subject-supposed-to-know," the object of transference love, someone taken to embody the authority once attributed to a parental figure.[25] This master subject (Lacan revealingly abbreviates it "SsS") is assumed to know what one wants, to know what is true. The fantasy of such a subject thus sustains the illusion that some perfect satisfaction of need and desire would be possible, if one could only attain to the knowledge of the SsS, the fantasy that underlies most ideological formations. Since subjectivity is itself an "unbearable discord" (Žižek 207) resulting from the existence within the subject of some remnant of the Real, that which has not been submitted to the Law (Lacan's "in you more than you"), the subject inevitably fantasizes that, in some external space outside the self (in some Other), his or her internal otherness could be overcome, in a reexperience of some earlier (but wholly imaginary) wholeness.

Transference, then, is necessary to the functioning of the symbolic; in order for one to discover or produce new meaning or belief, one must suppose it to be a repetition of an earlier authorized meaning. At the simplest level, imagine a child trying to learn language without the repetition that promises that *someone* is in control of all this otherwise-meaningless sound making. All meaning is thus constituted retroactively, as the reprise of a previous experience that only comes to have its identity as prototype through the emergence of such repetition.[26] But though the presumed knowledge of the subject-supposed-to-know is an illusion, Lacan is clear that the illusion cannot be circumvented, true knowledge reached directly, because knowledge in fact is *produced* by means of the error, as the effect of our assuming that some other, the transferential object, has already legitimized what we are only *re*discovering. We produce the truth of our own symptoms (personal or cultural) insofar as we define them to be *repetitions* of earlier, formative events; but in doing so, we actually construct those initial events *as* original(s).

This is the continuity and causal logic of history, always retroactively constructed, always an effect of the *Nachträglicheit*. And this is also why Lacan can insist that the repetition in transference is not actually mere repetition, something occurring *"in absentia, in effigie"*:

> The transference effect is that effect of deception in so far as it is repeated in the present here and now.
>
> It is repetition of that which passed for such only because it possesses the same form. It is not ectopia. It is not a shadow of the former deceptions of love. It is isolation in the actuality of its pure functioning as deception. (*Four Fundamental Concepts* 254)

The negation in this passage suggests that Lacan is defining transference *against* the grain of certain conventional and reductive understandings of it, and his point seems to be very close to Freud's claim that "all love is transference love." We must not understand what happens in transference to be any less genuine than the love (or ambivalence) that occurred prior to the occasion of transferential repetition. Transference is not just an imitation of something else that was real: it has its own reality *as* deception—as a certain kind of *resistance*—but in its earlier forms it was also deception insofar as it is reconstructed retroactively in accord with a faith in the illusory subject-supposed-to-know.

Why Modernism?

The emphasis on psychoanalytic theory in these opening pages reveals that this book is not strictly about the literature of modernism. But neither are the texts discussed in the following chapters arbitrarily chosen. As I mentioned earlier, the connection between psychoanalytic theory and ideological analysis in Žižek's work makes possible a reading of literary practices that seem to reject the very grounds of ideological criticism. The rejection of politics, history, and social responsibility often attributed to literary modernism thus becomes interpretable as a symptom, a particular manifestation of the "reaction-formation" Žižek discusses as intrinsic to culture itself.

The texts I talk about in the following chapters are useful for articulating a consciously ideological method of reading at least in part *because* they are supposed to be resistant, or at least unsympathetic, to such analyses. Modernism's formalist closure, extreme self-referentiality, and apparent refusal to acknowledge the importance of material circumstances constitute what many critics have read as its retreat from history, its efforts to deny precisely the importance of history's determination of modernism's "present."

In the charge most famously articulated by Georg Lukács in "The Ideology of Modernism" but reiterated with varying degrees of enthusiasm by many other writers, modernism is the literature of bourgeois decadence and late capitalist degeneration that fails to achieve greatness because of its political conservativism and social irresponsibility.[27] In a more recent construction, modernism "forces the work of art, the artist, the critic, and the audience outside of history . . . [and] denies us the possibility of understanding ourselves as *agents* in the material world, for all has been removed to an abstract world of ideas, where interactions can be minimized or emptied of meaning and real consequences."[28] Jameson, too, comments that, as an "expression of capitalism, and in particular, of the latter's reification of daily life," modernism is also responsible for programming us to accept the alienated and alienating social order we ought instead to be working to change (236).[29]

Jameson's theoretical equation of representation with some kind of propagandizing of the object of representation is problematic, to say the least. A more sophisticated understanding of modernism's apparent disregard for history would see it as motivated particularly *by* historical conditions, responsive to what Terry Eagleton calls the late nineteenth- and twentieth-century crisis in which "the bourgeois ideology of the sign as 'representational' is beginning to be called into question."[30] Interestingly, one of the phenomena of this crisis involves the degradation of language to mere instrumentality, a view that informs some of Lukács's notions of proper literary form. Among the other forces contributing to this representational dilemma are the rise of a middle-class, mass reading public with limited interests in high culture, the breakdown of collective beliefs shared by audience and artist, and the difficulty of reinventing such a framework or frameworks anew. Modernism, then, must be recognized, in the terms Eagleton uses to describe structuralism, as "both symptom of and reaction to the social and linguistic crisis" of the period. As such a symptom, it can also be read as an account of the conditions that require compensation.[31]

Modernism may, then, attempt to deny its own historically specific nature and to substitute for such a limited, determined identity the illusion that it reflects a permanent and universal condition of existence. The very attempts to do so, however, suggest the existence of the reaction-formation I referred to earlier: the *denial* of something that paradoxically speaks of its existence. In Jameson's words, again, modernism can be understood as "canceled realism, as a negation of 'realistic content' which, like a Hegelian *Aufhebung*, continues to bear that content, crossed out and lifted up all at once, within itself" (266).

The above construction reveals that, for Jameson, realism continues to embody the form of authentic social criticism; it is thus a kind of critical dead father whose authority manifests the critic's desire for some kind of full speech. I will argue, however, that the texts I work with call realist literary forms and ideologies into question by exposing the terms and mechanisms through which their apparent coherence has been achieved. By aligning their own coherence—admittedly fictional and thus limited—with that of the ideological fantasy that sustains culture itself, these texts produce a kind of "viral" effect, an "infection" of the closure of cultural forms. If literary coherence imitates the methods of cultural coherence, then it cannot help but suggest, through its "baring of the device," that cultural order derives from the same sources as the literary: the decision (though not conscious) to make self-referentiality and closure the ground of meaning. This project requires the repression of both internal and external challenges to the order's authority, and such repression is always readable, symptomatically, as evidence of something motivating the repression. These texts thus expose the lack in the Other at the root of the symbolic order and of ideology itself insofar as that lack, again, *motivates* the construction of systems to disguise such a lack. They thus indirectly engage the trauma that induces the symbolic in the first place.

But modernist literature is not just more clearly engaged with history than some have claimed; in fact, the ideology of modernism that Lukács and others have identified might in great part be the result of its critical canonization. Readers have often worked to simplify certain complications of these texts by reducing ambiguity, ambivalence, and polyvalency to unified and coherent themes.[32] By thematizing the subject's essential alienation, for example, critics often overlook much of modernism's equally important alignment of the subject with conventions of cultural discourse. By accepting the conscious doctrines of formalism, critics sometimes fail to see the text's valorization of form as a defensive maneuver that simultaneously destabilizes its privilege. By supposing that only mimetic transpositions of cultural reality and chronological time could produce a historically self-conscious critical realism, critics ignore the problem that a progressive view of history poses for modernism, and should continue to pose for us.

It is not coincidental, after all, that the modern genealogies that eventually displace natural or theological accounts of culture derive from a change in the status of the signifier in the material world. With the work of Hegel (at least as Žižek reads him),[33] Marx, Nietzsche, Freud, and Saussure, the idealism of Western culture, though never overturned, is questioned. The beginnings of materialist theories of culture, history, language, and the subject can be found in Marx's view that consciousness follows after the modes of production, in Saussure's assertion that the relation of signifier and signified is arbitrary, and in Freud's discovery of the mutually constituting conscious and unconscious functions. Implicit in these claims is the displacement of natural determinism with cultural determinism, and the growing recognition of the role played by language and other social discourses in that determinism.

As a result of these tentative revisions of the notion of representation, the orders available to modern writers that provide a hope of authorizing their own authority—the subjects-supposed-to-know—may be recognized, at least unconsciously, to be neither different from nor more trustworthy than their own writing. Although social orders still function as if they were absolute, their authority to name and thus legitimize the subject is revealed to be provisional. Just as the relation of signifier to signified is in flux, so is the relation of the subject as signifier of a social identity to the psychic processes it ostensibly reflects. If the founding of the subject requires placement within the signifying chain of some stable discourse, but the discourses of social authority no longer appear stable, then the subject is in trouble. This is the trouble that Lukács correctly intuits in his critique of modernism's antihumanistic and antiliterary impulses, and he disapproves of it.[34]

In the chapters that follow, I read a series of modernist texts with their critical representations, recognizing, with Jameson, the importance of acknowledging the forces that have determined my own readings of these works. My aim is to articulate the contradictory impulses of these works and to suggest that the disquieting attention to authority that provokes their struggles continues to provoke their critical recuperation. Each of the works I examine addresses at least one transferential order promising individuals coherence, closure, and perhaps most importantly, the opportunity to define their personal significance. But if much of modern writing grows out of and reflects an ambivalence about the ideologies implicit in these orders, that is not to suggest that it ever transcends those values' continuing power. What the books I work with can tell us about the Real sources of authority comes through their *resistance* to that knowledge, through the conflict that is transference.[35]

I believe much of modern writing can, for example, be characterized by its uncomfortable recognitions about the nature of sociocultural power. The persistence of any cultural system depends on its capacity to ensure its own coherence, to convince its members of its logic and comprehensiveness by normalizing or co-opting any challenge to it. To provide such assurances to its subjects, culture cannot acknowledge its own limited, provisional, and motivated systems of order. Like the languages that form it, culture must present itself to its members as a representational system of meaning that refers ultimately to reality, a Real Father, or subject-supposed-to-know such as God, nation, nature, or tradition, if not some actual parental figure. The power to provide this meaning, however, is never recognized to be a product of language, but is projected outside the symbolic, onto some authorizing Other, the transferential object.

This Other is constituted in the denial of the Real, of the fundamentally arbitrary origin of the Symbolic. In Lacan's terms, what makes such denial possible is a certain effect of signification that stops the slippage of one signifier into another. As Žižek explains, the "floating signifiers" of our language are "structured into a unified field through the intervention of a certain 'nodal point' (the Lacanian *point de capiton*) which 'quilts' them, stops their sliding and fixes their meaning" (87).[36] However, these nodal points must not be understood to consist of some plenitude or density of meaning; on the contrary, what characterizes them is precisely their status as "pure signifier" without a signified. The *point de capiton* is in fact only a "pure difference" (99). The ideological power of the *point de capiton* lies in a certain "error of perspective": the nodal point is, like zero, a place holder, but this mark of emptiness is perceived as evidence of a supreme plenitude (99).[37] This error is, of course, a motivated one: the assumption of the signifier's meaning promises its power to the one who believes.

Despite the fact that the nodal point is understood to be "[exempt] from . . . differential interplay," it is, as pure difference (99), part of a binary. To exemplify this point, Žižek comments on the meaning of *democracy:* "'democracy' is defined not by the positive content of this notion (its signified) but only by its positional-relational identity—by its opposition . . . to 'non-democratic' . . ." (98). The nodal points that end the undecidability of *mere* difference thus produce our crucial organizing binaries: genital difference, for example, is interpreted as the absolute opposition of male and female nature, the genitals the locus of the subject's natural inscription. Similarly, differences in skin color and facial bone structure come to be read as the *opposition* of white to other natures, the body's form a code that nature thoughtfully provides to help us understand and adapt to its intention. Even explicitly social codes, like money, are understood to be bound to some true nature of the subject: those who have money must also possess some quality that makes them deserve the social sign of power, while those who lack the signifier must similarly lack the quality of nature to which money merely *refers*. In every case, however, the belief is a resistance, facilitated by the *point de capiton,* to the nonsense of an accidental, nonoppositional, mere difference.

It is a truism to say that binaries are inevitably hierarchical. Hegel's theory of the emergence of human consciousness and the development of the master/servant relationship explains, however, why this is so.[38] Opposition, of course, is at the heart of the dialectic, but more specifically, the perception of *otherness,* Hegel says, is always threatening. Consciousness understandably seeks to eliminate such threats to itself, either imaginatively, by interpreting all otherness to be in reality an effect of consciousness itself (*I* am the source of the other, its reality is in me: in this sense, the *I* may be, for Hegel, the originary *point de capiton*), or materially, by destroying the other, killing or enslaving it, whether "it" is nature or other people. *Humanness,* Hegel says, emerges precisely as this desire to transform the world, to change nature from its status as given or found into something expressive, indeed, constitutive of the self: I look at something in the world and, recognizing its separateness from me, I experience anxiety, alienation. This alienation, however, is paradoxically productive, because it motivates me to perform the transformative act that brings my humanness into being: I negate the objective otherness of the other, and I turn it into something *else*, something that signifies *my* being, not its.

The more sophisticated version of this transformation occurs in the master/slave stage of the dialectic, in which the individual consciousness recognizes its own need to be acknowledged by an other like itself; transforming found objects and killing enemies cease to be effective means of expressing one's humanness, and the need for a living testament to one's power arises. Eventually, of course, even the slave becomes an inadequate measure of the master's self, though at this stage of the dialectic, Hegel seems to lose interest in the master, shifting his attention to the alteration in the slave wrought by his slavery. The dialectic of consciousness from this point on describes the transformations of a self that repeatedly recognizes its own enslavement in continually new forms: stoicism, skepticism, unhappy consciousness, etc. Within the dialectic, these inadequate manifestations of Spirit will eventually lead to the achievement of Absolute Reason, presumably in some form of Romantic philosophy. But as Žižek argues, taken as a process and abstracted from the ideological fantasy of perfectability, wholeness, what the *Phenomenology* really describes is consciousness itself as the perception of its own inadequacy, lack of mastery, enslavement—its *lack* of wholeness—regardless of historical transformations in philosophy, material conditions, and political and social institutions. Not that such transformations are unimportant, only that they may not be adequate to eliminate the lack that Hegel describes as constitutive of the subject: they may manage it differently, and some will cope with it better, more democratically, but they will not escape it. Such a rereading of the dialectic makes clear its status as precursor to Freud's theory of the oedipal complex, or at least suggests the extent to which Hegel and Freud (among other Western theorizers) responded to the shared recognition of a fundamental power struggle at the heart of human consciousness.

In both Hegel and Freud (and in Nietzsche too), this struggle is resolved through different strategies of renunciation, herein revealed to be itself a transferential effect: my renunciation of the object guarantees that there is somewhere a someone-who-has-not-renounced, someone who possesses the desired object, mastery, knowledge. In the oedipal complex, the redemptive nature of this renunciation is clear: it is structured as a *deferral* of the subject's desire for the mother to another time and space (another woman), a surrender redeemed by the subject's identification with the figure previously experienced as threat and rival, the father. What had heretofore *blocked* access to the object of desire is transformed into the promise of the object's eventual achievement: I cannot have her because Father has her, but someday I will become (a) Father. This identification makes possible the subject's further identification with the very structure that prohibits his desire, the Law embodied in the father as the first subject-who-knows (or perhaps the second, after the mother).

In Hegel, "renunciation" occurs in forms philosophically more sophisticated though no more psychologically complex. Stoicism, for example, the slave philosophy, emerges with the slave's recognition that his material powerlessness does not accurately reflect the reality of his spiritual equality with, indeed superiority to the master.[39] Unable to transform these material circumstances because of the master's greater wealth or physical strength, the slave nevertheless frees himself mentally; but this freedom involves *renouncing* the ultimately illusory material pleasures for the *other* pleasure of feeling better than both the master and one's circumstances. Once again, such renunciation is redeemed by its constituting the certainty that there is, somewhere, someone-who-is-truly-master, someone whose real mastery I merely emulate in my degraded condition. When this pleasure is eventually undone by consciousness's new recognition of its inadequacy (the physical world has been merely retreated from, not transformed), a new strategy (skepticism) arises, and on it goes.

This brief review of the early stages of the dialectic of consciousness reveals that Hegel constructed the *Phenomenology* around the enormous flexibility of the human capacity for coping with inadequacy, the perception of the lack in both the self and the Other. In Hegel, *negation* might well be less the name for Spirit's capacity to throw off inadequate manifestations and more the title of this imaginative resourcefulness, continually casting off one deficient rationalization after another, always capable of constructing the next. Similarly, in Freud, *negation* names the doubleness of psychic material that may appear to be absent, canceled, but that nevertheless survives as a force. *Negation* for both, that is, designates the repeated attempt to make a new start that is always inevitably a repetition—de Man's modernity—an attempt that grows out of the inescapable discovery of inadequacy at the subject's heart.

I believe that the works I discuss here manifest in different ways their discovery that cultural coherence is an effect of repressing and managing the lack that Hegel, Freud, Lacan, and other modern thinkers theorize. This discovery derives from certain real or potential lapses of or inconsistencies in that coherence. But while some of these texts address particular political or social problems in an explicitly critical fashion (Conrad's representation of European imperialism and Woolf's feminism, for example, are propositional attacks on oppressive cultural practices), these texts more radically enact *through repetition* nonpropositional analyses of cultural binaries. In so doing, they demonstrate the subject to be a function of the simultaneous resistance and capitulation of the individual to and within the cultural symbolic. As these writers begin to appropriate and deform discursive modes and conventions—altering, as Walter Benjamin described it, the modes of production—a secondary disruption may also occur in the exposure of the repressive mechanisms necessary to ensure cultural as well as literary or textual closure.[40]

These works do not offer up any particular truth that has been repressed by culture: that women are equal to men or Africans are as civilized as Europeans, for example. Such banal claims could not transform cultural stereotypes, let alone cultural practices, because they are determined by the same binaries of subject/object, culture/nature as the original statements to the contrary. They could thus not undo or even really challenge the binaries or the binary system itself.[41] Indeed, even if such alternative truths are at times manifested by characters or within the narrative's drive toward closure, they reveal not a real alternative to oppressive cultural myths but rather the symptomatic *desire* for truth as evidence of the transference, the construction of a subject-supposed-to-know.[42] In consequence, these texts demonstrate repression to be the mode of cultural truth. Within such writing, repression is not overcome, but its operations are revealed to be the means by which culture establishes its inside—that which is proper to it—by simultaneously producing the outside whose difference from and potential threat to the center ensures the center's status as good.

Love (or Hate) *Instead* of Knowledge

These texts thus perform their revision of discursive conventions by means of a curious imitation of them: writers reproduce the cultural systems they challenge, just as readers so often reproduce the structures they discover in their reading. As a subject attempts to dissociate him- or herself from the unsatisfactory symbolic order, to reject the dead father's authority, the establishment of the "new," original order occurs only as a duplication of the repudiated system. This is the negative transference at work in the reproduction of cultural and literary practice.[43] This may also be an example of what Žižek calls "choosing what is given," the psychic strategy by which we rationalize our own lack of power in the world by "'posit[ing]' as our own work what is given to us" (220). Žižek offers a Lacanian reading of the funeral rite to exemplify the nature of this formal conversion: "In the funeral rite, the subject confers the *form* of a free act on an 'irrational,' contingent natural process," death (219; Žižek's emphasis). But choosing what is given does not occur just in the cultural response to natural phenomena such as death; it occurs within culture all the time as individuals assume responsibility for the reality they discover around them, pretending that what is given to them is something they produced for themselves. Such a *pretense* is not purely psychological; it is carried out in the subject's imitative habits of thinking and acting, transferential repetitions of cultural models that paradoxically reinforce the subject's bondage to those models even as they pretend to a kind of autonomy. These texts, then, do not by and large seek to subvert cultural authority, even if they may be critical of it. Whether positive or negative, supportive or critical of existing power structures, they nevertheless almost always enact a transferential repetition of the form of that power; the important exception to this model occurs in Woolf's *A Room of One's Own*.

That exception leads me to another important point about the rationale for linking the four modernist texts discussed here. I have chosen these particular texts because they dramatize the modernist dilemma of authority in various yet characteristic ways. But these familiar texts are also important in part *because* of their canonical status, their role in actually defining and exemplifying, within a long critical tradition, the characteristic themes, styles, and problematics that constitute the various modernisms of the late twentieth century.

Remembering again Jameson's claim that literary texts can only be responsibly considered within the larger discursive frames of their critical appropriation, I have chosen to exemplify the transferential conflict in modernism by means of texts that in themselves have functioned for readers as transferential objects, repositories of authoritative knowledge, subjects that know and embody the truth of the modern. As Vincent Pecora has noted about his own choice of equally canonical texts in his recent study of modernism, despite our desire as critics not to "[encourage] . . . canonical narrowmindedness, . . . canons, like clichés, are often revealing in spite of themselves" if we work to "brush [them] against the grain" (6). The canon itself may be another version of the critical reading effect and as such revelatory of transference at yet another level of operation.

In addition, I must admit I have found these texts compelling in themselves as modernist stories, stories of modernist desire: as texts, these works seem to aspire to truth even as they dramatize the constructedness of that aspiration and reveal it to be an ideologically motivated one that perpetuates the modes of production of modern Western subjectivity.

Something else links these texts for me, something that in another of his works, *Looking Awry*, Žižek calls *legibility*. In the very difficult and elliptical texts of classic high modernism—*Finnegans Wake* and Pound's *Cantos*, for example—their very resistance to normal reading practices, their stylistic density, their illegibility, "functions precisely as an invitation to an unending process of reading, of interpretation."[44] The alienation effect produced by these texts alerts us as professional readers to the challenges they present, the pitfalls they threaten. The texts I work on, however, though at one time also perhaps alien to readers, have become through their very canonization examples of a certain already-understood phenomenon, "modernism." By comparison with Pound and Joyce, James and Conrad, Hemingway and Woolf are stylistically accessible, conventional, and highly legible: not just read*able* but *read*. But in this very availability, Žižek locates a certain "radical opacity"; something in the "overexposed character" of these works "blocks every essay of interpretation" (151). Certainly that does not mean that the texts have not been sufficiently or intelligently interpreted in the past, but only that their repeated appropriation by critics should make us see them as part of larger cultural and academic practices of self-definition whose familiarity can sometimes obscure their strategies.

I mentioned before that I have chosen these texts because they exemplify the phenomenon of transference in characteristically modernist ways. However, I do not mean to suggest that there are not significant differences among the kinds of transferential resistance and repetition represented in these four modernist texts. In fact, the chapters seem to me to move through several different attitudes toward and degrees of consciousness about repetition.

Heart of Darkness, the subject of chapter 2, contains a clear critique and repudiation of the Company's exploitative behavior in Africa. But the mockery of the avaricious and inept imperialists is not the real point of this story. That point emerges in the apparent *alternative* to the ethnocentric arrogance of imperialism that Marlow's journey to Africa makes possible. His narrative, that is, seems to embody an early modernist existential faith in the self-consciously constructed identity, in place of the Romantic-Victorian arrogance of the Company men. He thus turns from an inherited cultural delusion of white grandeur to the personally discovered truth of his individual vision. Marlow's confrontation with the raw and unmediated nature of the jungle, coupled with his construction of Kurtz as the *negative* subject-supposed-to-know—the subject who has discovered both his own social constructedness and the *lack* underlying the construction—provokes Marlow's theory of the "deliberate belief," which has come to be synonymous with the modernist "supreme fiction." But the novel does not simply replace the now-unacceptable political imperialism with a new imperialism of the subject. Marlow's first-person account displays the processes by which he has appropriated the inside/outside distinctions of his culture (and thus reproduced its exploitation of Africa) to construct his own "original" notions of the difference between self and other, man and nature. Political imperialism gives way to its private counterpart only to demonstrate again the subject's effective determination by—that is, imitation of—the order he believes he has resisted.

In chapter 3, whose central topic is *The Wings of the Dove,* I begin with a reading of James's critical analysis of *The Tempest.* Here, I offer a very explicit example of one form the reading effect so often takes in Western literary criticism. In this analytic piece, James turns the mystery of Shakespeare's personal life and strangely truncated career into a kind of aggression by the writer against his admiring reading public. Shakespeare, that is, becomes James's subject-supposed-to-know, the master in possession of the truth, and James's advice to future readers contains some explicitly parricidal tips. The reading of *The Tempest* that James provides appropriates its images and themes—of water, transformation and disguise, of power struggles and aging suicidal masters, for example—as a way of explaining not just how the text allegorizes Shakespeare's authorial intentions but also how one who wishes to be *like* the master must behave. The play thus becomes both a record of Shakespeare's desire and a blueprint for authorial desire for others. Coupled with his admiration of Shakespeare, James displays a very oedipal rage to escape the master's authority; but this drive can apparently be satisfied only in an *imitation* of the strategy James believes Shakespeare employed. One who seeks freedom from the tyranny of the Other must achieve it by becoming tyrannical master *to* an other, in this case, to James's readers.

The second part of the chapter considers how, in the novel, Milly Theale assumes a paradoxically authoritative position with her friends in London by turning her mysterious illness into a strategy for controlling others. This technique effectively limits their ability to manipulate her—or at least determines the shape that their relations to her will take. But the form of Milly's authority also effectively repeats the forms by which she herself has been determined. Her construction of her illness as a "family legacy" suggests the extent to which the cultural model of patrilineal descent—and the oedipal authority embodied in it—ensures its own stability. That order promises to each subject his or her opportunity to become a formal father figure if he or she obeys the order's laws. By accepting her determination by this patriarchal tradition—the family tradition of death from which she has so far been excluded—Milly achieves a certain coherence to her identity. Just as she believes the death of her family has inscribed her as impotent heir to the will of the other(s), so, in choosing to acknowledge her link to that tradition, she makes her sickness and death the means to power over the others who would exploit her for their ends. Milly's apparent difference from the worldly and cynical Londoners is thus undone by her repeating their impulse to dominate her, though in a less explicitly aggressive form than their exploitation of her: indeed, tragically, the clearest object of her destructive behavior is herself.

In chapter 4, I discuss how *The Sun Also Rises* represents a phenomenon related to that in *The Wings of the Dove*. Jake Barnes's narrative demonstrates how his impotence becomes a means to power over others. The affair with Brett enacts the Lacanian economy of castration and desire, revealing that his power over his lover derives from his capacity to evoke in her a desire that he will never fulfill. But the dialectic of castration and desire is not a purely psychological construct in this novel: the bullfight, intended, perhaps, to represent modern "man's" existentially authentic engagement with his mortality, contains its own repressed supplement to the lovers' discourse. The relation of matador to bull includes a parody of conventional representations of gender and power, the matador assuming the guise and function of "femininity" to destroy the "man" figured in the bull. Although Hemingway would no doubt wish to preserve the authenticity of the bullfight by suggesting that its signifiers (man and bull) actually betoken the opposition of culture and nature—or man and death—his representation of the ritual demonstrates the distinctions male/female, aggressive/passive, and culture/nature to be constructions organized around the *lack* of the Real, imaged first in Jake's castration and then later in the staged performance of risk in the bullfight.

The subject of chapter 5 is Virginia Woolf's *A Room of One's Own*, the second nonfictional narrative I analyze. This chapter focuses on Woolf's generic disruptions of the essay form, arguing that they engender a series of other strategic ruptures in our normative ways of thinking about writing, gender, and human subjectivity. The explicit and conventional feminism of the piece criticizes prevailing conceptions of the social role of woman, but then something else happens in the writing. As her critique of the patriarchy begins to repeat many of the maneuvers by which that "originary" order has appropriated the body as the transcendental signified, Woolf's writing offers a disruptive supplement to the primary discourse of gender. By strategically linking the obvious and self-conscious motives of feminism—anxiety and anger—to the never-questioned motives of the patriarchy, the text suggests that women's desire for the status of "subject" can only be fulfilled in the appropriation of the "other" as "opposite." In so doing, Woolf provides a radical critique, not just of the discourse of gender identity, but of the discourses of the subject and human nature as well.

From Marlow's *denial* of repetition in his explicit repudiation of his imperialist masters, to Milly Theale's repetition of a family dynamic *"chosen"* but perceived as inevitable (as in "choosing what is given"), to Jake's exploitative *complicity* in the simultaneous revelation and reinscription of power and gender binaries, to Woolf's deconstruction of these patterns and the subsequent unsettling of the power relations and closure they reinforce: these texts embody important differences in the functioning of transference in modernist narratives. What links them all is the revelation that transference arises out of a resistance to the knowledge that the Real Father is impossible. In the modernist repudiation of transcendent authority, we often see a negative transference, but it is still a transference, an indication of resistance to that knowledge. As such, it also formally reproduces the belief in a Real Father, even if that father has to be constructed as an alternative to the original. There is no cure for this situation of endless repetition, at least not as most of the texts I examine represent it; there is only the textually embodied fantasy that nevertheless exposes its own motive, the repressed recognition of lack in the Other and in the self.

However, these representations, *read together*, may suggest, even if they cannot define, another possible relation to the father, one also suggested by Barthelme in a passage from *The Dead Father:*

> Patricide is a bad idea, first because it is contrary to law and custom and second because it proves, beyond a doubt, that the father's every fluted accusation against you was correct: you are a thoroughly bad individual, a patricide!—member of a class of persons universally ill-regarded. It is all right to feel this hot emotion, but not to act upon it. And it is not necessary. It is not necessary to slay your father, time will slay him, that is a virtual certainty. Your true task lies elsewhere. (145)

The question is in what this task might consist. The notion of a possible resistance to resistance is taken up at the end of chapter 5 and in chapter 6, where I consider Woolf's nonpropositional feminism as offering the most positive construction of a human subjectivity *not* either wholly produced by or wholly reducible to resistance.

The metaphor of androgyny may look like an effort to repudiate—to renounce—difference and discord, but in fact it becomes a way to acknowledge such discord to be at the center of human consciousness. If this is the case, then at least one of these modernist texts depicts an alternative to the repetition of transference.

Chapter 2

The Ideologies of Romanticism in *Heart of Darkness*

> Africa proper, as far as History goes back, has remained—for all purposes of connection with the rest of the World—shut up; it is the Gold-land compressed within itself—the land of childhood, which lying beyond the day of self-conscious history, is enveloped in the dark mantle of Night.
>
> —Hegel, *Philosophy of History*, 1830–31

> The mission which the agents of the State have to accomplish in the Congo is a noble one. They have to continue the development of civilisation in the centre of Equatorial Africa. . . . Placed face to face with primitive barbarism, grappling with sanguinary customs that date back thousands of years, they are obliged to reduce these gradually. They must accustom the population to general laws, of which the most needful and the most salutary is assuredly that of work.
>
> —King Leopold II, 1898

The Legacies of Romanticism

The continuity of rhetoric in the two short passages cited above suggests with disturbing clarity how Romantic philosophy functioned as an ideological basis for the nineteenth-century colonial movements into Africa. Leopold's construction of the progressive imperative of Western expansion owes much, for example, to the interpretation of difference implicit in Hegel's identification of Africa as the preserved infancy of the world Spirit: as "the Gold-land . . . of childhood," Africa is both a repository of truth about human origins and a continuing challenge to the *adult* human impulse to transform the given into a sign of Spirit. This identification is further echoed in Leopold's comfortable certainty that the colonialist task includes the "development of civilisation" in the jungle where, presumably, the childish Africans had not yet gotten around to civilizing themselves. More abstractly but no less importantly, the Romantic notion of Spirit as the universal law that pervades all physical forms, uniting them as expressions of the world's general coherence, has apparently been extended to Leopold's belief that particular laws having to do with the importance of (Western) *work* in fact constitute general laws. Presuming such universality allows Leopold and others to justify their own transformative efforts in Africa as purely altruistic.[1]

In this chapter, I will trace a series of transformations in Romanticism to suggest how a model of authority and identity based in Hegel's master/servant dynamic structures both the novel *Heart of Darkness* and much of its reception, manifesting the patterns of resistance and repetition I have been associating with transference and the reading effect. For much modern literature and its criticism, one of the most important versions of Romantic philosophy emerges in existentialism. Consider, for example, the role alienation plays in forming the human subject in both philosophies. In the most optimistic reading of the dialectic of Spirit, the goal of human self-consciousness is to achieve freedom from the illegitimate determinacy of the material world, to realize that the subject/object dichotomy is actually a false one. But to achieve this consciousness, the imagination must dismember the world and force it to signify something other than its own unconsciousness. The dialectic is thus motivated by transformative impulses that are essentially aesthetic.

But this aestheticism masks some troubling implications. If human history is read as the account of Spirit's progress toward its telos—the realization of World Spirit—the present moment must always be understood as a superior, though not final, stage in the dialectic. Romantic philosophy defines as progress, then, what is in fact a justification of the status quo. Another person, an alien culture, can never be allowed to be simply *different:* rather, it must be interpreted as a defining other, a vision of the lost past guaranteeing the superiority of Western culture. For the Romantic imperialist, then, there may be no significant difference between the psychic dismemberment of nature that Hegel describes and the literal transformation of lands and peoples that imperialism undertakes: the second act would appear as the logical fulfillment of the first aesthetic impulse.[2] Importantly, both transformative acts occur in response to the alienation human beings experience in the face of nature's apparent indifference.

Existentialism, of course, rejects the idea that nature or anything else could guarantee the spiritual potential of the human. However, in a kind of negative transference, existentialism nevertheless encounters and redeems alienation in the discovery of death, the event that separates each person from all redemptive or transcendent structures. As such—and here is where the implicit idealism of existentialism emerges—death is paradoxically what brings "man" into being: it ultimately becomes the foundation of human freedom, of the responsibility to choose, and of the individual's capacity to authorize the meaning of his or her existence.[3] It is not difficult to see the symmetry between this transvaluation of death and the Hegelian response of protohumans to the blank indifference of the world: both involve the transformation of a threat to the human into something signifying—indeed, constituting—humanness itself. To the extent, then, that the subject's response to death effectively directs his or her understanding of experience, it also redeems the potential absurdity of existence, like the Romantic dialectic.

Perhaps no canonical modernist work displays more clearly than Conrad's *Heart of Darkness* the way a Romantic existentialism can simultaneously interpret and disguise the individual's relation to actual social conditions. This novel very directly locates Marlow's repudiation of his culture—or at least the culture of imperialism—within a striking representation of the stupidity, ugliness, and brutality that motivate his effort to cancel the external. The representation of Marlow's retreat thus includes the dramatic account of *why* he has tried to divorce himself from the Company and all that it represents (and all that represents it). More important, the novel presents this cleavage as a scene of social instruction: Marlow's oral narrative occurs while he is out sailing with friends who will presumably learn from his tale (as his readers often do) to share his contempt for modern European arrogance.

The novel, then, does seem to manifest something like an existential insistence on the individual's freedom and responsibility to define himself through his actions: in this sense, Marlow's quitting the Company and exposing its crimes, if only in his story to friends, constitute his self-construction, his refusal to be determined by the contingent actions of those for whom he feels nothing but contempt, those whose actions are inadequate to define his sense of self. However, at the same time, the novel allows us to see the limitations of the existential solution: Marlow's drive toward self-creation is determined by his *rejecting* external social conditions, not his transcending them.

The consistent pattern of reading he performs in his journey exposes the process of Marlow's self-construction. Throughout his experiences, he confronts and interprets a series of resistant and incomprehensible others—colonialism, the nature of the jungle, the natives, and Kurtz—without recognizing his own interpretive activity. Far from the unmediated perceptions of essential truth that he seeks, his visions are always culturally influenced constructions of the other motivated by a desire to protect the stability of the self that sees. Marlow consistently acknowledges the potential threat of the other's strangeness only to transform it into an assurance, now granted the authority of nature, of his own coherence. His readings, then, are manifestations of the unconscious symbolizing activity that makes up the dialectic of the Real and the Symbolic. Marlow attempts to objectify his own psychology and project it into the external world where it will appear as insurance of the self's propriety. Like the Romantic version of nature as the external guarantee of "man's" necessity, Marlow's reified tokens of self function as ordering principles for the experience that might otherwise seem horribly subversive.

Critics have been quick to recognize and articulate the idealist mystification of colonialism that the novel represents, but many have been equally quick to redeem the spiritual failures of the colonialists by celebrating Marlow's spiritual successes. Such a redemption depends on our willingness to shift attention from the global significance of imperialist excess to the humbler domain of the individual education: if Marlow cannot single-handedly overcome the Company's violations in the Congo, he can at least derive from its evil a clearer sense of his own humanity.[4] His exposure and repudiation of the Company's delusions of grandeur thus offer us an opportunity to become similarly educated. What we take from Marlow's account of his visions in the African jungle is a renewed perception of our own mortal limitations, limitations that may nevertheless become the source of greater self-consciousness and a sense of our responsibility to choose our demons: the deathly truth of the jungle over the papier-mâché illusions of the hollow Company man.

Such are the arguments, at any rate, offered by many of the novel's interpreters.[5] But while Marlow's narrative does reveal the large-scale brutality of the colonialist enterprise, it also manifests his inability to free himself from the assumptions that provoke the Company's activities. And I would further suggest that Marlow's readers, following his lead, have frequently repudiated the deluded egotism of a certain kind of Romanticism only to embrace its legacy in the ostensible realism of existential philosophy.

From the existential perspective, Marlow's adventures constitute a confrontation with his mortal contingency. Africa, that is, remains an image of "man's" origin, though it no longer promises the gratifying assurance of the logic of Western cultural forms, as Hegel might have seen it. Instead, that origin "suggests that a naked exposure of the human ego, unshielded by civilization and its self-contents, to a world of savagery presumed to be far beneath it is, in the long evolutionary run, only a baring of the soul to the most primally rooted impulses. To plumb the native is to come up against the innate, apart from all cultural or racial demarcations."[6]

For both the Romantic and the existentialist, then, the experience of and response to originary alienation become the organizing principles of all future engagement in the world. And to the extent that *Heart of Darkness* addresses those two distinct but related structures of philosophical and psychic understanding, it also exposes Marlow's own colonization of the jungle in his unconsciously imitative repudiation of the Company's and Kurtz's exploitation of Africa.[7] Marlow's narrative makes imperialism's motivated misconstruction of the alien culture both its object and technique of representation.[8] In demonstrating the interdependence of imaginative and political imperialism, the novel also lets us see that the motive of such activities is a traumatic encounter with the Real arbitrariness of cultural authority; and further, that this motive has both authored and been repressed by Romantic idealism, in all its various forms.

The Persistence of the Past

As an ironic version of the Romantic bildungsroman, Marlow's narrative reflects the waning capacity of this genre to represent the present moment, the present man, as an outgrowth of a coherent and stable genealogy. The journey into the Congo is for Marlow a trip into the "night of the first ages," a primal world ostensibly anterior to and more powerful than man's efforts to control it. It is thus, as he imagines it and as Stewart and others concur, a journey into the generic self. Marlow hopes that encountering the innate, originary nature of Africa might allow him a vision of the originary being of "man," which is to say himself.

His fascination with the origin is apparent as soon as Marlow speaks, in his first utterance in the novel. In the midst of the eminently civilized context of a yachting excursion on the Thames, surrounded by friends who are, with the exception of the unnamed first narrator, identified in the allegorical terms of their modern social functions—the Lawyer, the Accountant, the Director—Marlow remarks about "the biggest, and the greatest town on earth" that it too "has been one of the dark places of the earth" (Conrad 9). For Marlow, as for any good Romantic, the appeal of darkness derives from its mysteriousness, the terror of which motivates his rage to know it, to assert himself by mastering it. Interestingly, the absence of visual differentiation in darkness is a threat that simultaneously encourages the Romantic privileging of voice as a token of the peculiarly human transformation of the natural. Marlow's oral narrative will occur in the deepening darkness of the day's end; its authority to master its complacent listeners will be in part a function of the context that makes that troubled but coherent voice one of the only available means of humanist differentiation from the natural setting. As such, that narrative, anticipating and doubling the authority Kurtz's voice will exert over Marlow himself, is offered to its hearers—and to us—as a transferential repetition of the powerful experience Marlow himself had in the jungle. It is thus not surprising that so much criticism of the novel would appropriate its authoritative account of the "primal self" to become the source of critical authority.[9]

Although the great town of London would seem to have been already mastered and transformed, Marlow evokes it here not as a testament to the power of human civilization, but rather as a mark of the original alienation that motivated the work of humanizing. For Marlow, the tamed nature of London still speaks of the horror it used to be: "All that mysterious life of the wilderness that stirs in the forest, in the jungles, in the hearts of wild men, . . . the incomprehensible, which is also detestable. The fascination of the abomination" (Conrad 10). The incomprehensible is detestable, we presume, because it denies understanding by means of familiar conventions and thus threatens their authority. Yet Marlow would seem to agree with

Hegel's view that such a threat is the inevitable and necessary initial experience of alienation that precedes and provokes the aesthetic impulses of self-consciousness. Although it is the task of culture to negate the fascinating abomination of nature, culture always speaks to Marlow of its origin in this activity of aestheticizing repression. It is by so reading culture that Marlow maintains for himself his identity as "man."

Marlow's desire to go to Africa is thus identified as a desire to recapitulate that originary alienation and its resultant experience of primal self-consciousness. But when he recounts the history of that desire, he also reveals the impossibility of its fulfillment. His fascination with Africa is associated with his childhood passion for maps and for the geographers who produced them, men whose object was, Marlow says, knowledge rather than material gain:

> Now when I was a little chap I had a passion for maps. I would look for hours at South America, or Africa, or Australia, and lose myself in all the glories of exploration. At that time there were many blank spaces on the earth, and when I saw one that looked particularly inviting on a map (but they all look that) I would put my finger on it and say, When I grow up I will go there. . . . But there was one yet—the biggest, the most blank, so to speak—that I had a hankering after. (Conrad 11)

A means of charting the unknown through a representational system, maps assert the mastery of knowledge over a vast and unavailable world. As such, then, they are another manifestation of the aesthetic dismemberment of the natural. As a child, Marlow had liked to contemplate the blank spaces on the map because, in the mysteriousness accessible to him precisely because it was indicated by conventional symbols of mystery, these spaces were a source of imaginative freedom. The white space allowed for visionary flights, self-expression unconstrained by facts: the child could people and landscape the delightful blankness with whatever came to mind, paternally bestowing life on the otherwise dead space of the paper. Marlow says he would lose himself in his daydreaming. That familiar metaphor for the psychological effect of intense interest suggests, however, that what he lost was the conventional powerlessness of the child (and indeed of the adult). To efface that limited ego is to achieve a more significant self, one characterized precisely by its omniscient authority. Importantly, though, this ego is modeled on the authoritative example of those earlier heroic mapmakers, who, to the child, must have seemed the inventors of the landscape they represented. That is, Marlow's imaginative authority assumes here the familiar form of one already known, of the paternal explorers, and thus is not a mark of either freedom or originality.

The adult Marlow finds that the biggest of all blank spaces, Africa, has ceased to be a "blank space of delightful mystery" and has become instead a place of darkness:

> It had got filled since my boyhood with rivers and lakes and names. It had ceased to be a blank space of delightful mystery—a white patch for a boy to dream gloriously over. It had become a place of darkness. But there was in it one river especially, a mighty big river, that you could see on the map, resembling an immense snake uncoiled. . . . And as I looked at the map of it in a shop-window, it fascinated me as a snake would a bird—a silly little bird. (Conrad 11–12)

The implications of this transformation are curious. On the one hand, Africa's darkness here may merely signify its partial charting. No longer totally mysterious, totally free, it still continues to exert the fascination of partial knowledge, the appeal of rivers and lakes and names that, in their foreignness, seem to be the names of mystery itself. Africa might come thus to be seen on the map as a huge space of preserved and uncontaminated nature, as Hegel had seen it. Its fascination would be that of a foreboding but exciting challenge, as a snake's sly and incomprehensible movements would fascinate the bird that Marlow feels himself to be. In fact, the metaphor by which Marlow expresses the appeal of the continent suggests again his faith in the capacity of the origin—mysterious parental object—to speak its uncanny message to man. As the bird, evolutionarily descended from the reptile, might be fascinated by the snake's strangely familiar movements, so will Marlow eventually find himself drawn to and repulsed by the primal men from whom he believes himself descended.[10] His simultaneously positive and negative transference here obscures the deludedness of Marlow's (mis)understanding of Africa's difference from Europe.

But the darkness of the continent seems also to reflect Marlow's personal repression of his childish relation to Africa. He had filled up the empty vessel with signs of his own power and no doubt identified himself by means of his capacity to do so. He thus came into imaginative being as the author of the continent, its existence mirroring and confirming his own. In adulthood, however, he must repress his prior invention so that he may conceive of the journey to Africa as an opportunity to repeat the exploits of the explorers he had so admired as a child. Wishing to encounter and engage the unknown directly, without the mediation of the map's reductive representation, Marlow's experience will nevertheless still be mediated by his forgotten constructions of Africa, as well as by the cultural clichés about its barbarism. Its transformation from white to black, then, would seem to reflect the movement of the uncanny, Africa's metamorphosis from promise of omnipotence to threat of death. If Marlow were to remember his earlier invention of Africa, he would have to recall as well the impotence that had motivated his childish acts of self-deification and to recognize that the same impotence now motivates his adult quest for self. He might have to acknowledge as well that his earlier performance of power in relation to Africa had also been an imitation of other conventional forms of power. This he cannot or will not do. Thus, the previously comforting token of self, Africa has become uncannily appealing, the "ghastly harbinger of death" that Marlow must repress by unconsciously reenacting his discovery of the unknown, his invention of himself.

The location of Marlow's adult rediscovery of Africa further suggests his commodification of the unknown, an attitude not so different from the lust for material wealth he deprecates in the early Roman cultivators of London. As he looks at the map through the shop window, contemplating its seductive representation, he represses the clearly economic "frame" of his own aesthetic contemplation. Indeed, the form of the map itself—"untamed" Africa surrounded by images of conquered territory—repeats the spatial arrangement of the object in the shop window: the map surrounded by things already bought and things yet to buy. In both cases, Marlow represses the economic frame—window or imperialist conquest—that contextualizes and indeed *produces* the object of aesthetic contemplation.[11] He desires to possess the mystery as we all want to own the things held up for our admiring and envious glances in shop-window displays. And, like most of us, Marlow fails to realize that the apparent idealism of his desire is a production of the very economic lust he wishes to repudiate.[12] He "had a hankering after" Africa, he says, as we all hanker after objects whose desirability derives from the transference implicit in mediated desire: we want to own the things that signify the power possessed by our betters. In this case, however, Marlow does not recognize his rival as, at least in part, himself, the childish ego whose delusions of grandeur he wishes to experience again. And, as is always the case in any quest for origins, Marlow's will only bring him face to face with his own deathly belatedness, the fate of all fathers.

Marlow fails to recognize that the originary world he seeks does not exist except as the construction of his own belated culture. What he finds in the jungle is the confirmation of the forgotten self that he had already projected into it, a self determined in part by the Western assurance that its own forms must be the model of humanness, the culmination of an inscribed natural intention. Marlow's Romantic quest for man's origin thus masks, as it fulfills, the primary narcissism of Western culture.

But what Marlow mystifies, his narrative strategies reveal. The symbol of the self that is projected outward must always be read as a token of the anxious desire that prompts its construction: a desire to humanize a world that threatens to expose the contingency of the human. As a subject, Marlow comes into being by resisting the authority of an other that he thinks threatens to master him. However, his resistance effectively ensures that his freedom from the other will reproduce the form of the authority he seeks to escape. As the other's source in the subject's anxiety is disguised, it takes on the rigid authority of a natural truth. The dark undifferentiated oblivion of the existential abyss that Marlow thinks he has encountered ceases to threaten once it is named *the heart:* then it becomes the meaningful origin, the center, the wellspring of a life that is significant because of its conscious engagement with that heart.

Nature's Text

Marlow's description of the jungle provides some of the clearest evidence of his motivated repression and revision of the facts of his journey:

> Going up that river was like travelling back to the earliest beginnings of the world, when vegetation rioted on the earth and the big trees were kings. . . . There were moments when one's past came back to one . . . but it came in the shape of an unrestful and noisy dream, remembered with wonder amongst the overwhelming realities of this strange world of plants, and water, and silence. And this stillness of life did not in the least resemble a peace. It was the stillness of an implacable force brooding over an inscrutable intention. It looked at you with a vengeful aspect. (Conrad 35–36)

Despite his claims that this is a primal nature devoid of any vestige of the human, characterized precisely by its "overwhelming realities," Marlow unwillingly represents a personified world where vegetation "riots" and trees are the magisterial authorities of the natural "state." Even the absence of language or other sound in the jungle speaks of "an implacable force brooding over an inscrutable intention" that "looked at you with a vengeful aspect." The shift in pronoun, from the accurate "me" to the general "you," masks Marlow's revisionary representation of nature: he involves his audience in the experience he has mastered through his interpretation, displacing and thus universalizing his own anxiety to overcome it. And yet his words unfailingly undermine this performance of mastery: they expose not just his humanization of the scene but the motive for that humanization as the threat to his own significance posed by the oppressive growth of the jungle. Marlow's desire to provide an account of direct engagement with a nature untouched by culture or convention is thus thwarted, as that direct engagement itself has been thwarted, by the very language he must use to give the account. Since his language provides the terms by which he could conceive of this nature as culture's other, it inevitably reveals the textuality of perception itself.[13]

But Marlow's interpretive revision of the jungle reveals more than just the anxiety that prompts it. The interpretation itself invests in nature a particular, vengeful intention toward man. But the only objective intentionality one could ascribe to nature would be the life cycle itself in which the lives of individuals are subordinated to the preservation of the species and death is merely a means of ensuring the continuity of the process. This intentionality, were he to acknowledge it, would be understandably distressing to Marlow precisely because it denies him the elevated status, the difference from mere nature, that he is seeking.[14] It would reduce him to just another bit of organic matter, a transporter of DNA's protoplasmic home, ultimately no more significant than the fish or flower that will be subsumed by a process more powerful than itself. Thus, despite Marlow's insistence, nature's threat cannot be located in its possessing a particular attitude toward him: that acknowledgment of human difference is precisely the lack in the Other that must be obscured. It is nature's indifference to Marlow that so terrifies him.

Such indifference is precisely what Marlow represses in his representation of the jungle. More importantly, the representation achieves a reassuring recuperation of the human specificity nature has threatened. By revising the nature of that threat, Marlow also revises his status. If nature wishes to take revenge against him, then he must have committed some prior violation of its order. But the very capacity to do so would depend on his possessing a power akin to nature's: the power to differ from any other life-form, to resist the cycle's masterful reduction of him. According to Marlow, then, "man" comes into being as a criminal whose crime is his unnaturalness. In separating himself from the original unity with nature, he violates the order of the life cycle. Nature's desire for vengeance could only result from its recognition of that violation. In Marlow's view, humanness, or at least civilized humanness, occurs at the moment that the individual simultaneously discovers and repudiates his or her originary nature.

This is a seductive theory, certainly. But we must recall here the crucial contradiction in the reading of the jungle that makes this theory possible: the nature that founds the criminal specificity of the human is invented, not perceived—nature does not brood or accuse. And the invention is motivated by the subject's need to redeem his inevitably insignificant death. The nature that Marlow sets up as his own origin and then self-consciously repudiates is a text determined by his desire to account for nature's power; its dynamism cannot be literally commanded, but it can be translated into a system of signifiers that guarantees the challenged authority of the human.

A similar pattern of revisionary perception is at work in Marlow's characterization of the African natives as primal men.[15] Apparently uncivilized, uncultured, at one with the brooding force of nature, the natives exist prior to the act of criminal self-consciousness necessary to bring Marlow's "man" into being:

> The earth seemed unearthly . . . and the men were—No, they were not inhuman. Well, you know, that was the worst of it—this suspicion of their not being inhuman. . . . They howled and leaped, and spun, and made horrid faces; but what thrilled you was just the thought of their humanity—like yours—the thought of your remote kinship with this wild and passionate uproar. Ugly. Yes, it was ugly enough; but if you were man enough you would admit to yourself that there was in you just the faintest trace of a response to the terrible frankness of that noise. . . . What was there after all? Joy, fear, sorrow, devotion, valour, rage—who can tell?—but truth—truth stripped of its cloak of time. Let the fool gape and shudder—the man knows, and can look on without a wink. But he must at least be as much of a man as these on the shore. He must meet that truth with his own true stuff—with his own inborn strength. Principles? Principles won't do. . . . No; you want a deliberate belief. An appeal to me in this fiendish row—is there? Very well; I hear; I admit, but I have a voice too, and for good or evil mine is the speech that cannot be silenced. (Conrad 37–38)

As "prehistoric," the natives are "a black and incomprehensible frenzy" (Conrad 37), their sounds "a burst of yells," a howling, a "wild and passionate uproar," a "fiendish row." In their noisy but inscrutable furor, the natives would seem to be participating in some Dionysian ritual of rapturous self-effacement; or perhaps they have not yet achieved the individuation that would require effacing. Lacking the self-consciousness of civilized people, they are at one with the intentionality of nature. Though Marlow finds the dynamism of this display frightening and ugly, it is also appealing in what he imagines to be its directness. The inexplicable noise of the natives is "frank," even, somewhat abstractly "truth stripped of its cloak of time," the primal truth. The natives' appeal, that is, derives from Marlow's fantasy that they are an image of his own beginning, his own nature. The natives are a token of what the self once was and always is, in some essential sense. But though he finds his own truth in the natives' noise, Marlow's response is once again to *deny* that truth, to construct an alternative truth grounded in and thus determined by the one he is disclaiming: "I have a voice too, and for good or evil mine is the speech that cannot be silenced." The quality that distinguishes him from the natives is also that which binds him to them as his own origin: it is the voice that Marlow defines as the locus of the strange and criminal doubleness of human beings.

Once again, Marlow's discovery of his originary nature provokes the impulse to repudiate it. Acknowledging the voice to be what links him and the natives to a frenzied unity with the jungle, Marlow nevertheless makes that token of nature the source of his transforming power: he uses his voice to speak the "deliberate belief" that opposes the Dionysian scream of the Africans. The voice is thus what identifies him as natural, as possessing an origin or a necessary cause, but also what rescues him from bondage to the inevitable reductiveness of that origin. As Marlow defines it, his language is equivalent to the denaturalized voice and thus both source and signifier of his criminal unnaturalness. Again, his nature is defined as his willful violation—his *negation*—of nature. The deliberate belief of the civilized person is the repudiation of his or her originary being, the voice of nature now made to speak something other than bondage to the jungle. Marlow's premeditated intention to believe, to have faith in his difference, is in fact the production, not the discovery, of his difference from the nature that both authors and threatens him.

Again, however, Marlow's theory of voice depends on significant misreadings of the events that provoke the theory's construction. The primal people whom he identifies as his own origin are *not* primal, a reality evident in Marlow's mention and strategic repression of the "rush walls, [and] peaked grass-roofs" he sees from the boat (Conrad 37). These vestiges of the natives' transformation of the jungle must also be evidence of their civilization, whose difference from Marlow's own permits his denial of it. More importantly, though, the natives' noise is not the call of the wild Marlow imagines it to be: it is a language that he does not understand. Only his arrogantly maintained ignorance of their language, their cultural specificity, allows Marlow to translate these sounds into the familiar and reassuring signifiers of his own culture—to read them as his own natural history.

Marlow's valorization of voice as the source of his double nature recalls Hegel's characterization of poetry as the most spiritual mode of artistic representation. For both Hegel and Marlow, language marks the most sophisticated cancellation of determinate nature: it preserves its relation to nature in its capacity as sound, and yet deforms and transcends that nature to make it speak human self-consciousness. "Man" commits the crime that destroys him in his original unconsciousness.[16] In destroying that self, however, his crime also brings him to consciousness of the law of his own being. Hurling nature into the abyss, man experiences nature's disintegration in his own psychic transformation. And what he discovers is that his terrible freedom to commit the inconceivable act of patricide is not freedom at all but the fulfillment of filial duty. Marlow represents this knowledge as the dreadful burden borne by "man," at least by the one who is "man enough" to recognize and admit his nature. This discovery, however, repeats the Romantic reconciliation of nature and the human, the impossibility of which was supposed to have generated the discovery in the first place. Indeed, the gesture that Kant initiates and that Hegel brings to systematic completion—the assurance that the apparent separation of "man" from nature guarantees his necessity as that which brings nature to spiritual being—is merely recapitulated in Marlow's existential vision. Which is to say, once again, that the implicit Romanticism of Western imperialism is merely disguised and repeated in Marlow's imaginative colonization of the jungle and natives of Africa.

The Real Other

But the Real challenge of Marlow's narrative is not Marlow himself, but Kurtz. The European's uncanny strangeness generates an anxiety that can only be mastered by a mythology. And the process by which Marlow constructs that myth repeats the strategies he employed in his readings of the jungle and the natives. Kurtz is another resistant other whose initial strangeness is finally redeemed by Marlow's interpretive mastery. There is, however, one crucial difference: as a representative of Western culture in the midst of the abominable incomprehensibility of Africa, Kurtz should function for Marlow as an object of unambivalent identification.

Indeed, for much of the narrative, Kurtz fulfills this function, though initially the similarity between the two men is suggested to Marlow by others. The chief accountant, for example, first mentions Kurtz as "a first class agent" and "a very remarkable person" who has been marked by the Company's administration to rise high in its ranks (Conrad 22). But it is the brickmaker who expresses what will become for Marlow the common bond between himself and Kurtz, the "prodigy" who is "an emissary of pity, and science, and progress, and devil knows what else" (Conrad 28). "We want," says the brickmaker, ironically repeating the language of unnamed others, "for the guidance of the cause entrusted to us by Europe, so to speak, higher intelligence, wide sympathies, a singleness of purpose . . . and so he comes here, a special being, as you ought to know" (28). Marlow's surprise at that final clause is relieved when the brickmaker comments accusingly "You are of the new gang—the gang of virtue. The same people who sent him specially also recommended you" (28). Marlow knows that his membership in this "gang of virtue" derives from his aunt's misrepresentation of him to the Company as one whose motives are essentially philanthropic. But though he had earlier mocked his aunt's sentimental delusions about the Company's activities in the Congo, Marlow now seems to have forgotten that one's reputation need not accurately reflect one's intentions or behavior. Thus, he internalizes what began as an externally imposed and indeed a mistaken identification of the two men.

When the boat finally arrives at its destination, it appears that Kurtz is already dead. Marlow's extreme disappointment derives from the loss of an opportunity to confront what he now believes was an image of himself. This image, however, is confined to a fantasy about Kurtz's voice: "I had never imagined him as doing, you know, but as discoursing. I didn't say to myself, 'Now I will never see him,' or 'Now I will never shake him by the hand,' but, 'Now I will never hear him.' The man presented himself as a voice" (Conrad 48). In fact, the man has not presented himself at all, but has been represented, first by the Company's employees, and then by Marlow's imaginative appropriation of the information he has received. His fascination with Kurtz's voice would seem to derive from two sources: one, the general stories of Kurtz's eloquence—Kurtz's identity as voice has been inscribed by the many other voices that have spoken of him—and the other, of course, Marlow's own conception of the voice. Having elaborated for himself a complex theory of human speech as the simultaneous origin and violation of "man's" nature, Marlow now transforms Kurtz into a token of his own psychology. If "man" is the denaturalized voice of speech, and Kurtz "present[s] himself as a voice," then Kurtz's speaking would have confirmed the validity of Marlow's own deliberate belief. If Kurtz could only be found, his very existence would guarantee the transcendent truth of Marlow's discoveries in the jungle.

When Kurtz is found, however, Marlow realizes his double's terrible difference from the anticipated image, and he must perform a quick revision of his earlier reading of Kurtz. Marlow decides that Kurtz has disintegrated because he has failed to use his voice properly. Instead of recognizing the inherent danger of the jungle and thus insisting upon his difference from it, Kurtz thought he could master his surroundings. Marlow quotes Kurtz's speech, stressing the latter's tendency to preface every substantive with the possessive pronoun: "You should have heard him say, 'My ivory.' Oh yes, I heard him. 'My Intended, my ivory, my station, my river, my—' everything belonged to him . . . but that was a trifle. The thing was to know what he belonged to, how many powers of darkness claimed him for their own" (Conrad 49). Kurtz's arrogant claims of ownership, Marlow says, reveal his failure to have adequately resisted the jungle's appeal to him: "The wilderness had found him out early, and had taken on him a terrible vengeance for the fantastic invasion. I think it had whispered to him things about himself which he did not know, things of which he had no conception till he took counsel with this great solitude—and the whisper had proved irresistibly fascinating" (Conrad 57).

This passage exposes the strategy—the negative transference—by which Marlow protects himself from the personal significance of Kurtz's degeneration. In Marlow's construction, Kurtz had experienced the same attraction to the Dionysian chaos of the primal world that Marlow faced. Failing, however, to recognize the vengeful intention of the jungle, misunderstanding the challenge posed by the primal world, Kurtz thought he could claim dominion over it by a simple assertion of ownership. Kurtz, that is, used his voice to claim his bond to the jungle rather than to repudiate its hold on him. The vengeance wreaked on him by the jungle thus becomes the fulfillment of Marlow's earlier prophecy about its power: the jungle whispers to Kurtz his remote kinship with itself, his own natural wildness, and it succeeds in mastering him because his culturally induced arrogance kept him from actively resisting the fascinating call of the wild.

Marlow's timely redemption of Kurtz's fate culminates in his interpretation of the dying man's final words. The "soul that knew no restraint, no faith, and no fear" (Conrad 66) ultimately achieves all three and thus asserts his humanity, but only at the moment of death. For Marlow, Kurtz's cry, the horror, establishes his moral victory over the forces that destroyed him, forces integral to anyone's nature:

> He had summed up—he had judged. "The horror!" He was a remarkable man. After all, this was the expression of some sort of belief; it had candour, it had conviction, it had a vibrating note of revolt in its whisper, it had the appalling face of a glimpsed truth—the strange commingling of desire and hate. . . . It was an affirmation, a moral victory paid for by innumerable defeats, by abominable terrors, by abominable satisfactions. But it was a victory. (Conrad 69–70)

The victory, however, would seem to be Marlow's rather than Kurtz's. It is his characterization of the cry that links it so clearly to his earlier account of the genesis of the deliberate belief. Marlow's deliberate belief in his difference from his origin involves a self-conscious acknowledgment of his kinship with the wild. This truth can only be met by his own true stuff—the vocal assertion, that is, of his rejection of that bond. Marlow says to the natives, "An appeal to me in this fiendish row—is there? Very well; I hear; I admit, but I have a voice too, and for good or evil, mine is the speech that cannot be silenced" (Conrad 38). According to Marlow, Kurtz's cry says much the same thing: it involves "some sort of belief," it has "candour" and "conviction," it has "a vibrating note of revolt in its whisper" to repudiate the "appalling face of a glimpsed truth." In Marlow's canny interpretive ploy, the terrifying implications of Kurtz's collapse are redeemed by a translation of those last words that reinstates Kurtz as Marlow's double, now more impressively like him than before. Kurtz is saved at the end because he finally does what Marlow has already done: he recognizes his own nature in the jungle and uses that knowledge as the basis for his judgment and the motive for his construction of a new nature. If Kurtz's end is a representation of what happens to one who fails to read as Marlow does, then Kurtz's death and redemption ultimately do affirm Marlow's vision and guarantee the self he has discovered through his education: Kurtz really *is* the subject who knows, and Marlow too can become master in his admiring repudiation of the other man's example.

Reading Kurtz as Marlow has read him, however, does not exhaust the signifying activity of Kurtz himself. Another interpretation of him will reveal one more example of the transferential effect structuring the novel. In addition to the various accounts of Kurtz's eloquence offered by other characters, we receive two examples of Kurtz's language. Both quotations are short, but they contain evidence of Kurtz's own self-constructing behavior in Africa. The manager first quotes Kurtz as having said that "Each station should be like a beacon on the road towards better things, a centre for trade, of course, but also for humanising, improving, instructing" (Conrad 34).[17] Later, Marlow cites Kurtz's report to the International Society for the Suppression of Savage Customs: the Europeans, Kurtz writes, "must necessarily appear to them [savages] in the nature of supernatural beings—we approach them with the might as of a deity. . . . By the simple exercise of our will we can exert a power for good practically unbounded" (50). The problem Kurtz's language poses is the contradiction between the philanthropic claims of his official writing and speaking, represented above, and the later scrawled addendum to the report, "Exterminate all the brutes!" (51).

But no such contradiction exists. Kurtz's initial altruism toward the natives is clearly based in his assumption of white supremacy: he has the power to instruct others because of his own superior knowledge; he can "humanise" the natives only if they are not yet human, only if he possesses the power of a god. In fact, the natives can only be loved with such altruistic fervor because their presumed inferiority provides countless occasions for Kurtz to manifest his own natural superiority. Altruism again masks the reality of the will to power, in this case manifested in Kurtz's enactment of a master/servant relation with the natives.

Once in the jungle, though, faced with the practical reality of his unbounded power, Kurtz must also have recognized the arbitrariness of such power. Kurtz had wanted to be a real god, had wanted to believe that his practical power over the natives was derived from and authorized by some *real* spiritual superiority to the natives. His capacity to act out the role, however, destroyed the illusion that it had a foundation in anything other than his own imagination and the willingness of the audience to accept his performance. The apparently absolute freedom he experiences in the jungle, therefore, must also signify the tenuousness of the cultural conventions that were supposed to grant his power spiritual authorization and meaning.

Kurtz's problem is that, in the jungle, able to do anything he can imagine, he loses his faith in the Law of the Symbolic, and the result is psychosis. This Law is instituted for each individual early in life. For the infant just entering language and socialization, each experience of no, of prohibition, is an arbitrary trauma. Ultimately, though, these meaningless experiences get held together for the child by what Lacan calls "the name of the father," the father function: though not capable of understanding what links these prohibitions to one another, the child nevertheless takes comfort from knowing that *someone,* the someone-supposed-to-know, *does* possess this mysterious knowledge. Someone is in control, holding this otherwise meaningless world together. Faith in the totality of the world, its internal coherence, is thus paradoxically a response to the initial and permanent gap in meaning that *negation* introduces to the child; that gap sustains the illusion guaranteeing a transcendent logic.

For Kurtz in the jungle, this father function has disappeared: there is no longer for him a subject-supposed-to-know authorizing his work in Africa because the natives have made it possible for Kurtz to become such a master himself. Kurtz's madness derives from his having encountered the Real: not in any banal sense of the reality of African or human evil, but in the Lacanian sense of the Real as the unassimilable, the absence at the heart of the symbolic. Indeed, Kurtz's status within the native community seems to derive from an African myth or practice of which Kurtz—and we—have no grasp, no understanding. To the extent that the natives have come to signify Kurtz's discovery of his own contingency—a contingency that takes the paradoxical form of apparent mastery—he must quite naturally want to destroy them. It is this unmissed encounter with the Real that he names *the horror.*

But it is Marlow's authority to assess the meaning of Kurtz's fate that should concern us here. And that authority does not seem to be undermined even by the lie Marlow tells the Intended. Rather, the lie further identifies him as repository of the truth, since he does not dispense it except in the complicated context of the narrative. The passage in which Marlow explains why he hates lies suggests again the maneuver by which he affirms the transcendent presence of the truth he does not tell: "You know I hate, detest, and can't bear a lie, not because I am straighter than the rest of us, but simply because it appalls me. There is a taint of death, a flavour of mortality in lies—which is exactly what I hate and detest in the world—what I want to forget. It makes me miserable and sick, like biting something rotten would do. Temperament, I suppose" (Conrad 29). Two conflicting lines of reasoning converge in this account. Despite explicit claims to the contrary, Marlow suggests that he does consider himself straighter than the rest of us: the lie appalls him because he is by temperament, by nature, a truth-teller. Yet his language suggests another reason for hating lies; he says there is a "taint of death" in lies, "which is exactly what I hate and detest in the world—what I want to forget." The desire to forget death would not seem to be peculiar to Marlow's temperament, but the remark suggests a desire to forget something else that Marlow does not mention: the motive for lying.

There are perhaps two such motives: either the truth is dangerous and must be masked for purposes of protection, or the truth is unknown, and thus anything one might say would share equal claim to validity, would be equally a lie. Despite their significant differences, however, both motives share a common consequence: however effective a lie might be in convincing others, it remains a problem for the teller. The lie is an attempt at linguistic mastery that always remains a sign of the speaker's fundamental weakness, vulnerability, or limitation; and we are taught early on to detest evidence of our limitations.

Curiously, though, Marlow's lie to the Intended seems to escape this inevitable signification of limitation. His explicit motive for lying is a desire to protect not himself but the grieving fiancée, to leave her the solace of her mystified memory of Kurtz. As such, Marlow presents his lie as a kind of self-sacrifice: he gives up his own passion for truth to protect another. He suffers the painful consequence of the taint of mortality to preserve the saving delusions of the Intended. But in this clearly philanthropic gesture, Marlow also asserts his superiority over another. In fact, Marlow's altruistic act toward the Intended recapitulates Kurtz's inscription of the natives as objective other to his own subjectivity; it further suggests that our narrator's representations of women throughout the novel have functioned in much the same way as his representations of the other figures of otherness—the jungle, the Africans, and Kurtz.[18]

The context of the lie further demonstrates this recapitulation. As Marlow waits for the Intended in her drawing room, he notes that "The tall marble fireplace had a cold and monumental whiteness. A grand piano stood massively in a corner; with dark gleams on the flat surfaces like a sombre and polished sarcophagus" (Conrad 72). The unmentioned ivory of the piano keys, simultaneously alluded to and elided in the mention of the *marble's* whiteness and the *piano's* darkness, suggests again the mystified conflation of the economic and aesthetic missions of imperialism. Music, Schopenhauer's ideal of the transcendent, intransitive art, is here unconsciously, even resistantly, revealed to be the product of Kurtz's economically motivated plunder of Africa, a plunder not unlike Marlow's imaginative dismemberment of the jungle. The piano's resemblance to a sarcophagus suggests as well the *ressentiment* implicit in Western aestheticism: the idealist mystification of the will to power results in the literally flesh-eating brutality of political colonization.

For Marlow, the lie is both redeemed and redemptive because of its philanthropy. Its effect, however, is to confer on Marlow a specific identity as the one who possesses the truth, the one who knows: about Kurtz, about the jungle, about the endangered capacity of social conventions to hold back and master the power of the dark origin. The lie, as negation of the truth, will continually remind Marlow and his initiated audience of the truth he once denied. Indeed, it is the *denial* of the truth that marks it so clearly as true, just as it is the detestable threat of death that grants life its tragic significance. In this sense, Marlow does not acknowledge his own contingency at all; he represses and redeems it by turning his journey into a source of privileged authority, an authority modeled transferentially precisely on those whose delusions he has previously mocked or villified.

If such is the case, then the very capacity of this narrative to speak a truth depends on its production of a threatening obstacle to that speaking, just as the son's eventual achievement of authority requires the presence of the simultaneously threatening and promising paternal obstruction. And if the truth must be repressed in order to exist, to achieve presence as the denied or deferred other of that which can be spoken, then the Real heart of darkness in this novel would seem to be its language: it is in language that the repeatedly missed encounter with the Real occurs, which may account for why Marlow has to tell this story in order to make sense of—that is, miss the encounter with—his experiences in Africa. What, other than the story, is capable of authoring the significant difference between the lie and the truth, between Marlow and the other whites in Africa, between words and the realities to which they defer? In its inevitably metaphorical naming of a "heart of darkness"—"nothing" now transformed into the distinguished thing—the story holds out the threatening promise of its own authorizing other, that of which it is merely and essentially the dangerous supplement.[19]

As such, the truth the narrative tells is about how a new generation of modernist existentialists emerges from the resistance to—and recapitulation of—Romanticism, still the philosophical subject-supposed-to-know for many readers and writers alike. In this early modernist text, that is, the negative transference is explicit: Marlow repudiates the institutional authority of the Company and the uncontrolled personal power of Kurtz, but he fails to see how his own self-construction repeats the form of both. Imagining himself to have rejected all transcendent figures of authority—god, culture, nature, even human nature—Marlow nevertheless resists the Real knowledge his experience makes available to him in the figure of Kurtz. Although he rejects the particulars of Kurtz's actions, considering them to be evidence of the European's immoral lack of restraint, what Marlow appropriates from Kurtz is the ideal of a self that has perceived the terrible truth of its own aloneness and then transformed that terror into the source of his individual authority, yet one more version of the master/servant relation at work in the determination of both individual subjectivity and philosophical system.

In the following chapter, on James's *The Wings of the Dove*, Milly Theale's dependence on an oedipal model of authority links her experience to Marlow's, despite the profoundly different social and material conditions in which the two journeys of consciousness are represented. However, the more important difference, for my purposes, lies in Milly's apparently greater *self*-consciousness of her own "choosing what is given," her acceptance of the model of authority she has inherited. Here, the drama lies in the young woman's seeming understanding of her determination by the past. But Milly's knowledge in fact merely displaces the oedipal determination into her *body* as a strategy for disguising a more frightening determination. Her acceptance of the inherited disease, her subsequent acts of love, permit her to resist understanding what the novel so powerfully demonstrates: how her *desire* has been constructed through the patriarchal model of mastery, and what the satisfaction of this desire will cost Milly and others.

Chapter 3

Deathly Bequests in *The Wings of the Dove*

> Oh yes, you are right in saying that in a manner he has got more out of me than I out of him—and yet you are wrong. I have got out of him that I know him as if I had made him—his nature, his culture, his race, his type, his *moeurs*, his mixture—whereas he knows (as a consequence of his own attitude) next to nothing about me. An individual so capable as I am of the uncanniest self-effacement in the active exercise of the passion of observation, always exposes himself a little to looking like a dupe—and he doesn't care a hang.
>
> —Henry James

The Paternal Legacy

When Merton Densher asks Kate Croy exactly what her father did to have become so "impossible," he is making a request for information. Her response, however, provides a lesson in the power of uncertainty: "I don't know—and I don't want to. I only know that years and years ago—when I was about fifteen—something or other happened that made him impossible. I mean impossible for the world at large first, and then, little by little, for mother."[1] To Kate's suggestion that he can find out for himself if he really wants to know, Densher replies tactfully, "I wouldn't find out for the world, and I'd rather lose my tongue than put a question" (James, *Wings* 57). The young man's willingness to accept Lionel Croy's impossibility on such vague grounds as Kate can give him suggests his faith in her, but it also reveals his own social sophistication and moral refinement: he trusts the legitimacy of Croy's social condition, assumes a correspondence between that condition and the unknown truth, and refuses to engage in any ignoble search for gossipy details.

But Densher's wish to know the truth, even if admirably sublimated here, suggests the generally ambiguous and disorienting effect of secrets in Henry James's fiction. On the one hand, we may often feel as intensely as James's characters do a desire to know the simple facts—what Mrs. Newsom's company manufactures, what Vereker's figure is, what Maisie knows, or what Lionel Croy did. At the same time, however, we may also feel embarrassed by this desire, fearing it to be a sign of vulgar literal-mindedness. Since most of the secrets in James involve the violation of a social propriety—a petty crime, an illicit relationship—to require the specifics is to expose oneself as unaware of the general aesthetics of social order. To need to know the facts is to refuse the opportunity that a mystery offers, the chance to assert one's civil sophistication by analogically inferring its solution.

Perhaps this opportunity accounts for much of secrecy's power in James. For while Kate appreciates Densher's delicacy, she nevertheless identifies her father's mysterious dishonor as a treasured possession: "Then she sounded for him, but more deeply than ever yet, her note of proud, still pessimism. 'How can such a thing as that not be the great thing in one's life?'" (*Wings* 57). The effect of this on Densher is marked: he gives her "one of his long looks, and she took it to its deepest, its headiest dregs" (*Wings* 57–58). In this passage, the exchange of the secret constitutes a kind of mutual seduction: Kate makes Densher the gift of (non)knowledge, of a literal absence, really, and he in turn mirrors back to her her own appealing strangeness.[2] Kate's attractiveness for Densher, that is, derives in great part from his awareness that she possesses a secret depth, a layer of the illicit hidden beneath her remarkable self-possession and propriety. Indeed, the number of secrets that enter into the relation of the lovers encourages their formation of an elite and private community.[3] And as Kate is bound to her family by the secret of her father's crime, so does Densher become increasingly bound to Kate as the secrets they share proliferate.

Were Kate to know, after all, what her father's crime had been, it might prove to be a vulgar embarrassment. The ignorance that she passionately maintains, however, aggrandizes the disgrace and thus gives her otherwise accidental and unfortunate complicity in it potentially romantic consequences. For one thing, her father's secret gives Kate a sense of mission, the chance to dedicate herself to righting the order that he had upset, to reestablishing in her own life the honor that her father had sacrificed. In Kate's mind, Croy's offense has sullied the family name, cheapened its worth: but to perceive oneself as having fallen from grace is, luckily, to see grace itself as one's original and legitimate state. Without the crime and the restitution it makes possible, Kate would be merely the product of a vulgar family whose economic poverty adequately reflected its spiritual condition. In possession of the mysterious crime, however, Kate can imagine herself to be a victim of her father's temporary dissociation of herself from the honorable order she properly belongs to. As John Carlos Rowe has noted, Kate "is in quest of a fount for order and value that will revive her own history and provide her with an independent relation to the world"; she "longs to act in a salvatory manner."[4] Only her father's violation allows Kate to live as such a savior: only by locating that mission in her *father's* failure can she conceive of both her life and her purpose in life as deriving from the same paternal origin or fount.[5] Kate's relation to her father thus clearly manifests a negative transference: though she is very angry with him, she also locates all power in him. *He* has determined the family's fate, and to have power is in great part to *imitate* him, even if only by undoing, by negating, what he had previously done in his life.

The narrative gives this power an authorial dimension when it describes the literariness of the young woman's relation to her family history: "She hadn't given up yet, and the broken sentence, if she was the last word, would end with a sort of meaning. . . . It was the name, above all, she would take in hand—the precious name she so liked and that, in spite of the harm her wretched father had done it, was not yet past praying for. She loved it in fact the more tenderly for that bleeding wound" (*Wings* 22–23). Conceiving of her history as a broken sentence, a garbled and incomplete syntactical error, Kate can identify herself simultaneously as a subject in the already-existing familial predication and as the new author who will bring that predication to its proper conclusion. It is the name, after all, that Kate will take in hand, as any new author appropriates his or her inherited linguistic material to inscribe a new and authoritative story.

The name thus becomes an incarnation of Kate's task: as a patriarchal bequest (like the inherited shame), it speaks Kate's bondage to her father, her predecessor; but as a signifier, it simultaneously provides her with the material by which she can aggressively script her own difference from the bestower of that "bleeding wound." The name is for Kate a source of her potential freedom from the paternal failure, which is simply to say that Kate's capacity to be better than her father requires his failure. Thus, Kate must preserve her father's mystery because it bestows on her the ennobling identity as redemptive author of the family history; it is "the great thing" in her life, as the precursor's inadequacy must always be both the motive for and the origin of the young writer's triumphant modernity. And to switch roles, as Kate does here, from passive "grammatical" subject, subject to the dangerous whims of the failed father, to her new and powerful position as self-conscious author, is to transform impotence into authority. To represent her intention as the reinscription of some lost original intention is to become her own father.

The convergence of these authorial and genealogical metaphors begins to suggest more about secrets in James: though ostensibly the violation of some propriety that must remain hidden as protection of the social order, the Real secret may well be the absence of any proper or absolute authority that founds the social proprieties.[6] The mystery of her father's action makes Kate's authorial self-conception possible; analogously, it is perhaps the phenomenon of the secret, among others, that preserves cultural authority by simultaneously preserving central ambiguities, the fine line that distinguishes the acceptable from the impossible, the scripting author from the inscribed subject.

We have already seen one example of how a mystery functions to direct the behavior of an individual: Kate's family secret binds her to the father she would like to repudiate, but whose repudiation is impossible since she shares with him his name. By making that mark of shame something to be loved and redeemed, Kate turns her father's natural authority over her into the source of her own personal power, what she imagines to be her self-possession, obscuring the fact that it is necessarily an imitation of his power over her. But Kate's secret also becomes the source of her authority over another: Densher, whose life lacks the significant drama of Kate's, submits to her inscription of him in the plan to exploit Milly Theale, thereby enjoying for himself the possession of a compelling secret knowledge, as well as the authority that attends such knowledge.[7] If possessing a secret is the way to become a master (by making another a servant), then Kate's situation becomes clearer: she ensures her father's continued authority over her by devoting her life to the redemption of his failure, but, in compensation, she models her mastery over Densher on her father's example.

As I have already suggested, the secret's double bind does not operate only within the James text, as one of its themes; it is as well a strategy of James's authority over his readers. To give oneself up to James's fiction is, after all, a potentially unflattering experience: wanting to know the truth is to risk feeling exposed at the writer's hands. To avoid such unmasking, readers may be as willing as many of James's characters are to accept their determination by the mystery they can't resolve but can only exploit. Readers may be willing to work, as both Kate and Densher do, toward a further proliferation of the secret in order to achieve some power over others: they may make of the writer's domination of them the model of a displaced revenge against others. Readers, that is, may become critics.

The Master Lesson

In a critical piece written in 1907, after the publication of the three great works that would ensure his status as "the Master," Henry James paid tribute to another master with his essay on *The Tempest*.[8] But this essay is a strange and disconcerting one. It begins with a general attack on the bulk of the play's criticism, but then, rather than articulate the truths that previous critics have failed to reveal, James works hard to undermine any sense of certainty about Shakespeare's final composition. He works, in short, to produce a mystery.

James begins by insisting that any reader of Shakespeare must experience confusion above all else: the "effect of the Plays and Poems," he says, is "to mock our persistent ignorance of so many of the conditions of their birth" (297). But it is most of all in *The Tempest*, he claims, that uncertainties "hover before us in their most tormenting form" to leave us "baffled and exasperated" (297). Since most criticism fails to pay proper tribute to the play—this admission of bewilderment—James's intention is corrective: he characterizes its astute reader as baffled, confused, mocked, ignorant, rueful, resigned, tormented, and tortured.

If confusion is to be the mark by which we identify the intelligent reader of Shakespeare, then clearly we must all wish to be confused. Yet James also insists that this state must be overcome since it is detrimental to our proper appreciation of the play. The understanding that has been denied us, however, is not essentially aesthetic: it is a knowledge of Shakespeare the man. To appreciate the work, James claims, we must get as "generally near" the man as possible; to understand the offspring, we must know the conditions of its birth, or recognize its father. We must discover the *intention* that was ultimately fulfilled by the play's production.

The problem, though, is that the known facts of Shakespeare's life do not adequately explain how he could write a play like *The Tempest*. Indeed, says James, the "recorded circumstances" of Shakespeare's life "are only not supremely vulgar because they are supremely dim and few; in which character they but mock, and as if all consciously, as I have said, at our unrest" ("The Tempest" 310).[9] The very dimness of these facts implies for James that Shakespeare has purposely, mockingly, withheld something from us. After all, Shakespeare's powers declined, James asserts, only because he willed that they should: "Prospero has simply waited, to cast his magic ring into the sea, till the jewel set in it shall have begun to burn as never before," and the effect of this mysterious decision is to produce a "complete rupture, for our understanding, between the Poet and the Man" ("The Tempest" 305–6).

But the mystery is not so insoluble as James here implies; the solution inheres in the mystery's consequences. The effect of Shakespeare's willful withdrawal of himself, both literally, in his refusal to write again after *The Tempest,* and figuratively, in his art's refusal to reveal the man, is the writer's *power* over his reader, his possession of something the reader wishes to have. Who, James wonders, incensed at the affront to logic, would willfully silence himself at the height of his powers, powers unequaled by any predecessor? Who indeed, but the Father of psychoanalytic fame, the one without predecessor, who is, for the child imagining him, the incarnation of the Law and the impediment to the child's achievement of his or her own desire?

In this context, the "torture" Shakespeare's reader suffers is explicable as a manifestation of the oedipal drama: the father, unable to satisfy his own desire directly, does so indirectly by evoking it in another; or more specifically, by inscribing himself as the simultaneous object of and obstacle to the other's desire. I find support for this reading in James's account of the tantalizingly indirect presence of Shakespeare the man in his art: "The man everywhere, in Shakespeare's work, is so effectually locked up and imprisoned in the artist that we but hover at the base of thick walls for a sense of him . . . " ("The Tempest" 300). The artist is "amused with himself, that is with his art, with his power, with his theme"—but his art, his power, his theme, indeed he himself (all effectively synonymous in this parallel construction), also all apparently serve the same end: the refusal of the man. The play's art is thus its *seduction* of the reader, a dispossession effected by the play's promise of a hidden reserve whose presence can only be inferred from its being withheld.[10]

But in what does this seductive reserve consist? For James, *The Tempest* represents "the momentous conjunction taking place for the poet . . . between his human curiosity and his aesthetic passion. Then, if he happens to have been, all his career . . . the victim and slave of the former, he yields, by way of a change, to the impulse of allowing the latter . . . the upper hand" ("The Tempest" 301). Shakespeare's aesthetic power has already been linked to his capacity to confuse and torment his reader, to provoke in an other a desire for knowledge. Now, James suggests that the artist's own human curiosity about others became, through a transformation that he defines only as "a change" but that we might more specifically identify as an *imitation*, his passion to become the object of someone else's curiosity. Knowing, that is, how his own desires are evoked by the apparent reserve of others, the artist makes this self-consciousness serve his own will to power.

To become the consummate artist of *The Tempest* is to turn oneself into the sought-for object of value, a turn James says is made possible by the artist's sinking "into . . . the lucid stillness of his style" in a "plunge" that effects a mysterious and transformative "sea-change" ("The Tempest" 300–301); we should note here how directly James's analytic language derives from the play's themes and images. The play's style is thus one more means of Shakespeare's disguising and withholding his personal identity. But if the art of *The Tempest* is the refusal of the artist's humanity, it would appear to constitute as well a kind of suicide.[11]

James has now represented both the decision to stop writing and the artist's style itself as forms of suicide, means of the man's willfully removing himself from others.[12] But he also suggests that the writer hides himself *within* his subjects, the "old wives' tales" ("The Tempest" 304) that are merely *occasions* for the artist's deployment of the style that masks, veils, muffles, and perverts them: a subject, James says, is "Anything . . . that offered to sight an aperture of size large enough for expression and train to pass in and deploy themselves" ("The Tempest" 304). The Shakespearean subject is thus that which the artist hides with his style, but also that into which *he* enters to hide himself. This juxtaposition suggests that Shakespeare the artist functioned to hide Shakespeare the man twice: first within the play's subject and then behind the veil of style. Such burrowing implies the hidden presence of a hefty reserve.

The conditions of the play's composition, however, explain the motive for such deceptiveness: "concocted to meet a particular demand, that of the master of the King's revels . . . this, so far from interfering with the Poet's perception of a charming opportunity to taste for himself . . . the virtue of his skill, would have exceedingly favoured the happy case" ("The Tempest" 301). Despite, or maybe because of, the fact that the play was written under royal decree, according to the prescriptions of the King's representative, it lets the artist discover the extent of his personal power.[13] It is as if the artist's fulfillment of his imaginative potential—his achievement of mastery—actually required some paternal (indeed, imperial) impediment to his freedom.

In attributing to Shakespeare this motive for making a mystery of himself, James suggests a parallel between the work of the artist in *The Tempest* and his own work with regard to the maker of *The Tempest*. He points to the possibility that Shakespeare has become James's own subject, first to penetrate and then to disguise behind the veil of his own style. This identity is clearer toward the end of the essay when James criticizes those readers who deny the importance of understanding the man that Shakespeare was. Such a view, James says, "ignore[s] any impulse, in presence of Play or Sonnet (whatever vague stir behind either may momentarily act as provocation) to try for a lunge at the figured arras. In front of the tapestry sits the immitigably respectable person . . . while the undetermined figure, . . . who supremely interests us, remains as unseen of us as our Ariel . . . remains of the bewildered visitors" ("The Tempest" 306).

Again, we see the plays and sonnets characterized as hiding places for the provocatively stirring figure behind them. And a few pages later, James insists even more passionately on the need to establish a relation with that provoking creature behind the arras:

> How are we to arrive at a relation with the *object to be penetrated* if we are thus for ever met by a locked door flanked with a sentinel who merely invites us to take it for edifying? We take it ourselves for attaching—which is the very essence of mysteries. . . . An obscurity endured . . . one hour longer, than our necessity truly holds us to, strikes us but as an artificial spectre, a muffled object with waving arms, set up to keep appreciation down. ("The Tempest" 308; my emphasis)

As "the object to be penetrated," Shakespeare has become for James the Shakespearean "subject" par excellence: something to allow James's "penetration" and thus to muffle James himself as a potential subject of another's biographical interest, but also something to be further muffled by the veil of James's own mystifying style.

Perhaps this double muffling can help us account for the strange transformation undergone by the figure behind the arras. In the first passage, the figure who stirred provocatively behind his own veil was an object of veneration and fascination. Now, however, he has become "an artificial spectre, a muffled object with waving arms, set up to keep appreciation down." The significance of the hidden figure has shifted dramatically, as has "our" relation to him: no longer just interesting, or even attaching, he has become a trick, a diversion established to mislead us from the truth we seek more and more aggressively.

Readers willing to accept this trick, the "imposed view" of a necessary rupture between artist and man, nevertheless face an obstacle to their complacency. Such a distinction "exists only in the vision of those able to content themselves with arbitrary marks. A mark becomes arbitrary from the moment we have no authoritative sign of where to place it, no sign of higher warrant than that it smooths and simplifies the ground" ("The Tempest" 307). Earlier, James had described Shakespeare as accepting the "arbitrary marks" of the king's prescriptions only to transform them into the "sign" of his own authorship. Now, he is suggesting that we do the same thing with Shakespeare's bequest to us: turn the arbitrary marks of his obscurity from impediment to opportunity for our own assertion of mastery.

But the only way to manage this transformation is to solve the mystery of Shakespeare, an ambition that is becoming not just aggressive but downright hostile: "The figured tapestry, the long arras that hides [the man], is always there. . . . May it not then be but a question, for the fullness of time, of the finer weapon, the sharper point, the stronger arm, the more extended lunge?" ("The Tempest" 310). To avoid being infantilized ourselves, as critics of the past have been, we must take a more rebellious approach to our reading, one that will help us get at the man who hides himself. But if we can only touch the man indirectly, through the plays that are the figured tapestry hiding him, we must apparently sacrifice the plays to capture our prize. Even more disturbing: to plunge the point of one's critical sword through the arras is not just to destroy the tapestry. It is to get at the man only as Hamlet got at Polonius—by killing him.[14]

James has previously called the unilluminating facts of Shakespeare's life "dim ghosts" testifying inarticulately to the existence of a crime requiring solution and vengeance. Now, James becomes another of those ghosts, paradoxically most articulate as he announces the others' failure to direct our activity properly. In making Shakespeare's mysteriousness a crime against the reader, James directs critics of the future to retaliate by killing the hidden figure of the man, the source of our frustration. Yet the metaphor by which James gives this advice confuses it. In killing the man behind the arras, we take him for the king we sought to repudiate by our actions: we obscure whatever his real and potentially insignificant identity might have been. In our efforts to depose Claudius, we instead invest Polonius with the kingly authority we had sought for ourselves.

Through such actions, we would also fulfill what James implies has been Shakespeare's desire all along: to preserve his power over his readers by becoming the dead father of their desires. As James has chafed (and has worked to make us chafe) at his servitude to the master, now he appears to have caught on to the strategy by which Shakespeare metamorphosed his "human curiosity" into the "aesthetic passion" that would make him the object of another's desire. And in setting himself to the proliferation of the master's authority over others, James takes his metonymically displaced revenge for the crime Shakespeare committed against him.

James makes his analysis of Shakespeare both a tribute to and an imitation of the playwright's mastery of his pupil. The essay thus becomes a model of how one should read to preserve the authority of the author. But the author we read here is James; as his writing displaces that of the other master, announcing itself to be in direct line of patrilineal descent, James provides us with a seductive allegory of how to read *him*. However we choose to deal with the mystery of Shakespeare—through either infantile acceptance or adolescent aggression—we enact our bondage to his paternal authority. And since it is *James* who ensures our impotence to escape the master's dominion, it is also James who shares in his master's victory over us.[15]

James's account of *The Tempest* presents a paradigm of a culturally determined reading practice—a reading effect—that repeats both the promise and constraint inherent in the culture's model of subjectivity as deriving from the imitation of a prior master. According to this paradigm, the only way to achieve a significant identity is to claim it on the example of the patriarch, by doing to another what has been done to oneself, reenacting a new version of the master/servant relation. And James suggests that both men and women understand the possibility of authority in relation to the culturally determined oedipal model: women appear to be as much caught up in and therefore guilty of perpetuating the dynamic as men, as we saw in Kate's behavior and will see again in Milly Theale's. The culture, that is, preserves its own authority by offering acceptable outlets for each subject's will to power: it promises that each may earn the privilege of the parent if he or she follows the ordered terms of patriarchal law. In Lacan's account of the castration complex (which I will discuss in more detail in chap. 4), the mechanism of that appropriation and sublimation is revealed: "What analytic experience shows is that it is castration that governs desire. . . . Castration turns fantasy into that supple yet inexhaustible chain by which the arrest of the object-investment, which can hardly go beyond certain natural limits, takes on the transcendental function of ensuring the *jouissance* of the Other, which passes this chain onto me in the Law."[16] By delaying the satisfaction of his or her desire—temporarily renouncing it—in deference to the greater power of the master, the subject imagines that he or she will eventually be allowed to assume a rightful place in the chain of inherited authority.[17]

What James discovers and exploits in Shakespeare's final work, then, is a pattern of how authorial mastery can be achieved; in turning that pattern on us, his readers, he provides us with an allegory of how to read him. There is of course an alternative to entrapment in this double bind, an alternative James makes possible in his simultaneous *exploitation* and *exposure* of the authorial will to power. Instead of fashioning our reading on the example of James's explicit appreciation of *The Tempest,* we can question the secret as a device of that will. Such analysis requires that we recognize, as James does, the secret's origin in its effect—its production of another's desire—and not necessarily in some actually hidden value. But there is a certain sacrifice to be made in this kind of reading: if we give up our faith in the real existence of secret truths (like that of the father's mastery), we also lose our opportunity to exploit them for purposes of gaining authority over others and a sense of power in ourselves. It is as if the son were offered the chance to escape the oedipal struggle with his own father by acknowledging the dynamic's artificial conventionality, only to face as well the loss of the opportunity to win the battle by becoming father to another.

The difficulty of such a sacrifice is evinced by the fact that James himself, master of "the uncanniest self-effacement," nevertheless could not give up the model of selfhood he inherited both culturally and literarily. In his "Preface to *The Wings of the Dove,*" James remarked on the demands serial publication makes on the writer: "[W]hen not too blighting," he said, "they often operate as a tax on ingenuity—that ingenuity of the expert craftsman which likes to be taxed very much to the same tune to which a well-bred horse likes to be saddled."[18] And a few pages later in the Preface, remembering with some frustration his original intentions for the novel and his "failure" to have achieved those goals, James noted "Such cases are of course far from abnormal—so far from it that some acute mind ought surely to have worked out by this time the 'law' of the degree in which the artist's energy fairly depends on his fallibility. How much and how often, and in what connexions and with what almost infinite variety, must he be a dupe, that of his prime object, to be at all measurably a master, that of his actual substitute for it—or in other words at all appreciably to exist" ("Preface" 297). These comments should remind us of James's speculation that Shakespeare, too, found a liberating challenge to his artistry in the restrictions on his freedom posed by the King's representative. But the remarks also reveal that the artist's very existence depends on his encountering and then overcoming impediments to his authority. One must first serve the master if one is eventually to imitate and thus displace him.

Cause, Effect, and the Texts of Hysteria

> [I]f one wishes to deceive a man, what one presents to him is the painting of a veil, that is to say, something that incites him to ask what is behind it.
>
> —Lacan, *Four Fundamental Concepts*

The alternative that James suggests but does not fully exploit is the genealogical reversal that would locate the origin of something (in this case the secret) in its likely effect on others. Analyzing the historical production of the notion of the intention, Nietzsche discusses this paradox, arguing that prior to the modern age, "the value or disvalue of an action was derived from its consequences."[19] The inversion of such a view, in which the *origin* of an action determines its value, is, Nietzsche says, "the unconscious after-effect of the rule of aristocratic values and the faith in 'descent'" (*Beyond* 43–44). In this claim, Nietzsche makes explicit the culture's reliance on the patriarchal family and patrilineal descent as central metaphors for order in general; he also reveals the relation of patriarchy to aristocracy. If the father's intention determines the value of any offspring—literal or figurative child—that child in time becomes the successful or failed fulfillment of the intention. The child's identity is always derived, belated, secondary to the prior identity of the master-precursor.

In suggesting the basis and effects of the law of intention, Nietzsche further reveals the delusion the law depends on: the subject's faith in his capacity for self-conscious control over his intention, in his capacity to know himself. Analyzing the sentence "I think," Nietzsche says he finds "a whole series of daring assertions that would be difficult, perhaps impossible, to prove; for example, that it is *I* who think, that there must necessarily be something that thinks, that thinking is an activity and operation on the part of a being who is thought of as a cause . . . " (23; Nietzsche's emphasis). In his questioning of these assumptions, Nietzsche looks at the inadequacy of the "I" to stand for a true cause. Something thinks, but what? Can "I" control the thoughts that come into my consciousness, and if not, can "I" still claim to intend my actions? The "I," Nietzsche argues, is a symptom that allows us to live in ignorance of something else behind intention.

The orderly consequences of this delusion suggest its origin: the culture preserves its own authority over a subject by offering acceptable expressions of that subject's desire for freedom from the parent. We may conclude, then, as Nietzsche does, that it is the subject's authorial will to power that directs his conscious intention, but only as that will has been safely appropriated and channeled by the culture toward its proper manifestation. The will may be primal, but the subject is not: the causality of the will to power can only be expressed and therefore observed in its cultural manifestations, as signs of a prior authority.

This is precisely the dilemma that Marlow was faced with in *Heart of Darkness* and that James confronts in his reading of *The Tempest*. Clearly, the only means by which a subject in such a culture could hope to achieve any authority would be to claim it on the model of the patriarch. "He" must become the father to another offspring, even if he recognizes unconsciously his parent's inevitable determination of the desire or intention to become a parent in his own right. The subject can only achieve freedom by doing to another what has already been done to him or her—as Kate, understanding the authority of her father's secret, makes herself the rightful heir to his bequest by authoring the fawning Densher; as James, entrapped by his master, models the seduction of his readers on the example of his poetic predecessor.

I have already noted how Kate Croy and Merton Densher achieve their own authority at the expense of others: they make the apparent impediments to their freedom—Maud's economic seduction of Kate, Merton's lack of money and prospects—the very opportunities for apparently original self-assertion. But the dialectic of impotence and authority, secrecy and power, finds its clearest representation in *The Wings of the Dove* in the adventures of Milly Theale. Milly's illness—never named or even described except with regard to its ultimate consequence of her death—is perhaps the Jamesian mystery par excellence.

But Milly's death is not the only consequence of her disease: the heiress's sickness and dying have powerful effects on the lives and futures of her friends. It is, I believe, precisely in those effects, in Milly's unconscious anticipation of her illness's power over others, that we can discover the origin of the malady that kills her. But it is not just the other characters in the novel who are effected by their belief in Milly's illness. Readers have also apparently found ample reward for their faith in the deadly disease whose existence is supported by, I believe, very little textual evidence.

Part of that reward may be membership in the Jamesian community of believers, those whose knowledge does not depend on the vulgarly explicit piece of information. But in addition, of course, there is much extratextual evidence for believing that Milly is sick. We know, for example, that Milly Theale is modeled in great part on Minny Temple, James's beloved cousin who died tragically and very much against her will of the unmysterious disease tuberculosis. We know as well James's explicit comments about his intention for the novel in its Preface: the novel's central drama, he said, involved his heroine's concerted resistance to her fate, her "catastrophe determined in spite of oppositions. My young woman would *herself* be the opposition . . . " ("Preface" 290; James's emphasis). James intended, in short, that his heroine would really be dying of a real disease.[20]

But despite these clear announcements of clear intentions—Milly's to live and James's to kill her against her will—the novel does not quite, or merely, represent the plot its author planned. For just as there is much extratextual evidence for believing that Milly's illness is based on Minny Temple's tuberculosis, there is also evidence that James was familiar, in the person of his sister Alice, with the manifestations of psychosomatic illnesses in young American women. Jean Strouse's biography of Alice James provides ample demonstration throughout that James was remarkably aware of the causes and consequences of his sister's many illnesses. One of the most striking and poignant examples comes very early in Strouse's work, where she cites a letter that James wrote to Grace Norton in 1883, when Alice was almost thirty-five years old: "Try not to be ill," he counseled, "that is all; for in that there is a failure."[21] In fact, as Strouse notes, James actually wrote "future," though he no doubt clearly "intended" "failure." But again, despite conscious intentions, James's slip expressed a truth that both he and Alice no doubt knew by this time in their lives: the mental breakdowns she began to suffer at the age of nineteen did indeed become, if not her entire future, then an enormously powerful element of the life and identity she would possess for herself and others.[22]

Alice was not the only one who knew that being sick gave her power and a kind of moral superiority over others; Henry was also aware of this potentially seductive aspect of his sister's condition. Writing to his father in 1887, Henry sent Alice the message that the worse her health became, the greater Henry's concern for her: "only," Henry wrote, "if she takes that as an alleviation, she must not take it as an encouragement to sickliness" (Strouse 202). Here, Henry seems to recognize not just Alice's knowledge of her illnesses' effects on family relations, but also his and the family's participation in these exchanges: Alice's illnesses bound her to her family and bound them to her, love and guilt in this relation merely two sides of the same coin.

Perhaps the clearest indication of Henry's sympathetic understanding of Alice's illness occurs in one of his responses to her diary. Writing to William in 1894, two years after Alice's death, Henry says that the diary "puts before me what I was tremendously conscious of in her lifetime—that the extraordinary intensity of her will and personality really would have made the equal, the reciprocal life of a 'well' person—in the usual world—almost impossible to her—so that her disastrous, her tragic health was in a manner the only solution for her of the practical problem of life—as it suppressed the element of equality, reciprocity, etc." (Strouse 314). In acknowledging the practical usefulness of Alice's ill health, Henry registers his own conscious or unconscious knowledge of the origin and function of hysteria and other psychosomatic diseases suffered by so many people, particularly women, in the late nineteenth and early twentieth centuries.[23]

These observations about Alice James do not prove that James made Milly a simple version of his sister; rather, Alice's life and James's involvement in it suggest that, consciously or not, he knew a good deal about hysteria and other nervous disorders. I believe this knowledge inevitably made its way into his representation of the troubled young American woman Milly Theale. Whether he meant to or not, that is, James depicted an illness more confusing and less simply identifiable than the tuberculosis, cancer, or chlorosis that have been variously distinguished as Milly's killer.

Milly's Real Secret

The attention to Alice James's life should also make clear that I am not arguing that Milly has consciously invented her illness as a means to power over others: she does not, in my view, *pretend* to be dying. Her history, however, suggests that she has reasons, besides the existence of physical symptoms, for believing or even wishing herself to be ill. That this belief persists in spite of her doctor's contrary indications further suggests that Milly knows the potential benefits to be derived from illness: it will invest her with a certain authorial control over herself and those who surround her.[24]

She has good reasons for thinking so; Milly, we should remember, comes from a long line of dead people. The family history she recounts to Sir Luke is a chronicle of death and bereavement experienced many times over: "I'm a survivor—a survivor of a general wreck. You see . . . how that's to be taken into account—that everyone else *has* gone. When I was ten years old there were, with my father and mother, six of us. I'm all that's left. But they died . . . of different things. Still, there it is" (*Wings* 149; James's emphasis). There *it* is, Milly offers her doctor, as if this sad but vague account of deaths from different things nevertheless marks her as similarly doomed. Milly seems to think that she has inherited, along with her millions, her family's proclivity for dying.[25] The medical validity of this self-diagnosis is questionable, to say the least; it is made even less persuasive by the fact that her relatives have died, according to the narrator, of their "engagement" in a "high extravagance of speculation and dissipation" (*Wings* 113). They have apparently died, that is, of high living, something from which Milly does not seem to suffer.

There would not seem, then, to be anything particularly inheritable in Milly's family's fate, except Milly's sense that death itself is a family tradition from which she has so far been excluded. In her own words, Milly has been "left" by the others. This construction suggests the girl's interpretation of her relation to her family. Children frequently experience a parent's death as a kind of abandonment, punishment perhaps, for some wickedness. The death of an entire family, then, might feel to the survivor to be punishment for a very gross crime indeed—or to be an unfair punishment. Milly's survival appears to confuse her, evoking in her all the ambivalence that normally exists in any love relation, and even perhaps generating further ambivalence. She may feel, as she often appears to do, lucky to be alive, in love with life; but she may also experience anger and resentment at her isolation, the result of having been abandoned to an unrelated existence. Indeed, in her loneliness, Milly must occasionally feel what a power there is in leaving a loved one behind.[26]

To have been abandoned by those who should have cared for one is likely to produce anger and even a desire for revenge against the irresponsible loved ones; but to have derived great benefit from such abandonment, as Milly does, would perhaps make one feel guilty about the dead, as if one had unconsciously wished for the situation. How then to fulfill the seemingly mutually exclusive requirements of both revenge and atonement? Perhaps by means of the gradually increasing assurance that one is bound to lose everything, that one may not have it long.

This, I think, accurately describes the position Milly finds herself occupying in London. The genealogy of Milly's illness suggests both her double bind and the melancholic resolution of it. Her sickness begins as a vague misgiving Milly feels about her health during the period in which she quite naturally mourns her most recent familial losses. Only later does she elaborate that misgiving into the certainty that she is the recipient of a mortal family legacy—a mark of her descent from her forebears—that will fulfill several functions at once. By being sick, Milly punishes herself for surviving when no one else in her family did and simultaneously takes revenge on the irresponsible family by killing off the last member of the criminal clan. But since no relatives remain to experience the girl's abandonment of them, Milly's revenge risks becoming one more example of her own impotence. To fill the important role of the absent family, Milly makes her friends at Lancaster Gate serve as the substitute family who will witness and survive her own tragic death.

The complicated oppressiveness of Milly's isolation, the way it binds her in her own mind to death, is suggested by the changes that take place in her attitude toward her wealth, a sort of metonym for all the effects of having been left. Early in the novel, Milly appears relatively unconscious of her money, but such disregard seems to reflect more than mere naïveté about its social significance. Her fortune, again, has come because of death, and Milly may seek to repress that uncomfortable association. But her arrival in London makes such repression increasingly difficult, even impossible: her friends there continually speak of Milly's immense freedom, the combined effect of great wealth and no one with whom to share it.

Indeed, the education that Susan Shepherd provides for Milly, with the help of her London contacts, is all about the power of money. Susan is perhaps the first to think about Milly what the girl herself will later believe: that the American princess is effectively the offspring of a marriage between money and death. In the Alps, Susan remembers her first impressions of Milly: "She was alone, she was stricken, she was rich, and, in particular, she was strange . . . " (*Wings* 77). Even to the mystifying Susan, however, Milly's romantic strangeness is easily explicable as the result of her money: "if one were talking of the 'difference,' it was just this, this incomparably and nothing else, that when all was said and done most made it. . . . [T]he girl couldn't get away from her wealth" (*Wings* 85–86).

Educating Milly

At Lancaster Gate, the association of money and death is repeatedly brought home to Milly in the explicit or implicit responses of others to her. Kate's sense of Milly's remarkableness derives from the American girl's freedom, and Kate, given her own circumstances, could not help envying the history that had left Milly so much money along with "her black dress, her white face and her vivid hair as the mere last broken link" (*Wings* 113). Milly's white face and vivid hair, clear signifiers of her genetic connection to the dead, are accompanied by the other family legacies of black mourning dress and money. The troubling implications of the financial inheritance are confounded by the suggestion that money itself might have been a partial cause of the loved ones' dying, through their "high extravagance of speculation and dissipation." In Kate's reading of the situation, at least, Milly derives her freedom and power from what killed her family. And since Milly is pleased to "borrow from the handsome girl a sort of view of her state" (*Wings* 113), why wouldn't Milly also borrow from Kate the impression implicit in this representation: money is deadly?

Although Milly learns much from Kate, Maud Lowder also acts as an instructive figure for the American heiress. When Milly remarks to Susan, during a discussion of Maud's "taboo" on Merton Densher, "that they appeared all—every one they saw—to think tremendously of money," Susan points out ironically that "it came, as a subject for indifference, money did, easier to some people than to others . . . " (*Wings* 125). Comparing Milly's and Maud's attitudes toward money, Susan concludes that their difference derives from Milly's failure to have made a connection between her wealth and her will. Maud, on the other hand, "would impose her will, but her will would be only that a person or two shouldn't lose a benefit by not submitting if they could be made to submit. To Milly, . . . such far views couldn't be imputed" (*Wings* 125). Susan identifies here precisely the lesson Milly will eventually learn from Maud, a lesson that she has already begun to intuit from her family situation: money is a means of imposing one's will, in both senses, on others, of inscribing others in a plan of one's own invention.

But Milly receives an education in something more than the power of money from her London friends; she learns equally about the power of mystery. The American girl is struck by the kindness of her new acquaintances, but such benevolence also becomes an indication of some troubling lack in herself. Milly recognizes that others see her as transparent, easily explicable, almost a cultural cliché. At Maud's first dinner party, for example, Milly feels as if Lord Mark has seen through her to reduce her, not very flatteringly, to a national stereotype. Milly may silently resist Lord Mark's certainty that he knows her, writing it off to his benighted arrogance, but she still wants, at least initially, to escape from the context in which she is so easily decipherable, so reducible: she imagines two options, "one to leave London again the first thing in the morning, the other to do nothing at all. Well, she would do nothing at all. . . . She gave herself up . . . " (*Wings* 104). Once again, in Milly's construction, power lies in leaving, as others have so powerfully left her, surrender, weakness, and giving up in remaining.

Although Milly appears to give herself up to the authority of those around her, she is nevertheless irritated by her own failure to be interesting. Even her self-consciously offered confession that Kate's kindness to her is a function of pity does not succeed in gaining Lord Mark's attention. Milly may think that she is "content to be easy" as a means of keeping herself "in abeyance" with the others; but to think so is to imagine herself as having something interesting to hide from them. She might therefore like to be recognized as thwarting their desire to know, except that they have no such desire. Suggesting to Lord Mark that she is naturally to be pitied is already a sign of Milly's wish to engage the curiosity of another; that her admission of vulnerability fails to have any effect rankles with her. All the more important to her, then, that Kate alone, "one of his own species," would have the power to interest Lord Mark by resisting his powers of categorization. All the more reason that Milly should begin to feel her interest in the other girl piqued.

When Susan tells Milly of the forbidden relation between Kate and Merton Densher, Milly feels she has located the source of Kate's compelling reserve, her secret association with an unknown other: "[I]t now came over [Milly] as in a clear cold wave that there was a possible account of their relations in which the quantity her new friend had told her might have figured as small, as smallest, beside the quantity she hadn't. . . . " (*Wings* 120). Milly's altered sense of her intimacy with Kate derives at least in part from the American girl's own interest in Densher; Milly had no doubt felt an attraction to him when they had met in America and now feels some sexual rivalry with Kate. But the enormous curiosity she shows in Densher at this moment seems also to result from his association with Kate. Densher is identified here as the source of *Kate's* strangeness—the strangeness Milly has felt as both a challenge to and an exposure of her own transparency.

Kate's now-revealed capacity to keep something of herself in hiding, beyond or beneath her public representation, has on Milly the effect of making her friend seem "other," "not wholly calculable" (*Wings* 122), the result of which is to evoke a powerful curiosity in others. Having experienced and meditated on this effect, Milly herself now begins to take a certain pleasure in hiding things from others. Particularly, keeping things from Kate becomes the "beginning of a new sort of fun" for Milly, conscious as she has now become of the presence of "a still sharper reason for interest in the handsome girl" (*Wings* 122).

But what Milly unconsciously makes of Kate's reserve, what really constitutes the source of her fun, is suggested in the American girl's analysis and judgment of her own behavior toward her friend and "her own possible betrayals" (*Wings* 122). In feeling guilty of some disloyalty to Kate, Milly by extension judges Kate's secrecy toward *her* as a similar sort of betrayal. Now, however, she can take her revenge, becoming as complicatedly split, as other, as Kate has been. Despite Milly's attempt to match Kate's reserve, though, to achieve a certain balance of power in the relationship, there is still a significant difference in the effects the two women have on one another, at least in Milly's view. Milly may possess the knowledge about Kate that her friend has kept from her, but Kate does not know this; consequently, Kate cannot appreciate the extent of Milly's own capacity to hide things, and Milly still feels a certain failure in her own constructed ambiguity to do its job.

At Matcham, however, Milly begins to find a way to compete with Kate on more equal terms. This discovery occurs just after another demonstration of Kate's ability to hold herself in abeyance: "Kate had . . . the extraordinary and attaching property of appearing at a given moment to show as a beautiful stranger, to cut her connections and lose her identity, letting the imagination for the time make what it would of them . . . " (*Wings* 132). Kate's ability to appear as a mysterious stranger, with her "connections" cut, is itself her most "attaching property," one that draws others to her in their desire to establish some relation with her. And this capacity again derives from Kate's secret attachment to Densher. Through Densher's marked absence from Kate's company, Kate herself becomes a sign of something more, something disguised or withheld. In Milly's estimation of this situation, power becomes the result of one's strange attachment to something hidden, one's membership in a secret relation.

Milly, on the other hand, feels at Matcham what she has consistently felt with her London friends: their desire and ability to fix her in some stable, even allegorical capacity. Milly can be cast in such roles because of her weakness; the quality that prompts others to want to take care of her also makes her a conveniently malleable tool of the others' will. With Maud, for example, Milly feels trapped within "the enveloping flap of a protective mantle, a shelter with the weight of an eastern carpet"; and she is well aware that "an eastern carpet, for wishing-purposes of one's own, was a thing to be on rather than under . . . " (*Wings* 134). She may also be aware that the protective impulses of her friends depend on her failure to have any wishes of her own. It is, however, precisely this vulnerability that Milly will eventually turn to her own authoritative advantage, putting to inventive use the others' preconceptions about her. The "eastern carpet" of manipulative pity will come to function for Milly as

James said the arras functioned for Shakespeare: the veil of the girl's "style" will produce a hidden depth, formulated in rebellious reaction to the "prescriptions" of those surrounding and directing Milly's circumstances in Europe.

Milly finds perhaps her most powerful model for this metamorphosis in the Bronzino portrait that Lord Mark intends to use as another way of reducing her to a type. And as the others—Maud, Lord Mark, and later, Kate—consistently try to "match" Milly at Match-em, she will turn the tables on them, matching their interpretive efforts with an aggressive twist of her own. During and following her vision of the portrait, Milly discovers a value in her apparent neediness: she will use it to achieve a self-possession that again depends on her ability to dispossess others. Announcing to Milly Lord Mark's protective intentions toward her, the painting he shows her suggests as well how she might exploit her apparent simplicity in the service of a new, more interesting duplicity. Looking at the portrait through tears, Milly sees

> [T]he face of a young woman, all magnificently drawn, down to the hands, and magnificently dressed; a face almost livid in hue, yet handsome in sadness and crowned with a mass of hair rolled back and high, that must, before fading with time, have had a family resemblance to her own. The lady in question . . . was a very great personage—only unaccompanied by a joy. And she was dead, dead, dead. Milly recognised her exactly in words that had nothing to do with her. "I shall never be better than this." (*Wings* 137)

Lord Mark's intention to place Milly, which she has previously resented even as she has surrendered to it, seems now to offer her an opportunity to position herself. But the position the painting makes available to Milly is significantly mysterious, like the painting itself: the portrait is both "strange and fair," suggesting to the girl her own potentially "fair" or attractive strangeness.[27]

The rich and magnificent lady of the painting bears a superficial "family resemblance" to Milly because of her hair color, but she also possesses a series of other "family" resemblances: the woman is rich and bejeweled, and also, importantly, "unaccompanied by a joy," "sad," and "dead, dead, dead." In the portrait, then, Milly seems to find a sort of "objective correlative" for her own state, much as she had found in Kate's relation to the absent Densher an objective locus for Kate's reserve. What the portrait makes explicit to Milly is the unexplained and thus compelling textual gap between the woman's obvious wealth and potential for joy and her equally obvious but unaccountable sadness. Rich, tragic, dead: the woman becomes an externalized representation, a figural mediation, of Milly's previously disjunct family bequests. The painting images a meaningful association among death, money, and mystery as the forms of authority to which Milly has continually felt herself helplessly subject. By means of the painting, that is, Milly experiences an apotheosis of self-identification, discovering how she may best appropriate and revise the systems of authority that have heretofore authored *her* as a helpless victim. Through her transferential cathexis onto the woman in the painting, she will assume the guise of a compelling ambiguity to make her own disconnected legacies into the supremely logical mystery of the rich and doomed heiress of all the ages.

The comment by which Milly recognizes her relation to the painted woman is her first explicit exploitation of the portrait's lesson. She may of course mean that *this,* vague word, is the most she could ever hope to achieve, despite her best efforts to do better: certainly, Milly's friends and most of her readers interpret her meaning thus, in which case the *this* refers to the painted woman's *failure* to use her rich potential to redeem or escape her own suffering and death. It thus refers to Milly's victimization by forces beyond her control. But Milly may mean something quite different. If the painting has given her a clue as to how she can exploit her own apparent simplicity, she would have no need to be "better than this," than she is now. The woman's fascinating combination of wealth and tragedy, her suggestion of doomed potential and wasted future, has pictured to Milly the very apotheosis of the authority she wishes to exert over others.

In the exchange with Kate immediately following this episode, the portrait successfully directs Milly's new manner. Through her behavior, Milly produces an ambiguity that provokes Kate's curious interpretation of her: "[Milly] was herself saying that she was afraid she must go now if Susie could be found; but she was sitting down on the nearest seat to say it" (*Wings* 139). This gap between word and deed provokes a question from Kate about Milly's health. The long passage following presents Milly's internal response. Because of its compelling relation to the language of James's essay on *The Tempest,* I will quote it at some length:

> Thus it was that, aloft there in the great gilded historic chamber and the presence of the pale personage on the wall, whose eyes all the while seemed engaged with her own, she found herself suddenly sunk in something quite intimate and humble and to which these grandeurs were strange enough witnesses. It had come up, in the form in which she had had to accept it, all suddenly, and nothing about it, at the same time, was more marked than that she had in a manner plunged into it to escape from something else. Something else, from her first vision of her friend's appearance three minutes before, had been present to her. . . . "Is it the way she looks to him?" she asked herself. . . . It wasn't a fault in Kate—nor in him assuredly; and she had a horror, being generous and tender, of treating either of them as if it had been. To Densher himself she couldn't make it up . . . but her secondary impulse was to make it up to Kate. She did so now with a strange soft energy. . . . (140)

Milly is sunk here, has plunged into something as an escape from something else: her repeated sense that the relation to Densher is the source of Kate's superiority to her. Now, Milly plunges into what she imagines is quite intimate and humble, the sense of her own weakness compared to Kate's strength. But the extent to which being sick functions as more than an escape from Kate's power—the extent to which it is the origin of Milly's power over Kate—becomes clear from the manner in which Milly tries to make up to Kate for any disloyalty of her own.

Milly's intention toward Kate is again ambiguously phrased. From the context of these meditations, it would appear that she wishes to atone to Kate for any ungenerous resentment of her relation to Densher. But "to make it up" also means to create a fiction of some kind, and Milly's way of atoning to Kate is precisely to fabricate a kind of mystery about herself. She manages, interestingly, to produce the mystery by appearing to confide in Kate, but her confidences are partial enough to be more confusing, more challenging, even "attaching" really, than edifying. Milly first asks Kate to help her deceive Susan, a strange request from the girl who always seems so open and frank. She then asks Kate to accompany her to Sir Luke Strett's office. Since Kate does not know who Sir Luke is, Milly must identify him as the "greatest of medical lights" (*Wings* 140). If Milly wished to keep an illness a secret, Kate's ignorance of Strett would provide her with the perfect opportunity to do so. But Milly does not make such use of her friend's ignorance. Nor does she confide more directly any particular fears about her health. Instead, Milly chooses to remain oblique, elliptical, suggestive—so provocative about her condition, in fact, that Kate asks with a certain impatience "What in the world is the matter with you?" "as if it had been a challenge really to produce something" (*Wings* 141). And what Milly produces to meet the challenge is a further mystification of her situation, something like the germ of a story that casts Milly as tragic heroine and Kate as helpful but secondary *ficelle*.

Kate wants to know how Milly could keep an illness from her friends, to which Milly replies, "Well, if I am [ill], it must of course finally come out. But I can go for a long time" (*Wings* 141). Suggesting that she can keep whatever "it" is "in" for a long time, Milly demonstrates her capacity for secrecy, her own possible otherness to what she seems. She also speaks "with her eyes again on her painted sister's—almost as if under their suggestion"—almost, that is, as if modeling herself on the painted origin: "That will be one of my advantages" she says of her ability to dissemble: "I think I could die without its being noticed" (*Wings* 141). Here, Milly translates her own seeming void, her ability to escape notice, into a powerful possession, rather than the absence it might have seemed to be. With the painting's assistance, Milly has discovered an effective means of deploying her apparent weakness for her own purposes: she will wear it, obviously, as something to be ineffectually disguised by her generous protection of her friends from a painful truth.

Kate's reaction to this new strangeness demonstrates the success of Milly's authorial strategies: Kate is visibly held by the American and finds her extraordinary, as Milly had earlier found Kate. When Kate remarks on the curious timing of Milly's confession, however, Milly's response is again provocative. "What a remarkable time to talk of such things!" Kate says, and Milly replies "Well, we won't talk, precisely": that is, we will be silent and deny the knowledge we now share, but also, perhaps, "we won't talk precisely"; we will speak only imprecisely, suggestively (*Wings* 141). Both readings acknowledge Milly's effective retaliation for Kate's provocative silence.

For the first time, Kate has a specific reason to pity Milly, but the reason is nevertheless specific only in its absence: Kate knows only that there is something she does not know about Milly, and whatever it is would apparently explain things. For the first time, Kate has to acknowledge a certain plenitude to Milly's character, evident in her ability to keep something of herself in abeyance. Milly has finally produced the curiosity about herself that she had not been able to achieve before. Since this success follows Milly's study of the painting, however, it seems to be a reproduction—an example of transference—rather than an original construction. Once again, the narrative demonstrates that authority derives from the ability to withhold something of oneself from others who then seek to possess what they believe they have been denied: knowledge of or identity with the master. Milly learned this first from her family and then from Kate's example.

The others thought they had seen through Milly to the original type of which she is only a copy: though free, she is ignorant; though rich, she is weak and without a will of her own. Now, the painting provides her with a model for turning her apparent simplicity into a powerful duplicity, if not multiplicity. Out of these discontinuities of her peculiarly American character, Milly will construct another more compelling reading of the gap between her opportunities and her impotence to make anything of them. The pity for herself that Milly had earlier ascribed to Kate in her conversation with Lord Mark has now become a fulfilled prophecy, the terms of which Milly controls.[28]

At Matcham, Milly more fully elaborates the role her friend will play in the ensuing drama. Kate wonders why she alone of Milly's companions has not been spared the torment of worry, assuring Milly that she will not be able to bear what Milly may have in store for her. In return, Milly offers an invitation, even a challenge to what she has already identified as Kate's "brutality": "'Oh yes, you will. . . . You'll pity me awfully, but you'll help me very much. And I absolutely trust you. So there we are.' . . . [Milly] had wanted to prove to herself that she didn't horribly blame her friend for any reserve; and what better proof could there be than this quite special confidence?" (*Wings* 142). But the special confidence Milly makes to prove her confidence in Kate functions more as an introduction to a confidence game than as a real confession: though most readers will eventually indict Kate, not just for her scheme to use Milly's illness to her own advantage but for the special viciousness of betraying Milly's touching faith in her, it is Milly who establishes here the terms for all future dealings between the two women. Milly takes possession of herself by dispossessing Kate, and she achieves this precisely by authoring *Kate's* assurance that she can control Milly. The pity of others is no longer the hateful exposure of her own weakness but an invited tribute to Milly's mastery of their desire.[29]

The increasingly strong associations of illness and authority are suggested by Milly's exchanges with and interpretations of Sir Luke. In her first brief meeting with the doctor, to which Kate accompanies her, Milly receives an immediate impression that he will be her friend; this identification reveals just as immediately Milly's expectation of her new acquaintance, since we remember that "friends" are by their very nature those who pity her. Milly is taken by the physician's face and decides that "he looked, to her fancy, half like a general and half like a bishop" (*Wings* 143). This appearance of conventional paternal authority encourages the faith Milly is already willing to have in her doctor. More importantly, though, the authority of Sir Luke's face makes *it*, and not necessarily him, the object of her new "relation." She does not listen to the doctor's speech for his counsel to her but rather looks to his visage, whose signifiers are conveniently vague enough to mean whatever Milly needs or expects them to mean.

Her decision to treat the doctor as a source of unspoken communication to her reveals how Milly will control his diagnosis; but it also manifests her desire to be a figure of mystery and reserve. The new relation is, in a mere ten minutes, fraught with secrecy and strangeness, "an absolute possession, a new resource altogether" that Milly carries with her "under her cloak, but dissimulated" when she, smiling, greets Kate again. She makes her intention to "withhold" Sir Luke from Kate explicit when she denies her friend membership in the privileged relation. When Kate asks when their next appointment with the doctor is, Milly withdraws the privilege she had previously granted her friend: "'Oh, dear thing, now that the ice is broken I shan't trouble *you* again'" (*Wings* 144; James's emphasis).[30] Ignorant of the actual state of Milly's health, Kate will from now on be forced to infer from indirect evidence how "bad," or rather, how "good," Milly is.

As readers, we too depend on Milly's "compromising" relation to Sir Luke for evidence of her illness, though we also get what Kate does not: the narrative's representation of Milly's private ruminations. It is still true, however, that the only evidence of Milly's illness comes to us from *her;* confirmation is notably absent from the exchanges between the doctor and patient. The first explicit suggestion that the doctor has found something comes from Milly's *anticipations, before* her second visit, of what the doctor will tell her. Instead of feeling discomfitted and insulted at the thought of being found out, as she has felt before, Milly now feels comforted at Strett's acuity because she expects it to "give her something firm to stand on. . . . It would be strange for the firmness to come, after all, from her learning in these agreeable conditions that she was in some way doomed; but above all it would prove how little she had hitherto had to hold her up" (*Wings* 146). Milly had felt oddly grateful at being "placed" by the tragically foreboding Bronzino because her painted "sister" had helped her to discover in her unrelatedness an identity of authoritative potential. Similarly, the threat of doom now promises to hold her up, to give her ground, precisely by binding her to her "queer" family history—by marking her, that is, as the legitimate offspring of her departed progenitors.[31]

Even the doctor's failure to substantiate Milly's presumption of doom, then, does not weaken her confidence in it. Because she had decided earlier that something besides Strett's speech would be her source of information, she can now discount his words and attend to what she imagines to be the doctor's silent communication, hidden between the lines of his innocuous comments. In the course of the interview, Milly has the impression that Strett is "letting her, almost making her, talk" (*Wings* 147), and from this, she speculates that he is interested "in other questions beside the question of what was the matter with her" (*Wings* 148). But despite the various implications of Strett's attention, one of which is that Sir Luke finds *in* Milly's talk evidence of what is the "matter with her," Milly reads a very particular diagnosis: "the desire to let the patient down easily. When that was the case the reason . . . could only be, too manifestly, pity; and when pity held up its tell-tale face . . . what was the inference but that the patient was bad. He might say what he would now . . . and in fact from this moment she only wanted him to say what he would" (*Wings* 148). The pleasure Milly had taken in thinking that the doctor would find her out seems here almost matched by her pleasure in feeling that he keeps something from her. Sir Luke's failure to name Milly's problem both convinces her of its magnitude and permits her to define it as she wishes.

But there is again a strategy motivating Milly's interpretation. The doctor's desire to keep something from her is a sign of his pity, and pity now becomes the challenge to the patient's acuity. Milly's clear, coherent, and comprehensive interpretation of Strett's interest in her suggests something like a *determination* to be ill, despite all possible obstacles. That determination, having at its command the "devilish" subtlety of "the suspected, the suspicious, the condemned"—of the paranoid—can even *enjoy* the challenges proferred by the doctor's saying "what he would" (*Wings* 148). Apparently, nothing Sir Luke could say to Milly now would convince her that she is not ill, since any contrary indication would have to be read as evidence of his flattering wish to "let her down easily."

If the doctor's disguised verdict gives Milly "something firm to stand on," it is perhaps because being sick places her, as the painting had, so directly in relation to the "queer little history" that she has before now experienced as a mere "wreck" of abandonment. After all, being "reduced . . . to her ultimate estate" is perhaps to be reduced to her familial essence (*Wings* 155). In the same way that Kate sees her father's crime as both the temporary disruption of the family "intention" and the source of her own role as redemptive author, so will Milly's illness direct her life from now on. The illness first of all puts Milly in her rightful place as the heiress of a particular family legacy: it establishes her in legitimate relation to the order from which she is otherwise excluded. Placing Milly in that direct line of descent, the illness also redeems her difference as the broken link in the otherwise solid chain. She can thus expect, as Kate does, to complete the familial predication with a logical conclusion, the "full stop" of her own "last word."

But the illness will further give Milly a way to avenge herself by proxy on her family. We have already seen how Milly's portent of doom invested her with a power to dispossess Kate (the same strategy had earlier been effective with Susan in the Swiss Alps). Now the relation Milly feels between death—manifested as absence, reserve, refusal, withholding—and power becomes even clearer. According to the terms of Milly's family history, the difference between leaving and living is the difference between (their) power and (her) impotence. Milly's experience in London further corroborates her faith in this opposition; it suggests that power derives from the capacity to keep something of oneself back, hidden, denied from the other. Through Kate's example, then, Milly learns what her new friends have in common with her lost family: all deploy their authority against her.

And through her own experiments with Kate, Milly also learns that she can protect herself from such authority by imitating Kate's manner. The possibility of even greater authority lies in the conjunction of the two related strategies—secrets and death: Milly's secret reserve, her private inheritance from the family, will be death itself. Milly's illness will eventually end in her complete withdrawal, protracted long enough to allow her to find or make the surrogate family to survive her. At that last moment, death transforms her from impotent heir of the will of the other to powerful author of her own "will."

The Master Lesson—Part 2

Milly's success as an author of the other(s) is evident in the control she exerts over the fates of her friends. But in addition to diverting Kate and Densher, Susan and Maud, from their own authorial intentions, Milly manages to divert her other readers to serve her own self-constructive ends.[32] Although readers have not always agreed on the character of Milly, they have by and large avoided attributing to her anything like maliciously manipulative behavior.[33] Indeed, most have been struck by Milly's very "niceness," finding in this characteristic either a serious flaw or James's fully conscious representation of virtue's victimization by the wicked world. A few have found Milly complicit in her own victimization by others.[34] If, however, Milly is the real author of her own illness and demise and therefore of the drama whose absent center she is, she is also the effective author of many of the critical accounts of her. In constructing herself as an ambiguous "text," Milly depends on her readers—those at Lancaster Gate, of course, but also the readers of the novel—to believe in the logic of the sign: she requires us, that is, to assume that the *appearance* of a mystery necessarily betokens the real existence of a hidden substance.[35] Since Milly knows, even if unconsciously, how her own desires have been authored by the text of her family's history, and by the example of Kate's ambiguity, she can direct her "aesthetic passion" to take over her "human curiosity"; a real secret need not necessarily underlie the reader's frustrated interpretive activity, nor his or her eventual mastery of the truth.

Finding pity and morbid interest in Sir Luke's manner, Milly can conveniently dismiss the doctor's explicit and repeated suggestions that her illness may not in fact exist. Too often, though, other readers follow Milly's lead in ignoring the doctor's information, despite the fact that at least some of his language is available to us. Sir Luke, we learn, had been "softly amused" at Milly's account of her own courage in the face of her doom. He suggests the reason for amusement in his explicit advice to the girl: "You've an excellent spirit; but don't try to bear more things than you need. . . . Hard things have come to you in youth, but you mustn't think life will be for you all hard things" (*Wings* 149). In fact, when Milly promises to do anything he orders, Strett makes clear that her case requires no special behavior: "You say you can do exactly as you like. Oblige me therefore by being so good as to do it" (*Wings* 151).

But Sir Luke also tells Milly what she and her readers must not hear if they wish to preserve the possibility of membership in the Jamesian cult of the acute: perhaps her troubles derive from her expectations of, even desire, even need for them. He suggests that Milly dramatizes her losses as a means of compensating for them: Milly makes the dead serve her by making her life serve the dead. In her powerful familial transference, she insists on identifying her own future as the necessary causal outcome of the past, a past that is not exactly her own except as she has appropriated it.

When Sir Luke demonstrates some slight impatience at Milly's persistent questioning of his "prescriptions," she asks, in an interesting non sequitur,

> "So you don't think I'm out of my mind?"
>
> "Perhaps that is," he smiled, "all that's the matter."
>
> She looked at him longer. "No, that's too good. Shall I, at any rate, suffer?"
>
> "Not a bit."

"And yet then live?"

"My dear young lady," said her distinguished friend, "isn't to 'live' exactly what I'm trying to persuade you to take the trouble to do?" (*Wings* 151)

That Milly even asks whether she might be "out of [her] mind" may indicate her unconscious understanding of the doctor's "message" to her. We should remember, though, an earlier suggestion that Milly's problem may be psychological: Susan had briefly entertained this possibility during the trip through the Alps, wondering whether Milly's vague restlessness and sense of foreboding might be an effect of the girl's possessing "one of the finer, one of the finest, one of the rarest—as she called it so that she might call it nothing worse—cases of American intensity," "some complicated drama of nerves" (*Wings* 82–83). For Susan, however, this explanation had to be rejected because it was too coarse, and perhaps also because it would impede her own performance in the romantic drama of the princess. To protect that opportunity, Susan displaced the threat of Milly's nerves, in language very similar to that James used in his reading of *The Tempest,* with "an explanation that remained a muffled and intangible form, but that, assuredly, should it take on sharpness, would explain everything and more than everything, would become instantly the light in which Milly was to be read" (*Wings* 83). So too must Milly now dismiss any possibility of hysterical illness with the curious comment, "that's too good."

A mere drama of nerves, even the most intense, would disrupt the various lines of descent that produce and bestow authority within this narrative: from her family to Milly, from Milly to Susan and Densher and the novel's readers. And that, of course, would be too bad. Following her exchange with the doctor, Milly thinks to herself, "It was perhaps superficially more striking that one could live if one would; but it was more appealing, insinuating, irresistible, in short, that one would live if one could" (*Wings* 156). Here, Milly sounds much like James himself, contemplating in his notebooks various plot possibilities and recognizing the superiority of one over another. In fulfillment of Susan's prophecy, then, the explanation provided by Milly's inheritance of a deadly family disease is not just muffled, but becomes the very process by which Milly muffles herself behind the protective arras of mystery. In so hiding, she also becomes the master of her various readers who will fulfill their desires as they fulfill Milly's, reading her in the light of her willful obscurity.

And Milly discovers that she can best fulfill her own intentions by appealing to those of her friends. Again, she takes pleasure in deception, recognizing it to be expected of her now, especially by Susan. In keeping with her newly discovered role—tragic and mysterious—Milly acts the part necessary to ensure Susan's continued service to her own plans: "If one could only be Byzantine—wasn't that what [Susan] insidiously led one on to sigh? Milly tried to oblige her—for it really placed Susan herself so handsomely to be Byzantine now" (*Wings* 156–57).

But if Susan provides Milly with one clear incentive to mystery making, the Lancaster Gate crowd provokes Milly's greatest achievements of reserve. Before the evening Milly spends alone with Kate, Maud asks Milly to discover if Merton Densher has returned from America. In response, Milly experiences renewed irritation at her own secondary importance in relation of Kate: "It pressed upon her then and there that she was still in a current determined, through her indifference, timidity, bravery, generosity . . . by others; that not she but the current acted, and that somebody else, always, was the keeper of the lock of the dam" (*Wings* 166).

Kate is particularly interesting this evening because she makes what amounts to a confession of her own potential danger to Milly. As she defines for her friend the workings of London society, she expresses a certain contempt for American squeamishness about society's monstrous requirements: "It might, the monster, Kate conceded, loom large for those born amid forms less developed and therefore no doubt less amusing; it might on some sides be a strange and dreadful monster, . . . but if one had to live with it one must . . . learn how . . . " (*Wings* 168). In educating Milly to the monster's operations, Kate "gave away publicly . . . Lancaster Gate and everything it contained . . . gave herself away most of all, and it was naturally what most contributed to her candour" (*Wings* 168). Informing Milly not just of the potential danger of British "society," Kate identifies herself as a specific threat, warning her friend, "Oh, you may very well loathe me yet!" (*Wings* 171). Milly is taken aback by Kate's frankness, as well she may be: it is evidence of the control Kate still imagines she has over Milly and thus also testimony to Milly's insubstantiality in her friend's eyes.

But Kate's warning also initiates a kind of contract between the two women insofar as it insists on Milly's responsibility for what may happen to her. If she refuses her friend's advice "to drop us while you can," Kate implies, Milly effectively agrees to participate in whatever "uses" of her may be made by the London crowd. By so warning Milly, giving her a chance to "escape," Kate also attempts to thwart her own "plans," however uncertain they may be at this time, much as she had earlier done with her father when she offered to give up Aunt Maud to go and live with him. If Milly could escape, so could Kate. Kate's offer to "rescue" Milly is thus, like her offer to her father, not so much an act of charity as one of self-defense against Kate's intuition of what she may become if she enters this world of money and power.

Although Kate may appear to be entirely conscious of both herself and the world in which she currently lives, her life with Maud has posed for her a series of difficult choices and uncomfortable discoveries: that "material things spoke to her" and that "She had a dire accessibility to pleasure from such sources" (*Wings* 35–36). Kate has felt her own situation as a double bind: she can either surrender the pleasure of material things, the choice she half-hoped her father would offer her, or she can make "a general surrender of everything . . . to Aunt Maud's looming 'personality' " (*Wings* 36). By deferring the choice between equally unpleasurable surrenders, Kate hopes somehow to discover a way of having everything, surrendering nothing. Though she acknowledges to Densher the "danger . . . of doing something base" in her efforts to play against Maud, she also insists "I shall sacrifice nobody and nothing, and that's just my situation, that I want and that I shall try for everything" (*Wings* 60). Kate imagines that she may somehow achieve everything—Maud's money and marriage to Densher—if she can only avoid being "stupid" and "vulgar"; she imagines, that is, that she can author her fate by recognizing the generic conventions within which she must operate and by accommodating her actions, if not her desires, to their demands. Thus, in warning Milly of what to expect at Kate's hands, Kate hopes she may absolve herself of any guilt over possible uses Milly may serve.[36]

But Milly's response to this warning is strategic: her own apparent surrender to Kate's power actually alters the terms of authority between the two. In a tone of what we may imagine to be bewildered hurt, Milly asks Kate "Why do you say such things to me?": "Kate had stopped before her, shining at her instantly with a softer brightness. Poor Milly hereby enjoying one of her views of how people, wincing oddly, were often touched by her. 'Because you're a dove.' With which she felt herself ever so delicately, so considerately, embraced . . . " (*Wings* 171). Milly evokes here the reaction she has come to expect from others. Her question reinforces what Kate has already assumed about Milly, what she has in fact been attempting to warn Milly about: that her virtuous and trusting weakness will make her a pawn of others. In responding to Kate's warning with further evidence of her faithful naiveté, Milly offers herself for a sacrifice *almost* of her own invention.

But if Kate, calling Milly a dove, names what she imagines to be the girl's loving sacrifice of herself to the needs of her friends, Milly apparently interprets her new identity differently. She takes the title from Kate as an inspiration, "accepting as the right one, while she caught her breath with relief, the name so given her. She met it on the instant as she would have met the revealed truth. . . . *That* was what was the matter with her. She was a dove. Oh, *wasn't* she?" (*Wings* 171; James's emphasis). This name is a "relief" for Milly perhaps because it dignifies her problem by giving it a romantic title, but also because it confirms Kate's mystified faith in her knowledge of Milly.

What it really means to be a dove, however, is complicated by Milly's later exchange with Maud when the older woman returns that evening. As Kate leaves the room, Milly and Maud face each other alone and, "in the tone of the fondest indulgence—almost, really, that of dove cooing to dove," engage in a series of lying exchanges with one another (*Wings* 172). With the greatest candor, Milly tells Maud what she does not believe to be true: that Densher has not returned. In fact, she had been sure of his arrival as soon as Kate had entered the room at the evening's start. Further, if being dovelike is something Milly shares, even momentarily, with Maud, then the dove is not the sweetly self-sacrificing creature Kate imagines it to be. Indeed, the barracuda-like Maud intends to sacrifice exactly nothing in her achievement of her desires. Whether or not she imagines Maud to be taken in by her lie, then, Milly's first act as "dove" is to work her own will in the guise of accommodating the other.[37]

To be a dove, then, is to strategically work one's will by seducing and then appropriating the desire of the other who remains convinced of his or her actual authority. Milly had earlier been unfavorably compared to Maud because she lacked a motive, a "will" to direct her understanding and her use of her wealth. In exploiting Kate's understanding of what it means to be the dove, Milly effectively matches and even outstrips Maud's authority: even Maud is not willing to die to ensure her control over others, as Milly does.

Jamesian Innocence and the Will to Power

A significant shift occurs at about the novel's middle to reflect both the method and the consequences of Milly's determination of her appropriation by the others. In place of direct representations of Milly, the narrative provides increasingly distanced and mediated accounts of her, almost exclusively with regard to her effect on others. But Milly's withdrawal seems less anguished than some have claimed; with regard to its practical consequences, at least, it figures the young woman's successful sublimation of her merely human curiosity to her authorial passion. Providing an account of Milly's history and education in London, the novel also represents the genealogy of her aesthetic intentions. Much as James described Shakespeare masterfully withdrawing himself within his subject and behind the provocative disguise of style, so does he show Milly continuing to withdraw further and further within the Byzantine context of her Venice palazzo and behind her equally Byzantine dissipation. Hiding herself from the characters whose interpretive activity she provokes, Milly increasingly effectively directs their interpretation of her, much as James withdraws Milly from any direct access we as readers might have to her. The illusion she gives of having succumbed to Kate's plan ultimately becomes her triumph over the others, and perhaps James's triumph too.

For one thing, the effect of Milly's strategic withdrawal is to make her, in the fullness of her absence, the object of others' discourse. Increasingly, that discourse involves a series of struggles, almost of a critical nature, among those who wish to make possession of Milly a source of *their* authority, not just over her but over others as well. In the terms Kate uses in Venice, Milly begins to behave as if she possessed a "hidden treasure," at which point "the beautiful little eloquence" of "Milly's avoidances" becomes the challenge the others must take up to inscribe their own stories.

The promise of Milly's illness is first of all Kate's freedom from Maud. But Milly is also a source of Kate's growing control over Densher, one of the means by which she both seduces and deflects his desire. However, as the success of Kate's plan seems surer, Densher grows resentful over his status as a mere "occasion" for the struggle of wills between Kate and Maud: "the drama . . . was between *them*, them quite preponderantly; with Merton Densher relegated to mere spectatorship, a paying place in front, and one of the most expensive" (*Wings* 205; James's emphasis). Ultimately, the unflattering implications of Densher's role in this drama motivate his struggle for power with Kate, in which he uses Kate's dependence on Milly to overcome his lover's sexual resistance to him.

Even before the Venice tryst, however, Densher is caught up, only half-unwillingly, in the struggles over Milly. During the first dinner party that Milly misses, Maud and Kate tease Densher about having invented the American heiress he had met in his travels before she entered London society: "He met, poor Densher, these inquiries as he could, listening with interest, yet with discomfort. . . . [T]hey were talking, or almost, as if he had publicly paragraphed a modest young lady" (*Wings* 205–6). Densher does not wish to take credit for the invention of Milly, apparently having little interest in the American, but he nevertheless defends himself against the jealous Susan's challenge to his authority. Offended at the suggestion that someone else might be responsible for her personal "find," Susan accuses Densher of misrepresenting his relation to Milly: "You know nothing, sir—but not the least little bit—about my friend" (*Wings* 207). When his authority is impugned, Densher responds with a claim to privileged knowledge: "Remember, Mrs. Stringham, that you weren't then present" (*Wings* 207). The struggle between Densher and Susan is finally resolved when the two settle on the mutually flattering characterization of Milly: "She's beautiful, but I don't say she's easy to know" (*Wings* 208). Thus, they both derive advantage from knowing her at all.

In Milly's illness, Susan also finds the chance to redeem the authority that had been threatened by London's insistent appropriation of Milly. From her meeting with Sir Luke, Susan gains the opportunity to save her young friend. Like Kate, Susan does not want to know the specifics of Milly's secret sickness, and, like Milly, she is impressed with the good doctor's interest in his American patient. But, as she tells Maud, "He says it isn't a case"; "'It isn't, at least,' Mrs. Stringham explained, 'the case she believed it to be . . . when, without my knowledge, she went to see him. She went because there was something she was afraid of, and he examined her thoroughly—he has made sure. She's wrong—she hasn't what she thought'" (*Wings* 245). The practical Maud wants more facts, but Susan insists she has none: "I asked nothing . . . I only took what he gave me" (*Wings* 245). What Susan takes from the doctor, however, generous vessel as she represents herself, is determined by her desire to make her limited knowledge into a kind of power over someone else—in this case Maud.

Out of the tragic possibilities of Milly's case, Susan makes her old friend and rival subservient to herself and her plan: that Milly must be made to be happy by marrying Densher. Susan, that is, uses Milly to seduce Maud, paying tribute to Maud's capacity for handling everyone. And Maud is quite naturally willing to serve Susan since doing so will eliminate the only obstacle to her own authority: Kate's relation to Densher. Thus the two women conclude their bargain, as Susan imagines Maud understands it: "I'll help you for Milly because if that comes off I shall be helped, by its doing so, for Kate" (*Wings* 249).

Although Maud is distressed that Milly should have, for her cure, to settle for the insignificant Densher, she consoles herself with the thought that "One lives for others" (*Wings* 251): sometimes, she grants, one must accommodate one's enterprise to the needs of others. In its ironic ambiguity, her statement is richly expressive of both the motives for and the mystifications of the behavior of all the novel's characters. Each finds his or her authority in the subjection of an other to his or her will in a version of the master/servant relation. One lives for others, that is, so that others may be living testimony to one's effective authority. In transforming the other's "arbitrary marks"—and the untransformed other must always seem arbitrary to the subject—into a token of the self's inventive "taste," one becomes the consummate artist: not victim but master of the prescriptions of a potentially overwhelming world.

But despite the others' well-considered intentions to use or to provide for Milly, her own authority remains remarkably intact. The others depend absolutely on her for the success of their plans, the achievement of their mastery; her apparent self-abnegation therefore ensures their subjugation to her symbolic proliferation. The novel gives us its clearest image of the critic's irritating and yet inspiring bondage to his master in the figure of the writer Merton Densher. Such enslavement as he suffers can only be redeemed and made to signify something other than a childish impotence when it becomes the occasion for and the source of his mastery of others. It is Densher who gains the most from the lesson of his master when he makes Milly's "sacrificial" death the model of his own revenge against Kate.

In the beginning of his affair with Kate, Densher had admired her talent for life; eventually, though, Kate's plan and the power it gives her threaten Densher. As Milly had worried about her own lack of will, her own failure to be interesting compared to Kate's prodigious powers, Densher also comes to see Kate's success not as something they share but rather as an aggression against himself. This menace becomes an occasion for partial mastery of his lover when he forces Kate's sexual "sacrifice" to him by threatening to withdraw from her plans. But his real revenge on Kate occurs after the apparent fulfillment of their mutual desire, Milly's conveniently early death and her bequest to Densher of a "stupendous" sum of money.

When Densher repudiates the money, refusing even to know its amount, Kate asks accusingly "Can you only do it by doing it blindly?" Her question implies that knowing the sum might tempt Densher to accept it, but there is no danger that this would happen. Densher has already decided that the only way to redeem his participation in the plot to seduce Milly is to derive no benefit from its success. Laurence Holland suggests that Densher's repudiation reflects his genuine love and compassion for the American. Although Kate tries to convince him that accepting the bequest would fulfill Milly's desire to help him, Holland argues, "Densher . . . feels that to take the money would be to complete his betrayal of what the money symbolizes. To take the dim reflection and soil it with his lips would betray the impassioned love it represents . . . " (326). But even if the desire to atone for his treatment of Milly were Densher's only motive for refusing her money, this act would hardly constitute the moral victory Holland holds it to be. Densher's refusal of the money is an attempt to disavow his complicity in Kate's scheme; thus, his "selfless" act still signifies only the repression, not the redemption, of his previous moral choices.

But Holland's mention of "what the money symbolizes" raises the important matter of the significance of inherited wealth in this novel. Such wealth, for Milly (and for Kate in a somewhat different way), has been represented as instituting the heir's submission to the will of the other. For Densher, accepting Milly's money would further require him to accept what he has been passionately struggling to resist: his subjection to Kate's will and his impotence to be anything but what Kate wants him to be. It might appear here that Densher chooses freedom when he rejects Kate's continued determination of him; but refusing the money does not exactly free him from Milly. Milly has modeled her bequest to Densher on the example of her family's "gift" to her, thus fulfilling her need for a survivor and a recipient of her benefaction. Offering Kate the money he refuses, Densher now repeats Milly's gesture: his "bequest" to Kate is thus a sign of her failure to have mastered him. Densher achieves authority here by simultaneously paying tribute to and imitating Milly's sacrifice.

In duplicating the terms of Milly's behavior, in which the self-sacrifice merely screens one's self-assertion, Densher's choice betokens James's general concern with the problem of innocence. The frequent doubling of generosity and aggression in his work suggests this writer's understanding of the desire, the will to power, that constitutes human love. The situation is a familiar one in James's fiction: characters motivated by the most compassionate and well-meaning impulses inadvertently entrap the objects of their good intentions by encouraging delusions of security, self-consciousness, and self-control. Ralph Touchett, for example, incapable of the active life Isabel Archer dreams of, secretly bequeathes her the money that should enable her to live freely, as he cannot. Ralph's fear and illness keep him from risking, and thus perhaps losing, his independence, so he uses his money to "author" Isabel as a metonymic extension of himself. He "invents" her, with her assistance of course, to cope with his own ambivalence: he can live vicariously through Isabel because her freedom is his gift to her. The gift, however, makes Isabel vulnerable to exploitation by Osmond and Madame Merle, and so Ralph's generosity to Isabel ends up inscribing her as the unconscious dupe of those who are more sophisticated. She becomes exactly the fool that Ralph feared he himself might have become. In generously allowing Isabel to live out her fantasy of freedom, therefore, Ralph unwittingly ensures that she will actually live out *his* fear of impotence.

Similarly, sacrificing herself to John Marcher's aestheticized retreat from life, May Bartram gives her friend the confirmation of his self-construction that he needs. But her sacrifice is not total: being Marcher's companion also gives May an identity and function, a passion, that she otherwise would not have. The relation may seem mutually satisfying and nonexploitative, except that May eventually comes to recognize that "the Beast" is a self-destructive delusion that keeps Marcher from involving himself with life, and with May.[38] Despite her awareness, though, May protects Marcher's faith, even in her final meeting with him. Her protection may reflect May's belief that Marcher must come to this consciousness himself (which he eventually does, during his visit to May's grave), or from her fear that the knowledge would come too late to do Marcher any good. Whatever her motives, however, May's protection effectively binds Marcher more thoroughly to his delusion. Preserving Marcher's ignorance may be both generous and exploitative: May saves her friend from the painful discovery that he has wasted his life, but in the process she also inscribes herself as the one who knows what he does not, the one with strength to bear the truth. Ensuring that Marcher's discovery of his delusion, if it comes at all, will include the knowledge of her sacrifice to him, May also avenges and redeems her own apparent slavishness.

As these two brief examples suggest, living in sacrificial service to another requires that one live at the *expense* of that other. The same master/servant opposition resides at the base of both philanthropic and exploitative relations, since both depend on the ideal of a subject in autonomous possession of his or her selfhood. But to prove one's self-possession, one must act in the world, find evidence of one's identity by effecting others: to be a master, one must produce the slave. To be a slave, however, paradoxically makes one *author* of the master, as Hegel pointed out. The same desire for authority that directs the obviously manipulative and dehumanizing behavior of a Kate Croy also informs the apparently generous behavior of a Ralph Touchett, a May Bartram, a Milly Theale.

The master/servant dynamic that characterizes Marlow's relations with those he meets in the African jungle James now locates at the heart of "civilized" society, determining the form of love between friends, lovers, children and parents, the living and the dead. And the persistence of the model of selfhood implicit in the dynamic ensures the perpetuation of the social structures and identities that characters sought to escape through their much vaunted self-consciousness. Kate loses Densher and remains bound to her aunt's authority, but worse (or better), she must also acknowledge her failure to "have [had] it all," to have sacrificed nothing in her striving for satisfaction. Densher loses both Kate and Milly and can only delude himself with fantasies that perhaps he really did love the dead girl. Milly, of course, loses everything.

What the narrative reveals is that both the self-assertion and the self-sacrifice are efforts to prove that the self exists with the power to make itself known by its influence on others. The subject who believes in a difference between the two simply finds one more path to confirmation of his or her identity. But the self we believe in and act as if we possess is as much a bequest, an inheritance from the dead, as Milly's millions. It thus binds us equally thoroughly to the will of the ones we imagine to be without predecessor. In Milly's positive transference onto her family, she apparently chooses the impotence that in fact has inscribed her very desires for power, authority, control. In the following discussion of *The Sun Also Rises,* we will see Jake Barnes's apparent acceptance of his imposed impotence effectively exploit and obscure the false binaries that the master/servant relation rests on.

Chapter 4

Lovers' Discourse in *The Sun Also Rises:* A Cock and Bull Story

> L——d! said my mother, what is all this story about?—A COCK and a BULL, said Yorick—And one of the best of its kind, I ever heard.
>
> —Laurence Sterne, *Tristram Shandy*

When Gertrude Stein called the group of expatriates in *The Sun Also Rises* "a lost generation," she identified the challenge this novel would continue to pose for its readers: how to make loss the source of some kind of gain. This challenge has not been particularly difficult to meet. Since the logical possibility of loss requires the prior existence of a presence or integrity, loss must also signify the possibility of recuperation. Critics have generally made the articulation of that second possibility their own imperative: whether this novel represents loss as personal or cultural—Jake Barnes's castration or the postwar disruption of national coherence—it does so to inscribe the promise of a particular kind of redemption.[1]

Leon F. Seltzer epitomizes the critical response to what he calls "the opportunity of impotence" in *The Sun Also Rises:*

> Impotence in *The Sun Also Rises* . . . describes, paradoxically, not man's deficiency but his amazing potentiality. For impotence can actually promote the scrupulously measured detachment that is itself the key to happiness—a happiness that can survive solely through the "distanced involvement" with reality. . . . By not "spending" almost the whole of his mental and emotional energies on a single love object, man may invest his abundant resources into wresting from reality its best possible bargain and, successful, satisfy his natural appetite for the infinite variety that life has—and has always had—to offer. Such are the prerequisites to human fulfillment.[2]

The paradox of impotence as Seltzer represents it would seem to be identical to the paradox of existential philosophy, whose influence on most readings of this novel is clear.[3] Like Seltzer, existentialism requires that the individual detach him or herself from the artificial constraints of external reality, embrace the terror of mortality, and thus discover that death is the author of freedom. By acknowledging the limits of his or her power to affect the world—limits figured by mortal contingency—the individual may paradoxically achieve a certain kind of authority over the self.[4] Impotence is thus prerequisite to human fulfillment because it provokes the individual to repudiate the false conventionality of the life of "bad faith" and to choose self-consciously "the fate that governs his own values" (Seltzer 10).

For all its posing as courageous realism, however, the existential project is a supremely romantic one that effectively returns "man" to the center of a humanistic universe. In locating the meaning of humanness in individual freedom and responsibility, existentialism divorces the subject from all forces of determination, except the inevitable death. All meaning is constituted by the individual; all the physical or material conditions of life are inadequate to define him or her. However, it is precisely this rejection of the materiality of existence that has led contemporary critics to locate existentialism's determination in the ideologies of traditional humanist idealism. The existentialist faces what he or she presumes to be the physical reality of death only to idealize it. In confronting the loss of absolute order to the world, existentialism constructs a new absolute—absolute negation. As Derrida has pointed out, "Negativity has always been determined by dialectics—that is to say, by metaphysics—as work in the service of the constitution of meaning."[5] The existential transvaluation of death's negativity renders existence not prior to essence, but the means to essence. Death is thus the foundation of existentialism's negative metaphysics, which Lacan argues "grasps negativity only within the limits of a self-sufficiency of consciousness which . . . links to the *méconnaissances* that constitute the ego, the illusion of autonomy to which it entrusts itself."[6]

Though it is true that Hemingway's novel incorporates the false dilemmas of existential philosophy—dilemmas that depend on a belief in the autonomous ego of Western idealism—it just as seriously subverts those dilemmas by revealing the romanticism that sustains them. This novel, perhaps even more clearly than *Heart of Darkness*, inscribes the existential redemption of death and impotence within a dynamic fundamental to Western culture: the masculine oedipal complex and its institution of what Lacan calls the dialectic of castration and desire.

In chapter 1, I suggested a similarity between Hegel's master/servant relation and Freud's theory of the oedipal complex. In chapter 2, I looked at the relation between the idealist version of Hegelian alienation and the existentialist transformation of that notion. Here, I would like to point out the striking parallels between the child's passing of the oedipal complex and the existentialist's response to death. As the child enters the alienating world of language, "he" is forced to identify himself symbolically, by means of the "I," and thus "loses" the illusion of autonomy produced by the mirror stage. To account for the loss of his apparently previously unified ego, the child must make an interpretive leap: he decides that the father has taken the mother away because he possesses something she does not—the phallus. The child thus interprets the father to rationalize the loss he cannot avenge or overcome, but also to redeem the potential arbitrariness of the father's greater physical power. It is this *méconnaissance* that will, through the phenomenon of the transference, continue to determine all the subject's future relations to cultural power structures. By symbolically castrating himself—displacing his desire for the mother into his identification with the father—the child ensures that he too may someday become a father: "What analytic experience shows is that . . . it is castration that governs desire. . . . Castration turns fantasy into that supple yet inexhaustible chain by which the arrest of the object-investment, which can hardly go beyond certain natural limits, takes on the transcendental function of ensuring the *jouissance* of the Other, which passes this chain onto me in the Law."[7] The deferral inherent in castration allows the subject to enter the Law of Fatherhood.

Similarly, the existentialist, faced with the death of God and the absence of immanent meaning in the world, imagines that the only obstacle to his or her own divinity is mortality. Death is thus transformed to account for the loss of power and to invest an otherwise meaningless life with its tragic significance. As the child's deferral of bliss organizes his experience by directing it toward the eventual recuperation of autonomy, so does the existentialist's "detour" of death allow him or her to enter the Law of the Individual, to redeem the immanent meaning that was lost when God's death ensured his or her own. Renouncing God, that is, the individual becomes a god of sorts, just as the child overcomes the threat of the father only by imitating his master. Existentialism and the castration complex thus function as strategies of deferral that both depend on and produce the subject's faith in the existence of a subject-supposed-to-know: both construct the possibility of a transcendent ego by defining the obstacle to autonomy as the signifier of what lies behind it. The difference between the two strategies is that the transference in the conventionally successful oedipal complex is a positive one—the subject continues to believe in and to wish to embody the father's authority—whereas the transference in existentialism is a negative one. Feeling abandoned by all transcendent powers, the subject seeks to satisfy his need for an SsS by modeling himself on the most transcendental subject of all, while simultaneously repudiating the existence of that master-subject.[8]

What both the child and the existential hero fail to recognize is that the castration they attempt to overcome does not in fact exist, at least not in the literal form in which it is usually understood: it is a *méconnaissance* produced by the binaries of Western culture, whose confirmation of the positive values of life, phallus, and father depends on the negatives of death, castration, and child (something Nietzsche seemed to understand in *The Birth of Tragedy*).[9] Both strategies repress the arbitrariness of the subject's will to power by deferring it through a structure naturalized by culture. And, like both the child and the existential hero that he has come to represent, Jake Barnes depends on similar strategies of deferral to transcend his impotence. Incorporating several modes of self-representation—the writing itself, the affair with Brett, the ritual of the bullfight—Jake's narrative simultaneously exploits and exposes the strategies of deferral that underlie these and all signifying systems. What is crucial to the success of each mode is that the structure that supports its signifying power not be fully interpretable: it must exist as the promise of a meaning that cannot be adequately represented. Each system of self-representation thus preserves the illusion of a certain reserve or plenitude that can only be intuited from the signifiers that defer to and from the ineffable truth of Jake's self.

The Scene of Writing

The narrative style itself is one manifestation of this strategy of deferral whereby truth is constituted through the assembly of lies, hints, or half-truths. Jake's writing, characterized by its understatement, evasiveness, and absence of subordination and transition, seems constantly to be withholding the very pieces of information essential to a true understanding of the story.[10] Hemingway himself revealed the motive of this style when he described its effects in another of his stories. "Out of Season," he says "was a very simple story . . . and I had omitted the real end of it which was that the old man hanged himself. This was omitted on my new theory that you could omit anything if you knew that you omitted and the omitted part would strengthen the story and make people feel something more than they understood."[11]

In this very explanation, the omission of the logical subordinate conjunction between clauses functions to obscure Hemingway's simultaneous definition and exploitation of this authorial means to power: "the omitted part would strengthen the story" *because* it would "make people feel something more than they understood." That is, the writer's *obvious* omission of certain important facts makes readers aware that something is being withheld, that the writer refuses to expose the truth. Like Milly Theale's behavior in *The Wings of the Dove,* this style succeeds because it seduces readers: by exposing, indeed, *producing* a gap in readers' knowledge, inscribing readers as impotent slaves to the master author, the story evokes a desire to be like the author, to possess his or her knowledge and power. But to master our own impotence, readers must acknowledge the inadequacy of the words we read to represent the truth we want to know: we must read "below the surface," a metaphor for reading that suggests the existence of an invisible true text beneath the deceptive one we see. The narrative thus becomes a means to the truth it hides, almost an initiation rite preceding membership in a secret club. The text becomes the way we earn our right to know the story's truth. However, as we fill in the narrative gaps so conveniently exposed to our view, we also become complicit with the text, committed to its ideal of a hidden truth. That we must, as readers, temporarily castrate ourselves, defer our possession of that truth until we have earned it, legitimizes the mastery we hope eventually to achieve.

The hidden truth of the novel is all the more seductive because it appears to be a deeply romantic one. The narrative's refusal to speak directly of the war and the wound—its evocation of those topics only as "the unspeakable"—invests them with a potent and compelling fascination. When Georgette, the hooker Jake picks up for "sentimental" reasons, makes advances to him in a cab, his refusal is cryptic:

> She touched me with one hand and I put her hand away.
> "Never mind."
> "What's the matter? You sick?"
> "Yes."[12]

Sensitive readers will likely concur with Georgette's and Mark Spilka's interpretation of Jake's response: "Everybody's sick. I'm sick, too" (Hemingway, *The Sun Also Rises* 16). By refusing to acknowledge the specificity of his wound—to name it—Jake effectively generalizes it, transforming it into a metaphor for the plight of modern man, the "venereal disease" Spilka defines as the death of love in the postwar world.[13]

A similar ellipsis occurs when the topic of the war arises. Georgette wants to know what is really wrong with Jake:

> "I got hurt in the war," I said.
> "Oh, that dirty war."
> We would probably have gone on and discussed the war and agreed that it was in reality a calamity for civilization, and perhaps would have been better avoided. I was bored enough. (*Sun* 17)

Jake's reduction of the war to a series of tired clichés, the boredom that suggests serious understatement, serves paradoxically to elevate the war's significance. Its actual importance to Jake and to the world is so exaggeratedly minimized here that we know we are to take heed: that which cannot be spoken must be the center of Jake's, and therefore our, concern. Jake's defamiliarization here rescues both the war and the wound from their status as banal if unfortunate truisms;

it is the elision of their real significance that makes these issues take on the status of truth itself.

Jake's desire is clearly to withdraw from bondage to his wound: he wishes to avoid the culturally determined significance of a castrated man. However, in retreating from the world that would make him a horrible joke (Jake?), a figure of the uncanny that can only be displaced by laughter, Jake still remains bound to the loss he seeks to transcend. His strategic displacement of the literality of his castration allows him to invest that senseless mutilation with the function of an initiation into some fundamental truth. By making the wound serve him as the source of his mysterious and compelling tragedy, and as the source of his personal and narrative authority, Jake consequently serves the ideology that makes young boys want to go to war in order to join the ranks of the initiated.[14] This is the same ideology, we might suspect, that inspired Jake's decision to fight on the Italian front, the same ideology that all good stories about the horrors of war are bound to serve. If Jake were really able to perform the significant transvaluation of his castration that he thinks he wants—if he could cancel the determinacy of the inscribed meaning of castration to achieve a certain skepticism toward it—he might be able to effect a real transformation of the significations of the phallus in Western culture, which would be a radical revision indeed.[15] But that would be another story.

And besides, Jake's narrative is perhaps not so bound to the dominant ideology as I have suggested (and as many other critics have insisted, though not in so many words).[16] Or if the novel is bound to the ideology that valorizes war and its consequent mutilations as the initiation into the horrific truths of manhood, it at least suggests the dependence of that ideology on the master-servant relation.

The narrative's deferral of the truth it wishes to announce is part of a certain code of ethics. The suffering of these characters need never be directly spoken since it is simply but clearly betokened by their diversionary tactics: week-long drunks, multiple sexual escapades, financial profligacy, even a regular and ritualized confrontation with death. The foolish romantic Cohn, who speaks what all the others feel ("He can't believe it didn't mean anything"), is mocked and finally ostracized for behaving badly when "he had a chance to behave so well" (*Sun* 181). That is, given the perfect occasion for displaying his tortured stoicism, Cohn renounces his chance in favor of the expressivist mode. Cohn cannot believe that his affair with Brett meant nothing, and, in insisting on its importance, he reveals that indeed it did mean nothing. The others, though, maintain the illusion that their suffering is significant by continually representing themselves as survivors of a tragedy they can neither name nor overcome. Brett's comment about Cohn makes explicit what is suggested throughout the narrative: one can only behave well if one receives the opportunity to suffer stoically. One can only be tragic if one has experienced a great loss. If one does not actually possess a deep secret whose denial bestows meaning and purpose on one's life, one can perhaps create that opportunity by imitating the form of a loss.

Bill Gorton ironically but accurately characterizes the power of the secret when, speaking to Jake, he catalogues the clichés about American expatriates: "You don't work. One group claims women support you. Another group claims you're impotent." Jake responds: "No . . . I just had an accident": "'Never mention that,' Bill said. 'That's the sort of thing that can't be spoken of. That's what you ought to work up into a mystery. Like Henry's bicycle'" (*Sun* 115). The allusion here to Henry James, a writer who also had an "accident" and who mastered most consciously in his writing the power of the secret to evoke fascination and desire, suggests that Jake also participates unconsciously in the "working up" of mysteries as a means to power over others—and perhaps over himself as well.

Jake's exploitation of the power of omission presumes that the unconscious is a buried or hidden depth beneath the surface layer of consciousness. His notion of denial thus differs substantially from Freud's; among other things, Jake always assumes that he knows the truth that he omits. According to Freud, however, repression occurs not as burial but as disguise. Displacement, condensation, jokes, and negation are all familiar modes of disguise by which the repressed may reside within consciousness in unrecognized form: "Thus the content of a repressed image or idea can make its way into consciousness, on condition that it is *negated*."[17]

Jake's narrative, not surprisingly, explodes its own "false" unconscious by clearly enacting the motives for and the means of its mystification of the reader. Early in the story, Jake returns home after his reunion with Brett, a meeting that has evoked his doomed desire for her:

> Undressing, I looked at myself in the mirror of the big armoire beside the bed. That was a typically French way to furnish a room. Practical, too, I suppose. Of all the ways to be wounded. I suppose it was funny. I put on my pajamas and got into bed. I had the two bull-fight papers, and I took their wrappers off. (*Sun* 30)

The passage consists of an associative series of displacements involving wrapping and unwrapping, negation and exposure. Jake "unwraps" his body to reveal the wound that marks a substantial revision of his own bodily "furnishings." Looking at himself, however, he comments on the layout of the room; he displaces his attention from his body to the scene surrounding or framing his body, suggesting that the comments that follow reflect his perception of his own appearance. He calls the room "typically French," the provincial American's equation of the foreign with the exotic. But more interestingly, he calls the arrangement "practical." The cryptic reference to the exotic utility of the room's furnishings is followed by the equally evasive mention of the wound, the indirect "of all the ways" implying that Jake's way must be the most outlandish, the most "exotic" imaginable.

Again, the construction of an unspeakable occurs, but this time in a context that reveals its strategic motive. The juxtaposition of bed and mirror is practical because it reminds Jake regularly, whenever he undresses for bed, of his disfigurement. That dialectical relation of exposure and negation, of seeing and not seeing the wound, is necessary to transform the castration from threat to promise. Like the castration itself, the arrangement of his room becomes a means by which Jake provokes his own desire: he must regularly see what is not there, since its "not-thereness" founds him, establishes him in the full presence of a castrated man. And he must see himself at the most propitious time for evoking his sense of himself as one who desires tragically: when he gets into the bed he would like to be sharing with the forbidden Brett.

Although Jake denies his obsession with the wound when he calls it funny, a remark intended perhaps to compel admiration for his stoic forbearance, that obsession is clear: the room itself has become a shrine to the full presence of the missing god. Such is the complexity of Jake's relation to his mutilation. The loss of his capacity for a "normal" sexual life is truly a horror to him, but that horror is simultaneously cherished and exploited as the origin of Jake's new tragic specificity. This much seems obvious, given the fact that sexual satisfaction would certainly not be impossible for Brett if she were to live with Jake. The refusal of either these characters (or the readers), however, to acknowledge the sexual alternatives to traditional coitus seems evidence of an almost willful repression, repression that, on the readers' part, shows further complicity with Jake's construction of himself and Brett as tragic figures.

Lacan's notion of the *sinthome* may be relevant here. Žižek says the "symptom as *sinthome* is a certain signifying formation penetrated with enjoyment: it is a signifier as a bearer of *jouis-sense*, enjoyment-in-sense" (*Sublime Object* 75). According to Žižek, the *sinthome*, which he exemplifies by reference to two stories of wounds (Kafka's "A Country Doctor" and Wagner's *Parsifal*), is a signifier "not enchained in a network but . . . penetrated with enjoyment, . . . by definition 'psycho-somatic' . . . a terrifying bodily mark which is merely a mute attestation bearing witness to a disgusting enjoyment, without representing anything . . . " (76). Jake's wound is certainly not psychosomatic in the conventional sense, anymore than it is the source of a conventional kind of pleasure. However, even as a real mutilation, it seems to function as a kind of signifier, pointing toward the pleasure Jake takes from the mastery the wound makes possible for him. Without the wound, that is, both Jake and Brett would have to face the banality of sexual frustration or the inadequacy of sexual satisfaction without any redemptive context. Again, Žižek explains with regard to Amfortas's wound in *Parsifal:* "in so far as it sticks out from the (symbolic and symbolized) reality of the body, the wound is 'a little piece of the real,' a disgusting protuberance which cannot be integrated into the totality of 'our own body,' a materialization of that which is 'in Amfortas more than Amfortas' and is thereby . . . destroying him. It is destroying him, but at the same time it is the only thing which gives him consistency" (*Sublime Object* 78). In Jake's case, we might add that the consistency afforded him by the wound is what distinguishes him from most of the rest of the novel's characters. Jake's wound thus gives access to a certain pleasure in which the arbitrary pathos threatened by castration—literal or metaphorical—is redeemed to the extent that it provokes a dramatic performance of manliness. His loss is a magnificent gain: like the existential hero, like Pedro Romero, Jake loves his enemy because it identifies him as a warrior. The end of the passage finds Jake rewrapping himself in his pajamas and his bed, which he shares with the unwrapped bullfight papers. The representation of the bullfight now becomes the substitute object of Jake's sexual desire, identifying that strangely sexual ritual as yet another of Jake's means of self-representation.

Lovers' Discourse

More directly, however, the passage suggests the role of the dialectic of castration and desire in Jake's relation to Brett. In the never-consummated love affair, Jake once again redeems his castration by making it the source of his mastery of Brett, evoking in her a desire that he will never fulfill. As Lacan reminds us,

> It is because he has not seen Socrates's prick, if I may be permitted to follow Plato, who does not spare us the details, that Alcibiades the seducer exalts in him the . . . marvel that he would like Socrates to cede to him in avowing his desire. . . .
>
> Such is the woman concealed behind her veil: it is the absence of the penis that turns her into the phallus, the object of desire. . . .
>
> Thus by showing his object as castrated, Alcibiades presents himself as he who desires . . . ("Subversion of the Subject," in *Ecrits* 323–24)

But though Jake may master Brett's desire, he does not quite master his own. No Socrates he, Jake cannot be satisfied with his capacity to control the desire of the other; he must continually evoke his desire for her by sending her off with other men, "pimping" for her to create his own sense of loss and jealousy. Jake depends on the presence of a third party, his rival, to maintain or mediate his desire; the lovers' discourse thus remains a stable source of desire and of the tragic identity inscribed by that desire.

Brett is of course the perfect love object for Jake precisely because she cooperatively affords so many opportunities for rivalry and its consequent evocation of desire. Collecting lovers, finding pleasure in the growing ranks of her sexual conquests, Brett can nevertheless be counted on to return to Jake, depending on him to define behavior that might otherwise seem sordidly promiscuous as a manifestation of her tragic desire for the only man she could never have. Brett's romantic history suggests that her desire has always depended on a master/slave dynamic: she married her husband after "her own true love" had died of dysentery during the war, thus effectively mastering her desire. Michael, her present fiancé, is also someone she "nursed," as he mentions in the context of her "looking after" the wounded Romero: "But she loves looking after people. That's how we came to go off together. She was looking after me" (*Sun* 203). Similarly, her relationship with Jake began when she served as a volunteer nurse in the English hospital where Jake was sent after his injury. All her lovers, though, are too easily mastered, too easily made dependent on her. Like the dead man, only Jake, her current "own true love" (*Sun* 55), remains an appropriate object of desire since he allows the maintenance of their dialectic: she must continue to want him because he can never be "possessed" (at least according to the very conventional standards of this couple), and his love for her legitimizes the economic nature of their arrangement.

Jake actually says as much when he explains to Brett how he feels about their relationship:

> ". . . what happened to me is supposed to be funny. I never think about it."
>
> "Oh no, I'll lay you don't."
>
> "Well, let's shut up about it. . . .
>
> "It's funny," I said. "It's very funny. And it's a lot of fun, too, to be in love."
>
> "Do you think so?" Her eyes looked flat again.
>
> "I don't mean fun that way. In a way it's an enjoyable feeling." (*Sun* 27)

It is fun to be in love when one will never have to risk the degeneration of the love relation, when one will never be forced to experience the lapse of desire in its "fulfillment." Under such circumstances, one feels one's love object to be a compulsion, the fated and essential complement to one's being, rather than a mediated occasion for the experience of desire.

The success of this relationship depends precisely on its capacity to withstand the threat of satisfaction. It thus perpetuates the delusion that the two lovers are victims of a fate beyond their control. But the control they exert is nevertheless apparent:

> She was sitting up now. My arm was around her and she was leaning back against me, and we were quite calm. She was looking into my eyes with that way she had of looking that made you wonder whether she really saw out of her own eyes. They would look on and on after every one else's eyes in the world would have stopped looking. (*Sun* 26)

From whose eyes could Brett look out at Jake so dependably if not from his own, her vision here determined by Jake's power to author her as one who desires? She can be counted on to continue looking on "after every one else's eyes in the world would have stopped looking" because she is the stable mirror of his own image. After all, looking into Brett's eyes to see what she sees, Jake would of course see only his own reflection: he masters her by effecting her castration in imitation of his own.[18]

Jake's fury at the homosexuals who accompany Brett to a nightclub becomes clearer when we recognize the power his castration confers on him. His rage is not resentment over the homosexual's willing abnegation of the conventional heterosexuality Jake has been denied by his accident. Rather, it results from the serious threat the homosexual man might pose to Jake's privileged relation to Brett. The homosexual is the only other male figure who might be able, like Jake, to evoke in Brett a desire that he would refuse to fulfill; indeed, the homosexual lover might even be preferable to Jake, who does not *refuse* to satisfy Brett's desire but is physically unable to do so. If anyone might displace Jake and his authority over Brett, it would be the homosexual man, so his response is fury over the superior composure of the gays (*Sun* 20).

What Jake requires in the way of an effective mediator to his own desire is someone who can temporarily replace him by becoming Brett's lover. Such a displacement is necessary because the temporary gratification of Brett's sexual desire will simply convince her that the true object of her desire remains unpossessed. Brett's lover's sexual potency is thus requisite to ensure his impotence and Jake's continued mastery of her. Jake further maintains his mastery by choosing the figures who will supplant him. Even as he announces his wish that the two of them could live quietly together, Jake's manipulation of Brett is clear:

> "Couldn't we live together, Brett? Couldn't we just live together?"
> "I don't think so. I'd just *tromper* you with everybody. You couldn't stand it."
> "I stand it now."
> "That would be different. It's my fault, Jake. It's the way I'm made."
> "Couldn't we go off in the country for awhile?"
> "It wouldn't be any good. I'll go if you like. But I couldn't live quietly in the country. Not with my own true love."
> "I know."
> "Isn't it rotten? There isn't any use my telling you I love you."
> "You know I love you."
> "Let's not talk. Talking's all bilge. I'm going away from you, and then Michael's coming back." (*Sun* 55)

Brett's apparent willingness to give Jake up, for both their sakes, simultaneously ensures the preservation of their bond: her companion at San Sebastian will be Cohn, whom she has met through Jake and who is thus associated with her forbidden love. Cohn's displacement of Jake will only remind Brett of what she is denied and will further guarantee her eventual return to her author.

Jake is even more clearly to be seen authoring Brett's desire for Romero. What might appear to be her natural or inevitable fascination with the handsome young man who performs his dangerous task so gracefully is in fact a product of Jake's careful maneuvering. Like Pandarus's describing Troilus's exploits as if he were a character in a romance, provoking Criseyde to ask confusedly "Who yaf me drinke?" Jake composes Romero's romantic persona.[19] The matador again is already clearly associated with Jake: the trip to Pamplona is Jake's yearly pilgrimage to his "holy land," and he is marked by Montoya as one who possesses the ineffable *aficion*. If Brett falls in love with Romero, then, it is at least partially in imitation of Jake's own passion for the boy. However, Jake carefully encourages Brett's interest:

> Brett sat between Mike and me at the barrera. . . . Romero was the whole show. I do not think Brett saw any other bullfighter. . . . I sat beside Brett and explained to Brett what it was all about. . . . I had her watch how Romero took the bull away from a fallen horse with his cape, and how he held him with the cape and turned him, smoothly and suavely, never wasting the bull. . . . She saw why she liked Romero's cape-work and why she did not like the others. (*Sun* 167)

Brett can see no other bullfighter because Jake will not allow her to. The parallels between Jake's mastery of Brett's vision here and the matador's mastery of the bull reveal the particular strategy by which Jake transfers Brett's desire toward Romero: he makes her see the matador as the seductive master of the beast's desire, thus establishing the link between himself and Romero as figures of authority.

The Bullfight: Another Scene of Writing

The parallels suggest an even more curious link between the bullfight and the affair with Brett, however. Jake's representation of the bullfight depends on and perpetuates the same mode of interpretation that underlies his representation of castration. Jake transcends his impotence, that is, only by repressing its textuality: now, similarly, he naturalizes the bullfight. According to Jake, Brett instinctively recognizes the superiority of Romero's capework, while he merely explains to her the technical skills involved in manifesting that superiority. The artifice of the capework, as absolute as the artifice of Jake's mastery of Brett, is denied here when Jake identifies the ritual's conventions as mere tokens of the greater natural truths they hide. Depending on both Brett and the reader to remain committed to the ideal of the hidden truth, Jake can thus represent the bullfight as the formal and legitimizing account of his own struggles with castration.

Jake's representation of the ritual is, not surprisingly, fraught with the same sort of mysteries that we found in his constructions of the wound and the war. The ritual is a secret with something shameful attached to it, the disguised evidence of which provokes a desire for membership in its cult. Jake's relation to Montoya is based in their shared knowledge of the unmentionable truth:

> [Montoya] always smiled as though bull-fighting were a very special secret between the two of us; a rather shocking but really very deep secret that we knew about. He always smiled as though there were something lewd about the secret to outsiders, but it was something that we understood. It would not do to expose it to people who would not understand. (*Sun* 131)

What is secret or shameful about the ritual cannot be spoken, however; it can only be figured by the very unpleasant, but certainly not mysterious element of the goring of the horses during the fight. That horror, ostensibly a token of a deeper and more significant one, is repeatedly referred to, though always in the form of the negative: "'Don't look at the horses, after the bull hits them,' I said to Brett. . . . 'There's nothing but that horse part that will bother you, and they're only in for a few minutes with each bull. Just don't watch when it's bad'" (*Sun* 162). Jake's insistent negation of the horses' importance grants their otherwise gratuitous misery its symbolic status. By producing the illusion that something is *omitted* from the fight, simultaneously displaced and represented by the sacrifice of the horses, Jake also produces the illusion of the ritual's secret meaning.

Indeed, Jake suggests that there is no exact translation, in any language, for the ritual of the bullfight:

> [Romero] was anxious to know the English for *Corrida de toros,* the exact translation. Bull-fight he was suspicious of. I explained that bull-fight in Spanish was the *lidia* of a *toro*. The Spanish word *corrida* means the running of bulls—the French translation is *Course de tareaux*. The critic put that in. There is no Spanish word for bull-fight. (*Sun* 173)

If there is no Spanish word for bullfight, then the English name for the ritual is somehow inaccurate, inadequate to the ritual itself. The problem of translation here, however, suggests the maneuver by which Jake further mystifies the already-mysterious ritual. The Spanish *Corrida de toros* is a metonymic displacement in which one element of the ritual—the initial running of the bulls through the town to the bull pen prior to the fight—stands for the entire thing. Similarly, the English bullfight metonymically identifies the significance of the total ritual by means of its final element. Jake implies that language—*any* language—is incapable of representing the reality of the bullfight, that all the terms used to name it are evasions of its actual meaning. They may circle around the performance itself, evoking or suggesting aspects of it, but they cannot define what it really is. Only partial names can escape the repression that surrounds the fight and suggests its ineffability. The ritual is thus evoked precisely as the unnameable: the secret that is the ritual can be performed, and perhaps even intuitively understood by some spectators; but it is by nature alinguistic, primal, anterior to all representational systems. It is its own origin.

Jake wants us to feel the bullfight as a constant and unchanging mystery that escapes the reduction of any language, even the language of the culture in which the ritual originates. In fact, however, the difficulty of translating the meaning of the bullfight into another language lies in the fact that the Spanish signifiers *Corrida de toros* refer to other signifiers in the Spanish culture, signifiers that have taken on the status of signifieds; the Spanish signifiers to which the name of the ritual refers do not necessarily exist in Anglo-American culture.[20] Again, it is by denying the cultural specificity of the ritual that Jake represents it as a fundamentally unchanging, universal, and essential mystery whose significance can only be intuited by the initiate.

One goes to the bullfight to experience its secret as one's own, but Jake complicates the spectators' expectations when he describes Belmonte's failure to fulfill them:

> People went to the corrida to see Belmonte, to be given tragic sensations, and perhaps to see the death of Belmonte. Fifteen years ago they said if you wanted to see Belmonte you should go quickly, while he was still alive. . . . When he retired the legend grew up about how his bull-fighting had been, and when he came out of retirement the public were disappointed because no real man could work as close to the bulls as Belmonte was supposed to have done, not, of course, even Belmonte.
>
> Also Belmonte imposed conditions and insisted that his bulls should not be too large, nor too dangerously armed with horns, and so the element that was necessary to give the sensation of tragedy was not there, and the public . . . felt defrauded and

> cheated. . . . He had expected to compete with Marcial and the other stars of the decadence of bull-fighting, and he knew that the sincerity of his own bull-fighting would be so set off by the false aesthetics of the bull-fighters of the decadent period that he would only have to be in the ring. (*Sun* 214–15)

The "tragic sensations" that one attends the fight to experience are a delicate commodity: they depend on the illusion of the matador's natural and spontaneous daring. The goal of the ritual is a presentation of the matador's sincerity, and the failure of that achievement leads to decadence. Clearly, the terminology Jake employs here, evoking a Wordsworthian romantic aesthetic, conflicts with the earlier implication that the bullfight is not a representation, but a presentation of the thing itself. The supplementarity of the ritual that was previously denied is here acknowledged, but only as something that must be disguised if the bullfight is to achieve its intended function. Tragic sensations occur only if the matador's performance is good enough—that is, deceptive enough—to create the illusion of unstudied and natural courage.

The essential but repressed artificiality of the ritual is also apparent in the matador's attitude toward his symbolic opponent. The relation of matador to bull is ostensibly one of rivalry, each desiring to master the other by destroying it. It thus looks like a ritualized representation of that stage of Hegel's dialectic of consciousness preceding the more sophisticated master-servant relation. But in order for the matador's desire for mastery to be provoked by the bull—granted a legitimate ground in courage rather than appearing as wanton destructiveness—the bull must be a particularly dangerous opponent. As Romero says, "The bulls are my best friends" (*Sun* 186) because they make his bravery possible; it is the actual threat they pose to his life that invests his otherwise-artificial behavior in the ring with something approaching authenticity. That real threat also provides the spectators with their opportunity to witness tragedy, as Belmonte's disappointing evasion of the threats reveals. Only a dangerous bull can make the matador a real master—of the bull, of the spectators, and of himself.

But the bull is oddly chosen to play its role in this allegory of "man's" confrontation with his own contingency: the animal is not a natural threat to people; it does not, as the lion or wolf might, pose the wild hunter's threat to human domestic order. In fact, the bull is itself a domestic animal, and one that must be further domesticated for the purposes of the bullfight. The animal, carefully bred for a particularly unintelligent viciousness, must be *created* as the matador's enemy. If the bull is a token of anything in particular, then, it would have to be a pure but nevertheless unnatural physical energy or aggressivity devoid of rationality or even animal cunning. Or perhaps what the bull actually represents is the enormous resourcefulness of human narcissism, the ingenuity of which is demonstrated in this quite cunning transformation of a very strong and stupid beast into the terrifying and malignant enemy essential to the warrior's existence.

In fact, according to the passage detailing Romero's mastery over the bull (*Sun* 167), the animal must actually be seduced into attacking the matador; all the elements of the fight involve goading, pricking, taunting the bull into making its direct attack on the matador rather than on some other figure in the arena. The bull's artificially induced aggressivity is initially without a particular object: it wants to destroy anything or everything or perhaps even nothing. Romero's handling of the visually impaired bull makes his role as seducer clear:

> After the first two passes with the cape Romero knew exactly how bad the vision was impaired. He worked accordingly. . . . Nothing very fine could happen with a bull that could not see the lures. . . . With the bull who could not see the colors of the capes, or the scarlet flannel of the muleta, Romero had to make the bull consent with his body. He had to get so close that the bull saw his body, and would start for it, and then shift the bull's charge to the flannel and finish out the pass in the classic manner. . . .
>
> Out in the centre of the ring, all alone, Romero was going on with the same thing, getting so close that the bull could see him plainly, offering the body, offering it again a little closer, the bull watching dully, then so close that the bull thought he had him, offering again and finally drawing the charge and then, just before the horns came, giving the bull the red cloth to follow with that little, almost imperceptible, jerk. . . . (*Sun* 217–18)

To make the bull attack him, the matador must behave in a curiously sexual, even feminine fashion: dressed in physically confining clothing—tight pants and heavily decorated tight jacket—carrying the large skirtlike cape, the matador performs a series of intricate dancelike steps in front of the bull, offering his body, teasing the animal into charging, and then at the last minute pirouetting away, deflecting the charge to the flannel. The description of Romero's activity sounds suspiciously like that of a woman arousing a lover's desire: both forms of seduction involve offering the body, provoking the pass, and then capriciously denying satisfaction until the lover has been sufficiently worn down by his own frenzied desire, readied for his final sacrifice to the beloved.[21] Just as Brett's desire has been authored by her master-castrate, so is the bull made to desire the mastery of his own author. We should remember here Lacan's description of woman, the cultural castrate whose status as the fetishized phallus, object and signifier of desire, occurs by virtue of her lack of the penis: "Draw attention to this absence in a more precise way by getting her to wear a pretty wig and fancy dress, and you, or rather she, will have plenty to tell us about: the effect is guaranteed 100 percent, for men who go straight to the point" ("Subversion of the Subject," in *Ecrits* 322–23).

The relationship of matador to bull would seem to involve a bizarre sexual parody: the bull, made to play a role of conventionally aggressive masculinity, confronts the matador who is disguised as feminine seductress. The two engage in a struggle in which the "man" apparently holds the advantage, but "woman" masters her rival by provoking "his" desire to master "her." Here, the vulnerable passivity conventionally attributed to woman becomes her strength—her aggression, actually—against the man who goes straight to the point, in this case, the point of the matador's sword:

> Out in the centre of the ring Romero profiled in front of the bull, drew the sword out from the folds of the muleta, rose on his toes, and sighted along the blade. The bull charged as Romero charged. Romero's left hand dropped the muleta over the bull's muzzle to blind him, his left shoulder went forward between the horns as the sword went in, and for just an instant he and the bull were one. . . . (*Sun* 218)

The matador—master as castrate as woman—fulfills for the bull precisely what is the desire of every subject: the gratification of "his" desire in the master's gratification of "her" own. The subject's desire for the master and "his" desire to be for the master what "she" desires are fulfilled simultaneously: from behind the folds of the skirt (and some other folds might be imagistically evoked here) that veils the potentially horrifying absence, the master withdraws the phallus, becoming again, just for a moment, the phallic mother. But master and subject become one only at the cost of the "total expenditure": the end of the subject's specificity, the achievement of "his" *jouissance,* "his" return to the origin beyond the pleasure principle.[22] And if the subject of this ritual is a particularly heroic one, if "he" defers this ultimate *jouissance* long and tragically enough, the highest compliment will be paid in another manifestation of the total expenditure: a symbolic castration will occur in the cutting off of small appendages, like tail or ears, from "his" body. Derrida asks, "Would a woman be able to captivate us . . . whom we did not credit with knowing how to employ the dagger . . . skillfully *against* us under certain circumstances?"[23] The bullfight suggests that she would not.

Of course, this interpretation of the bullfight is antithetical to everything the ritual seems "intended" to stand for in Hemingway's novel, but that is what makes it interesting.[24] What the ritual apparently wishes to represent—humanness as some version of a hardy existential *machismo* engaging a mortal fate—simultaneously represses and inscribes another unwished-for representation: the mastery of culturally constructed masculinity by culturally constructed femininity. The signifiers of the ritual—matador and bull—seem intended to refer to the given and thus necessarily true signifieds of man and nature, or man and death. What they in fact refer to are other signifiers, masculinity and femininity. The bullfight is not a translation of an absolute code into cultural language; it is not the originary enactment of a taboo truth. It reveals what Jake's narrative has revealed throughout: that the subject is constituted by an imaginatively constructed other who confers that subjectivity by threatening it. Whether that other is castration, death, the father, or the bull, the subject *must* discover that opponent, in a repetition of a cultural model, in order to legitimize his or her own will to power. But the existential subject, caught in a negative transference, must resist the knowledge of his or her imitation of that model to preserve faith in the self's autonomy.

The ritual of the bullfight subverts more than the autonomy of the subject, existential or otherwise, however. Romero's transvestism suggests that, like Jake, the matador must behave like a woman to produce the effect of masculinity. Jake's narrative would thus appear to define power as fundamentally feminine. But this does not make sense: even if Brett possessed the same power that Jake and Romero have, the novel does not represent her mastery of men as a respectable victory over worthy opponents; it does not endorse her authority as it clearly does Jake's and Romero's. The logical contradiction of feminine power could only be resolved if the male protagonist's transvestism were understood as a temporary but necessary deferral of his achievement of masculine autonomy, as it clearly *is* understood within the Western oedipal dynamic. A woman's femininity, on the other hand, is a permanent and irredeemable sentence that cannot be transcended. In this sense, femininity figures the threat that the man must embrace to overcome. However, the bullfight as Hemingway represents it still poses one challenge to this particular resolution of its allegory: the matador may become a "woman" to prove his manliness, but the opponent he overcomes is "man." The question remains: why does the bullfight depict the symbolic destruction of man by woman? Is this "man" who must be overcome merely the father who blocks the subject's access to the desirable mother, or is the allegory more complicated than this?

Perhaps we can account for the anomaly by recalling the multiplicity of all the ritual's signifiers. The matador requires the artificially constructed significance of the bull to signify something about himself. Similarly, both participants in the ritual figure a certain doubleness in themselves: the bull manifests the binary human/animal, while the matador himself doubles the mutually exclusive (yet also mutually constitutive) meanings of "male" and "female." He figures, that is, the coexistence of the structures of difference—male/female, aggressivity/passivity, reason/passion—that the patriarchy has divided into binaries to form its own natural basis. If the hierarchy of those polarized differences is now inverted so that the guise of femininity is associated with a certain kind of powerful aggressivity, the ritual may suggest a couple of things about the codes of patriarchal culture. On the one hand, the inversion indicates that the distinctions on which the patriarchy depends are arbitrarily, or conventionally, ascribed to biological men and women. As Shoshana Felman has argued, "the substitutions of woman for man and of man for woman, the interchangeability and reversibility of masculine and feminine manifest a discord which subverts the limits and compromises the coherence of each of the two principles."[25]

Even more interestingly, however, the ritual may suggest why patriarchal culture has repressed the artificiality of its own category of castration. Again, to quote Felman, "If femininity becomes indeed a signifier of castration, it is by no means . . . the embodiment of *literal castration,* the literalization of the figure of castration . . . but rather . . . castration as a differential process of substitution, subverting, on the contrary, literality as such" ("Rereading" 41; Felman's emphasis). "Castration" in this context still signifies loss, but that loss must be understood as the power of certainty, of proper meaning, of literality, all absences that characterize the Real. The strategy of castration is to pretend that the danger is of a *literal* loss and so to make possible, in compensation, the belief in a *literal* phallus, signifying the merely temporary deferral of such a possession. Again, we see the transformation of the Real through the symbolic.

But in its dependence on woman to signify a stable principle of castrated otherness—the permanence of a loss a man may transcend—the patriarchy invests her with a curious power that might be quite improperly employed, like the dagger, against the man who embodies the patriarchy's authority. If the bullfight represents woman as the castrating enchantress, a version of the *vagina dentata,* it must also suggest that the value of the phallus depends on that toothy threat: it thus inscribes woman as author of the presence she threatens. But "she" is *already* a transvestite, a substitute signifier that can only refer to the presence she defers. According to the bullfight, then, woman's power to destroy man is not quite the power to castrate him: it is rather the signifier's power to castrate the very myth of castration, a knowledge that existentialism works as hard as does Romantic philosophy to obscure.

The authority that existential philosophy confers on the subject derives from a negative transference: it consists in a *denial* of the existence or legitimacy of any and all founding models of the self. That denial works, however, by granting the individual precisely the form of authority (or self-authorship) that had previously belonged to the transcendental structures of God or human nature. Unlike Milly Theale's almost grateful summoning of her oedipal family legacy, the existential subject as represented in Conrad's Marlow and in Jake Barnes resists the knowledge of his own debt to the dead father, thus preserving a fantasy of his freedom. Having run away from a mad old man who seemed to think his authority were a gift from the gods, the son discovers by sheer hard work that he is himself a master, and much better for not being arbitrary but based on a *real* power—it just happens to *look* like the old man's.

What distinguishes the version of this subject in Hemingway from that in Conrad is the former's representation of femininity as a figure for the subject's originating anxiety, his founding trauma. Again, Hemingway may intend to represent Jake's heroism as deriving from his ability to be a man despite the war's transformation of him. But what the narrative demonstrates is the lack of any *real* foundation to the idea of manliness—woman is not, after all, prior to man—just as there is nothing real at the base of either fatherhood or mastery, only the Real. The foundation of each identity is trauma, and only in projecting the resulting anxiety into the world as a threat does the illusion of the subject's origin become convincing. The question we might ask now is how the knowledge of such "resistance to knowledge" could be made productive: of another subjectivity, another kind of authority. In the next chapter, I will consider how Woolf's *explicit* recognition of the artifice of gender may allow her to resist the resistance at the heart of transferential repetition in Conrad, James, and Hemingway.

Chapter 5

The Strategy of Androgyny in *A Room of One's Own*

> It is not necessary to slay your father. . . . Your true task lies elsewhere.
> —Donald Barthelme, *The Dead Father*

In "Women's Time," Julia Kristeva describes the modern history of feminism with regard to two attitudes that have characterized women's relations to the patriarchy. The choice women frequently feel faced with is either to accept the values of the dominant culture and to conform to its practices—to succeed on its terms—or, on the other hand, to reject those values and construct a "counter-society" as an alternative to the one that has traditionally locked women out of positions of authority.[1] The problem, as Kristeva points out, is that there is less difference between the two positions than one might have imagined or hoped for. Women who accept the terms of power as they are conventionally defined and seek to gain that power for themselves not only reproduce the power structure's oppression of others; they also legitimize the notion that such oppression is essential to the individual's achievement of personal success and significance. But those who reject traditional power structures and attempt to establish counter-societies that avoid such exploitation *also* end up reproducing something about the order they are rejecting: if not the *content* then the *structure* of that oppressive system is carried over into the new system's dependence on the inside/outside, good/bad, included/excluded oppositions. The two attitudes toward authority implicit in these two different feminist goals might fairly be seen as versions of the positive and negative transferences I have been considering throughout this book. In the first position, one resents being excluded from enjoying such power oneself even as—because?—she accepts the terms of power relatively uncritically. In the second mode, she rejects the legitimacy of that which has rejected her, but ends up reproducing the structure of exclusivity in her alternative order. What the two modes share is a faith in wholeness, in the possibility of a return to a moment prior to loss or sacrifice, either through attaining mastery in male terms, or through discovering a new, nonmale mastery.[2]

Not surprisingly, Kristeva's essay describes what she calls a third generation of feminism, consisting in a kind of non-*Aufhebung* that would combine participation and nonparticipation, assimilation in and transformation of the existing power structures, without the synthesis that would overcome the differences between the other two behaviors. What this third mode would entail in practical terms remains somewhat abstract in Kristeva, but one of the interesting things about it is that it avoids any supposition of psychic harmony as the possible attendant of socialization. Kristeva argues very strongly against the belief that the human subject can emerge without experiencing sacrifice or loss: "In this sense, and from a viewpoint undoubtedly too Hegelian, modern feminism has only been but a moment in the interminable process of coming to consciousness about the implacable violence (separation, castration, etc.) which constitutes any symbolic contract" (203). The first two generations of feminism have worked, in different but related ways, to resist the knowledge that such violence is at the root of the human.

Kristeva, by contrast, accepts the psychoanalytic notion that castration is constitutive of human subjectivity, but she redefines the term in a move that by now should seem familiar. Castration refers in a general way to the *losses* that found the subject, rather than to the singular loss (or threat of loss) of the penis that (en)genders males and females. Kristeva, then, like Kaja Silverman and Shoshana Felman, preserves the term that has at times been used to reduce or denigrate women but revises its significance to make it productive in the feminist critique of patriarchy. In so doing, these writers (along with others) may be enacting the "third practice" Kristeva calls for, the simultaneous participation and nonparticipation in dominant cultural systems. The end of such practice is in fact a nonending in so far as it involves a transformed mode of being for the subject, but one marked by a struggle: to "[*interiorize*] . . . *the founding separation of the socio-symbolic contract*, as an introduction of its cutting edge into the very interior of every identity whether subjective, sexual, ideological, or so forth. This in such a way that the habitual and increasingly explicit attempt to fabricate a scapegoat victim of a society or counter-society may be replaced by the analysis of the potentialities of *victim/executioner* which characterize each identity, each subject, each sex" (210; Kristeva's emphasis).[3]

The Strategy of Androgyny

Virginia Woolf understood very well the difficulty of nonassimilation, how hard it is to criticize the oppressive practices of the powerful without simultaneously seeking that same power (to oppress) for oneself. As the daughter of a middle-class family in turn-of-the-century England, she knew firsthand what it meant to be an *effect* of contradiction: privilege and security on the one hand, exploitation and circumscription on the other. Responding to the simultaneous frustration and opportunity inherent in such contradiction, *Three Guineas* presents a feminist practice that acknowledges and exploits the subjective position of middle-class women to resist that subjectivity. This practice requires a certain knowledge of and intervention in history: women need to turn the "four great teachers of educated men's daughters—poverty, chastity, derision, and freedom from unreal loyalties"—into the means of transforming their social status and indeed their own senses of themselves.[4] Such a strategy may sound similar to the one Nietzsche claims is at the root of the Judeo-Christian tradition: to cope with what they could not change, Nietzsche argues, the slaves simply inverted the values that had been imposed on them by their stronger masters. Thus, what the masters called bad—the slaves—the slaves redefined as good, and what the masters called good—themselves—the slaves named evil.[5] Although he admits that such a redefinition of values is creative, Nietzsche despises what he considers the life-hating *ressentiment* and impotence motivating this example of transvaluation, preferring himself something more literally violent to this mean-spirited game of words.

Woolf, however, manages to avoid falling into either *ressentiment*—the myth of the counter-society, in Kristeva's terms—or literal violence, in part because of the language she uses to describe her feminist practice. As Marie-Luise Gättens has argued, "the names as well as the qualities themselves are bound to keep the memory of the patriarchal imposition alive. History here operates against a false reconciliation. . . ."[6] This redefinition of terms, that is, does not presuppose that the new meanings of the old words actually arrive at some natural truth that had previously been obscured. Rather, in preserving but revising these old terms, Woolf (like Kristeva and others) does two things: she admits her determination by cultural forces she does not control, but she also recognizes and exploits the instability of both language and history for transformative purposes. In the following chapter, I will consider how the feminist strategy in *A Room of One's Own* works to theorize "the subject" in terms very close to those of Lacanian psychoanalysis. In so doing, the text may also achieve a relation to cultural authority that escapes the transference we have encountered before.

My use of the term *strategy* in the title of this chapter derives from Derrida's definition of the term:

> In marking out *differance,* everything is a matter of strategy and risk . . . because no transcendent truth present outside the sphere of writing can theologically command the totality of this field. It is hazardous because this strategy is not simply one in the sense that we say that strategy orients the tactics according to a final aim, a telos or a theme of a domination, a mastery or an ultimate reappropriation of movement and field. In the end, it is a strategy without finality.[7]

Instead of announcing itself as the move toward a truth determined by some order outside of language and history, Woolf's feminism-as-strategy offers itself explicitly as discourse—a mode of language—that is not commanded by some meaning external to it. As strategy, feminism does not attempt to master or refute the other discourse of gender identity; instead, it engages that primary discourse in a dialogue to analyze the grounds of *its* authority to determine sexual identity. In refusing to assert itself as a replacement for the traditional patriarchal discourse, such feminism supplements, in Derrida's sense, that primary set of signifiers to dislodge their hold on truth and to reveal them as part of a specifically motivated and historical power structure.

In *A Room of One's Own,* Woolf exploits the very belatedness of feminism as a source of its power. Because feminism is so explicitly *defensive,* so rooted in anxiety, its motives so obvious, it can prompt a reconsideration of the motives of the primary discourse of gender, motives that are always denied to be motives and perceived as truth. Woolf's feminism thus deconstructs not just the phallocentrism of Western culture but also the faith in the unified subject as master of his or her own meaning. As such a deconstruction, *A Room of One's Own* does not proceed by contesting the claims of phallocentrism, but rather by reenacting phallocentrism's appropriation of the authority to define gender. As a repetition of an earlier act of such symbolization, this text subverts the primacy of the transcendental signified—the phallus—without necessarily attempting to replace that arche-telos with another.

In *A Room of One's Own*, the speaker never refers explicitly to the body, dealing with that fact of nature only as it has been already commandeered by cultural conventions to produce feminine stereotypes. She deals with the body, that is, as a signifier that has been *made to mean* rather than as something that means in itself. Her attention to the term *woman* thus incorporates a sophisticated understanding of how signifying systems ultimately gain truth-value as a function of their capacity to ensure coherence. The speaker treats the term *woman* as an ideological quilting point, in Lacan's terms, and by detaching the signifier from the systems that ultimately grant it its meaning(s), Woolf's text begins to demonstrate the ideological function of gender in our culture.

Readers who see Woolf as participating in, even initiating a tradition of feminist analysis of literature respond to the explicit intention in the text to rewrite, revise, or reappropriate a literary history that has excluded women. And certainly one impulse in the narrative is to rediscover a missing or repressed tradition of the woman writer. That impulse manifests itself in the ironic discussions of the social and familial contexts that produce women as social figures. Woolf seems to want to say two things about those contexts. First, that if we understand the structures that produce women as social entities, we will see the limitations placed on them and understand why most women do not write or have not written. But the second thing Woolf says in her revision of history is that in fact women *have* participated in its production: though the work of women has not always been considered aesthetically valuable, it informs us of the conditions in which women lived that kept them from producing such "art." These women, Woolf says, have either been ignored by a literary tradition defined by men, or held up as proof of the inferiority of women. And Woolf counters that repression by calling attention to and naming the writers whose absence from or denigration in conventional history now speaks of *its* limitations.

But Woolf does not want to talk about the tradition of women writers simply because it has not been done before. Her interest in that history is motivated by a desire to account for the present—1929—status of women in general and of women writers in particular. And to account for the status of one's class is to account for oneself as a member of the class. So Woolf's revision of history in *A Room of One's Own* displays political, social, professional, and personal impulses toward self-assertion that clearly respond to the various modes by which culture denies feminine power and potential. And yet, that feminist self-assertion is not an end in itself: it exists to be overcome by another state defined in the final chapter of the text.

The discussion at the end of the narrative of the writer's ideally "androgynous mind" has invited many readers to conclude that Woolf offers a deceptively simple and simplistic account of the creative process. The apparent intent of this section of the narrative is to argue for the necessary unity of the creative intelligence, its imperviousness to distracting and divisive emotions such as anger and fear. The speaker locates her meaning of the term *androgynous* in an analysis of Coleridge's, who, she says, "did not mean, when he said that a great mind is androgynous, that it is a mind that has any special sympathy with women. . . . Perhaps the androgynous mind is less apt to make these distinctions than the single sexed mind. He meant, perhaps, that the androgynous mind is resonant and porous . . . that it is naturally creative, incandescent, and undivided."[8] This discussion of the term *androgyny* follows the text's long, explicitly feminist analysis of the state of the woman writer, an analysis that involves a certain anger, albeit ironic, at the cultural constraints on women and the work they can do.

In rejecting sexual partisanship and its attendant resentment, the above passage moves away from the previous efforts to specify the feminine and toward a discussion of the danger, for any writer, of a sexual consciousness. The speaker says,

> It is fatal to be a man or woman pure and simple; one must be woman-manly or man-womanly. It is fatal for a woman to lay the

> least stress on any grievance; to plead even with justice any cause; in any way to speak consciously as a woman. And fatal is no figure of speech; for anything written with that conscious bias is doomed to death. It ceases to be fertilised. (*Room* 108).

The meaning we ascribe to Woolf's androgyny is thus crucial since, as Herbert Marder points out, "The idea of androgyny makes its appearance here as a corrective for the excesses of feminism."[9] Our reading of mental androgyny, the state the writer strives to attain after passing through the necessary phase of perhaps embittered feminist consciousness, will determine the way we understand the feminist argument itself.

But the manner in which the term *androgyny* has been glossed by critics contributes, I think, to the over-simplification of Woolf's argument.[10] For most readers, the androgynous mind is one in which the opposing male and female principles unite harmoniously to produce creative potential. Nancy Bazin, representative of many critical perspectives on androgyny, writes,

> In *A Room of One's Own,* [Woolf] suggests that every mind is potentially bisexual. But she finds that among writers, and particularly among her contemporaries, most men tend to develop only the analytic "masculine" approach . . . and most women only the synthetic, "feminine." . . . In her opinion, however, to be truly creative one must use the "whole" mind. . . . [T]he greatest writers are "androgynous": they use and harmonize the masculine and feminine approaches to truth.[11]

Marder concurs with Bazin's analysis of androgyny: "Wholeness—integration of personality—is the ultimate goal, and the symbol Virginia Woolf uses to represent this ideal condition is the androgynous mind, the mind in which masculine and feminine elements attain a perfect balance" (3). Marder's version of the masculine and feminine elements does not differ much from Bazin's: he equates the masculine with reason and the feminine with imagination (4). Marder also believes that "Virginia Woolf saw the universe as the scene of an eternal conflict between opposites, corresponding, roughly speaking, to masculine and feminine principles" (125). According to both these critics, it is the achievement of the androgynous mind to reconcile the split between these naturally opposing factions of the male and female principles. Again, in Marder's words, mental androgyny is a "resolution . . . [that] puts an end to discord" (109).

Two things become clear from these representative readings of the androgynous mind: the first is that these critics seem themselves to believe in the reality of the natural male and female principles; or if *they* do not, they are at least willing to argue uncritically for Woolf's belief in them. However, the more important link among these critical views of androgyny is the assumption that Woolf describes by that term a state of mental harmony, wholeness, integration.[12]

Of course, Woolf contributes to that impression since she uses the words *harmony* and *unity* in her discussion of androgyny. But I would suggest that such notions, though present, are themselves at war with other equally striking implications of the passage. And because of that conflict, I would further argue that the term *androgynous mind* is rendered incapable of referring to the harmonious fusion of any male and female principles in the individual, however those principles might be defined. Rather, the term is forced, against its will perhaps, to point to the existence in the mind of a fundamental principle of otherness, a principle figured by Woolf in her use of the terms *male* and *female*.[13]

This view of the subject is consistent with Lacan's claim that otherness is proper to the ego. The psychoanalytic experience, he argues, "leads us to oppose any philosophy directly issuing from the *Cogito*."[14] In rejecting the *cogito,* Lacan further refutes the existence of an autonomous subject able to be directly conscious of itself. Indeed, Lacan denies that there is any unified object of which the subject might actually be "self"-conscious. The "mirror stage" as he defines it occurs when the infant is able to recognize his or her own image in a mirror; this event inaugurates a constitutive alienation in the child, a function of the gap between the image he or she sees of a totalized and coherent bodily form and the reality of the child's bodily fragmentation and dependence:

> This jubilant assumption of his specular image by the child at the *infans* stage, still sunk in his motor incapacity and nursling dependence, would seem to exhibit in an exemplary situation the symbolic matrix in which the I is precipitated in a primordial form, before it is objectified in the dialectic of identification with the other, and before language restores to it, in the universal, its

> function as subject. . . . But the important point is that this form situates the agency of the ego, before its social determination, in a fictional direction, which will always remain irreducible for the individual. . . . (2)

The fictional direction of the ego results from the illusion of its autonomy that is produced by the mirror image. The child, seeing itself reflected, "mis-recognizes" itself, identifies with that image of totalization; but the image itself is an image of an other, something that the child is not, and not a reflection of the child's actual state of incapacity and vulnerability. The ego, then, is from the very beginning a representation of the self that is necessarily a misrepresentation, a function of what Lacan calls the "*méconnaissances* that constitute the ego" (6). As Anthony Wilden points out more explicitly, "The ego is an *Idealich,* another self," and it is fundamentally "an alienated self": "Lacan's *moi* corresponds to the internalization of the other through identification. . . . The *moi* is thus another, an *alter ego.*"[15]

The principle of otherness that Lacan defines and that Woolf alludes to is not oppositional, however. That the terms *male* and *female* have been read in Woolf as referring to a natural dualism is a function of the cultural insistence that male and female nature (if indeed there are such things) are opposed to one another, that sexual *difference* is actually binary. Woolf, on the contrary, never refers to nature, and instead suggests by the terms *male* and *female* the coexistence in the subject of disjunctive and "dis-unified," but not necessarily oppositional, forces. Since she never defines the meaning of sexual difference except insofar as that difference has been interpreted culturally, the terms can be taken to signify *difference* itself, in a far more complex sense than "polarity."

Thus, the male and female powers within the brain or soul, which readers have tended to understand as the given principles of rational aggressivity versus intuitive receptivity, must be defined less systematically. In fact, the discussion of the androgynous mind should make clear that it is precisely the cultural notion of polarity within sexuality that the speaker wishes to undermine. The androgynous mind, she writes, is "less apt to make these distinctions than the single sexed mind"; the androgynous mind is "naturally . . . undivided." One might even point to the negation in "*un-*

divided" to suggest the existence of multiple forces (including negation) in (as) the subject. The terms used to describe the androgynous mind need not refer to some wholeness or integration of opposites, but rather to a mind constituted by many forces that resist either unification or absolute separation. A writer who refuses to make sexual distinctions, in this sense, would be questioning the culturally determined significance of difference and rethinking that signification as plurality rather than as polarity. In doing so, she might also be "[retreating] from sexism (male as well as female) and, gradually, from any kind of anthropomorphism," as Kristeva characterizes the practice of third-generation feminism (Kristeva 210).

The speaker's discussion of the possible existence of "two sexes in the mind corresponding to the two sexes in the body" offers an image further in conflict with any explicit statements about harmony:

> I went on amateurishly to sketch a plan of the soul so that in each of us two powers preside, one male, one female, and in the man's brain, the man predominates over the woman, and in the woman's brain, the woman predominates over the man. The normal and comfortable state of being is that when the two live in harmony together, spiritually cooperative. If one is a man, still the woman part of the brain must have effect, and a woman must also have intercourse with the man in her. . . . It is when this fusion takes place that the mind is fully fertilised and uses all its faculties. (*Room* 102)

Juxtaposed with and therefore complicating the claim of harmony here is the prior acknowledgment of hierarchy. More interestingly, however, copulation, suggested here by the terms *intercourse* and *fertilised,* becomes a metaphor for mental creation.

And yet, the sexual act, whether procreative or not, is *not* a harmonious union or fusion of bodies, however pleasurable it may be. *Fusion* implies a joining that overcomes the distinctions and boundaries of individuality, a true unification, as that produced by melting or liquifying. Sexual intercourse, on the other hand, despite its romanticization or spiritualization, entails the penetration, partial and temporary, of bodily parts in a relation whose aftereffect might be a sense of harmony but whose occurrence depends precisely on bodily differentiation, on the *friction* deriving from simultaneous contact and separation. Following out the terms of the metaphor, then, imaginative creativity happens as a result of the encounter within the subject of at least (but not necessarily only) two differing forces, rather than in a state of tranquil unification of opposites. This encounter does not involve the writer's conscious thinking of herself as "woman," but it may involve the friction between her socially produced sense of wholeness—her ego as a representation of womanliness—and the ego's own otherness to that in the self that it represses. The (mis)representation of the self, asserting its completion and closure, confronts something in the self that exceeds the representation of woman and that, in exceeding, must ordinarily be denied.

Although the speaker calls this a "marriage of opposites," she never grounds that mention of opposition in any account of male and female polarity as real; the phrase therefore can refer to the culturally produced sense of opposition in the subject that must be overcome in favor of some other experience if creation is to take place. Read thus, the terms *male* and *female* are divorced from the cultural constructs that provide them with distinct and opposing referents and, in being so divorced, refer to an unspecified difference. Categorized oppositionally, such difference is appropriated by culture to signify two sets of polarities: male/female and self/other. But these polarities do not inhere in the structure of difference itself; rather, it is the need to overcome mere difference that motivates the illusion of polarity.

But this reading of the androgynous mind does not exhaust the activity of *A Room of One's Own;* its explicit feminist argument still poses some problems. I would agree with Marder that a feminist doctrine, however defined, is not the aim of the essay. A feminist practice, however, might be. One could argue, as most readers seem to have done, that the feminist consciousness represented by the text is simply a necessary phase through which the woman writer must pass in order to achieve the state of asexual or bisexual consciousness. In that reading, feminism is an instrument, a technique of consciousness-raising about the nature of the cultural wrongs done to women and of inspiring women as individuals and as a group to overthrow the oppression of cultural conventions so that they can reach some position of human legitimacy. But to read Woolf's feminism that way is to interpret it more systematically and more sentimentally than the text allows. The explicitly propositional feminist arguments of the narrative, however true they may be, are not really offered as truth by the speaker. At the same time, they are not to be romantically subordinated to some notion of essential humanness.

As a nonpropositional discursive operation, the text's revision of history and gender is not wholly determined, at least not oppositionally, by the social practices under examination; it thus does not require the speaker to suggest that some ultimate transcendence of cultural conditions must take place if women are to write. This supplementary revision of history occurs in the text's appropriation of discursive practices to make them say something other than what propositional language is intended to let (or make) one say. The appropriation results in certain cultural discourses, particularly the discourse of gender identity, rupturing from within. The text thus uses its language less to say something than to say something other.[16]

The question the writer in Woolf's position must face is how she can use language to write her difference from that which language determines her to be. She cannot say propositionally anything other than what a propositional structure allows, an assertion or a negation, both of which remain inscribed by and within the very binary opposition male/female that she wants to question. But by breaking the structural laws of the conventional predication, she can begin to let language act in such a way that, while it does not produce anything definitive as statement, reveals the repressive mechanisms of propositional language.[17] What gets exposed in this writing, the repressed, is of course not a stable truth that has been denied by culture. Rather, it is the *fact* that this repression occurs continually in the restraining of certain activities to which every utterance is prone—the activities of signifiers' straying or wandering from their conventional meanings in the continual acknowledgment and evasion of the Real. That wandering, controlled by language's formal mechanisms and organized into a stable duality, assertion or negation, determines our categories of thought precisely in so far as it is *not* acknowledged.

In the text's foregrounding of this activity of language, which its writing enacts in the strategic disruption of conventional narrative expectations, the problem feminism addresses does not dissolve. As a coherent and systematic discourse, however, feminism is subjected to the same disruption that all cultural discourses begin to undergo. Recognized in this text as a mode of language, an attempt to appropriate the authority for determining sexual identity and to announce woman as a legitimate subject of being, feminism becomes a metonymic displacement of another discursive practice based in its interpretation of the body's significance.

The particular strategy implicit in Woolf's use of the term *androgyny* lies in the word's own proper doubleness: it is impossible to say whether androgyny means two become one—in which case it argues for the harmony that critics have suggested and thus reveals Woolf's desire to recuperate feminine difference into an essentially human whole—or one become more—in which case it suggests the fundamental multiplicity of the subject, as I have claimed. But the very existence of such a word in the vocabulary, and its significant placement in this text, point to a principle of language that will be exploited throughout the narrative.

The word *androgyny* gives a single, simple name to an entity that is itself confusing: the human being in whom sexual characteristics or organs of both sexes are simultaneously present. The etymology of the word—andro-man plus gyne-woman—mirrors the physical reality of androgyny: it names the condition as the spatial juxtaposition of differences, without providing any indication of the precise relation of those differences (other than contiguity) or of the meaning of that juxtaposition. As such, the word is already explicitly a metaphor, since it names a state of strangeness by combining the names for states that are familiar. Who, though, is the androgyne: a man with feminine characteristics; a woman with masculine; a creature both male and female; or a creature that in being both somehow becomes neither? It seems impossible to say; and yet the word, in naming such a state, reduces the plurality of androgyny's possible significations. Or perhaps it does not, since the singleness of the name nevertheless refers to something that is itself absolutely undecidable.

The word *androgyny* is even further in conflict with itself. In the discourses of botany and zoology, androgyny refers to a plant or an animal that, possessing the sexual organs of both male and female, carries out reproduction without the involvement of another member of its own species. But the human androgyne certainly does not have this literal self-sufficiency. Whether it could fertilize another or be fertilized by another, it is unable to inseminate itself; and usually hermaphrodites are unable to reproduce at all, in either male or female roles. Thus, in having the organs—the visible signs or markers—of both sexes, the androgyne can function biologically as neither. Woolf, however, in accord with a whole tradition, seems to want to use the term figuratively to describe a state of mental self-sufficiency, a state in which the mind impregnates itself to produce imaginative offspring. So a term that literally refers to a state of sterility is used here to signify a state of consummate fecundity.

I find no resolution to the problem of androgyny's conflicting significations, except for the fruitful notion that the word can be made to refer to a simpleness only at the cost of repressing other, equally valid possibilities of meaning. If those other possibilities do not necessarily contradict the single meaning ascribed to the term, they still converge on that singleness from many directions to make it part of a complex of differences, a complex that in being repressed nevertheless still presses against any single meaning. So the coherence of the term *androgyny* depends on the power of its discursive context to put out of play any significations of the term that conflict with the desired meaning.

In *A Room of One's Own, androgyny* seems to be presented as an end, in both senses of *conclusion* and *goal:* the issue arises at the end of the book, and it is offered as a desirable state to be achieved after a certain struggle: it is thus the text's telos. And yet, its complexity as a term must also complicate its ostensible function in the text. Seeming to want to close on a notion of wholeness and stability, the essay instead offers an end that refuses its duty. Androgyny functions discursively as a conclusion that denies the possibility of ending—ending, that is, the questioning of itself—but that also refuses to mark a new beginning, because all we are left with is an old word and its old confusions. Refusing as a term to resolve the meaning of bodily differences, the idea of androgyny also refuses to resolve the different strands of this text. So the text closes by continuing its own activity, at least insofar as that activity involves a struggle with, and in, the notion of androgyny.

But *androgyny* may have other ramifications too: if we as a culture know so clearly the meaning of the terms *male* and *female,* why can't we resolve the meaning of the juxtaposition male/female? What effect does the undecidability of that spatial contiguity have on the two terms so juxtaposed? Woolf does not wait until the end of her essay to begin the strategic displacement of the terms of sexual identity, but in fact starts her writing on a note of estrangement: "When you asked me to speak about women and fiction I sat down on the banks of a river and began to wonder what the words meant" (*Room* 3). It would seem both logically and physically impossible to sit down on the *banks* of a river, since such a feat would involve straddling the river itself, literally sitting in two or more places at once. But the impossible physical act nevertheless suggests a feat of psychic flexibility that the speaker defines as both possible and desirable.[18]

The Evasions of Certainty

Even more disruptive of the announced purpose of her essay, however, is the speaker's confusion about her topic. Why should she wonder about these words, we wonder; and if we do not immediately put down the book, our wondering doubles the speaker's. We wonder at her, but also, against our will perhaps, with her, curious as to what her wondering will produce. *Women* and *fiction,* terms that belong to the discursive orders of gender and literature, should immediately evoke for one using them a process of code recognition. But in her attention to the meanings of those words, the speaker unsettles *their* stability and, by extension, that of the codes themselves.

This defamiliarization of the words *women* and *fiction,* their estrangement from the contexts that provide them with clear and distinct ideological, if not natural referents, may occur for the speaker as a function of their juxtaposition. As a relation, however, "women and fiction" still has some contextual stability, and the conventions of that discourse are sketched out in at least two of the four possibilities the speaker mentions: "The title women and fiction might mean, and you may have meant it to mean, women and what they are like; or it might mean women and the fiction that they write; or it might mean women and the fiction that is written about them; or it might mean that somehow all three are inextricably mixed together and you want me to consider them in that light" (*Room* 3). The fact that there are at least three possible referents for the phrase *women and fiction,* though that alone suggests the multiplicity of signification, interests me less here than the particular interpretations that the speaker offers. The second and third are not problematic, and the fourth would not be if it were not for the presence of the first suggestion. But the statement that women and fiction might mean "women and what they are like" clearly violates the context of this essay, identified as a lecture presented by a fiction writer to a group of college women.

And yet there the suggestion is, on the first page of the text: what women are like may be a fiction, and you, her audience, may have intended this meaning to be addressed by the speaker. The notion itself is logically absurd, but ascribing the intention to her audience is even crazier; our reasonableness is thus violated along with the conventional relation of women and fiction and the convention of the lecture itself.[19]

But those violations all seem to share a common effect: to point to the term *women* as a sign in discourse that receives its meaning from its context and from its relation within that context to the other signifiers surrounding it. By divorcing the term from its most obvious referent—female people—and by locating the term in a different relation to a certain mode of language, the speaker begins to suggest that the meaning of the term itself is altogether a matter of conventions; and further, that those conventions are all fictional. That is, women as sign is a fiction, or a series of fictions, written by culture; if the term refers to the fictional object "women and what they are like," then culture itself would seem to be the primary fiction in which all other fictions are subplots. And because "you" want her to talk about this, "you" also are implicated in the unraveling of subjectivity that will result.

This interest in the relations between and among different fictions—women, literature, and culture—however, does not seem to be motivated by a desire to find a truth to replace the lie. In fact, the aim of truth is immediately bracketed: "When I began to consider the subject in this last way [the three meanings combined], I soon saw it had one fatal drawback. I should never be able to come to a conclusion. I should never be able to fulfill what is, I understand, the first duty of a lecturer—to hand you after an hour's discourse a nugget of pure truth" (*Room* 3). She cannot come to a conclusion—resolve the issue of women and fiction—and she cannot provide a truth: but the two failures are synonymous since the end of the lecturer is to end with truth. So the speaker will give a lecture, marked as failure from its inception, on a topic her audience could not possibly have intended.

These mistakes, however, have the function of marking out a series of expectations not generally recognized as such until they are violated; only then can we contemplate what should have come with respect to its difference from what did come. And the speaker seems locked into this difference; the goal of her own speaking shifts, or is displaced, according to the topic she chooses. That goal is no longer truth, cultural or some alternative to it, but something else:

> All I could do was to offer you an opinion upon one minor point—a woman must have money and a room of her own if she is to write fiction, and that, as you will see, leaves the great problem of the true nature of woman and the true nature of fiction unsolved. I have shirked the duty of coming to a conclusion upon these two questions—women and fiction remain, so far as I am concerned, unsolved problems. (*Room* 4)

The parallelism between "the true nature of women" and "the true nature of fiction" links the paradox of the second construction—the truth of fiction—onto the first—the truth of women—and thus continues the representation of women as a sign without any relation to truth. But more importantly, the two apparent aims of discourse, truth and conclusion, have been supplanted by opinion and unsolved problems, which is to say that they have been replaced with continued discourse.[20]

Before discussing the particular opinion offered, I want to look at the speaker's account of how that opinion will be developed, since the method has ramifications for conventional reading practices. She says, "One can only show how one came to hold whatever opinion one does hold. One can only give one's audience the chance of drawing their own conclusions as they observe the limitations, the prejudices, the idiosyncrasies of the speaker. Fiction here is likely to contain more truth than fact" (*Room* 4). In thus identifying "the speaker"—herself, of course, but apparently any speaker—as limited, prejudiced, idiosyncratic, she more significantly demands that readers assume some responsibility in relation to this text. In place of quiet and confident reception, the speaker calls for an interpretive activity in which we attend not only to what the speaker says but also to what she does not say: the speaker's motives, history, repressions, blindnesses. Thus the speaker is defined as one who, incapable of offering a truth in any ideal sense, cannot even tell her own truth directly. Truth, in its now-limited sense of the writer's truth, is produced in the relation between the writing subject and her other: the speaker, despite her apparent willingness to display herself openly and frankly, using language that represses what might conflict with the explicit argument of the text, and the reader, constantly reading against the grain of that explicitness, on the lookout for the unspoken forces producing the text and perhaps speaking more truth than the text itself.[21]

Reminding the reader of certain conventions of the fictional mode even as she subverts them for her own purposes, the speaker announces her provisional status as speaker: " 'I' is only a convenient name for somebody who has no real being" (*Room* 4). If this speaker has no real existence, then she is free to say anything, since none of it will have any direct connection to reality. But this statement about the "I" as a linguistic convention applies to realms other than the literary; given the earlier discussion of androgyny and its implications for the status of the autonomous ego, this attention to the "I" as linguistic shifter, democratically available to, indeed constitutive of, each who would speak, undermines the positivism about the subject as real, true, and natural. It thus further undermines any "I's" authority to speak truth. If "I" is not real, what can "I" say but something equally provisional, equally a function of linguistic and other cultural conventions?[22]

The Master's Rage

"I," then, sitting in two places at once, confused by simple words, begins to think about her topic. But rather than tell us what she thinks and argue, logically or not, for its validity, the speaker hides it from us, disclaiming its importance and saying only "I will not trouble you with that thought now, though if you look carefully you may find it for yourself in the course of what I am going to say" (*Room* 5). Not in *what* she will say, but in the *course* of her saying will we find the thought that motivates the movement of the text; so that movement itself becomes our interest, replacing the conventional end of reading—the discovery of some kind of textual and argumentative closure—with process.

Indeed, closure seems to be of much concern to the speaker. The opinion she offered earlier—that a woman must have money and a room of her own if she is to write fiction—begins an analysis of the cultural forces that close on the individual and, in so doing, produce him or her as a subject. The opinion, as many critics have pointed out, certainly subverts the conventional romantic claims of the spirituality of artistic activity, its transcendence of material concerns. But it does not, as some have also argued, assert that a writer writes out of the freedom he or she derives from fulfilling those material needs. To have money of one's own does not make one free: rather, it strictly if differently binds one to the signifying structures of culture. It may free one from a literal dependence on a specific supporter, father or husband, but that achievement, however comforting, still marks one as dependent: in addition to depending on money for survival, one also depends on one's money to signify to others and to the self that one has attained a particular, socially defined status.

Similarly, to have a room of one's own does not make one free: the room is in another house, ostensibly belonging to father, husband, or landlord, so one's space is necessarily circumscribed within a larger structure that does not belong to the individual (this would be true even if one owned one's house). The terms *money* and *room*, then, are metaphors that suggest that a woman who possesses such marks of freedom is necessarily dependent on the signifying practices of culture, over whose significations she has little control, to assert her culturally defined independence: to own objects that function as signs of one's power paradoxically marks one as *owned by* the signifying systems or codes to which those objects belong. But these metaphors also reveal that the goal of personal freedom is as deluded for men as for women. Social identity is a function of linguistic and cultural power structures, like money and property, which cannot be overthrown or commanded. And, in giving one the illusion of autonomy, ownership may be particularly dangerous. If one no longer feels the need to be suspicious of the circumscribing powers of cultural codes, one is the more easily deluded by them: one may become willing to fight to conserve the closure that preserves one from having to participate in the construction of oneself (or perhaps from having to see how the self has been constructed). While the speaker suggests here that women need to assume less marginal social roles, she is careful in her choice of metaphors to avoid implying that one can ever actually be independent of the orders that mark one as belonging to a particular culture and class, to say nothing of gender.

The disadvantages of social centrality become more apparent in the analyses of Oxbridge and Fernham, the men's and women's colleges the speaker visits. The juxtaposition of the two institutions is often interpreted as exemplifying the injustice of the educational system to women. This injustice is certainly at issue, though its treatment is ironically skewed by the attention to the so-called freedom of the members of powerful male institutions. The primary difference between the two colleges lies in the quantities of money expended on the former and the lack of funds allotted to the latter. But the economic division does not parallel absolutely a division into desirable and wretched states. Once again, the speaker enters into a dialogue with the signifying structures of money and property to decenter them.

Wandering about the grounds of Oxbridge, wondering about the topic "women and fiction," the speaker gets chased off the turf by an indignant Beadle for literally treading on the male prerogative: only the fellows and scholars can walk on the grass; women are not allowed (*Room* 6). The encounter with this sexually motivated restriction makes the speaker lose her train of thought: "What idea it had been that had sent me so audaciously trespassing I could not now remember" (*Room* 6). The idea that led to the transgression of this conventional law is lost, repressed by the result of the transgression, a reprimand and the reestablishment of the law. But the very fact of the repression, the idea gone into hiding, suggests what its nature must have been—transgression itself. The impulse to transgress is already implicit in the speaker's introductory remarks about women and fiction, and the location of her present reverie makes her activities even more transgressive: she is, after all, on the grounds of not just a college, a center for acculturation, but a *men's* college.

Her experience of repression is doubled when, losing the original idea, the speaker makes a trip to the library where she is again repulsed by a male guardian. Those two acts of transgression and repulsion are separated by another experience, however. Following the encounter with the Beadle and preceding that at the library, the speaker continues to wander amidst the peace of Oxbridge, where "the roughness of the present seemed smoothed away; the body seemed contained in a miraculous glass cabinet through which no sound could penetrate, and the mind, freed from any contact with facts . . . was at liberty to settle down upon whatever meditation was in harmony with the moment" (*Room* 6). Such is the freedom of a mind admitted to the august institutions of the male college: one is as if encased in a "glass cabinet through which no sound could penetrate," like a specimen of one of the "rare types" preserved by the university (*Room* 8). That spirit of peace, ending a certain sensory reality, mirrors another, more permanent kind of peace. And it is to end this deathlike quietude that the speaker commits the second act fated to result in repulsion: she intentionally provokes another confrontation with "facts."

The locus of extremely powerful repressive forces, Oxbridge soothes the mind by closing it off from anything that might challenge it, anything out of "harmony with the moment."[23] Not terribly much, however, could be in harmony with this moment. The peace of Oxbridge, and the forces necessary to produce it, are here revealed to be seductive and dangerous. And yet the speaker continues to wander around, like the return of the repressed, continually knocking against the forces that repel her but that, in repelling her, acknowledge the power of her impulse to disrupt.

Deciding not to risk another rejection, the speaker stands outside ("But the outside of these magnificent buildings is often as beautiful as the inside" [*Room* 8]), and contemplates the church:

> An unending stream of gold and silver, I thought, must have flowed into this court perpetually to keep the stones coming and the masons working. . . . [A]nd when the stones were raised, still more money was poured in from the coffers of kings and queens and great nobles. . . . And when the age of faith was over and the age of reason had come, still the same flow of gold and silver went on . . . only the gold and silver flowed now, not from the coffers of the king, but from the chests of merchants and manufacturers. . . . (9)

Despite historical, religious, and philosophical shifts, despite changes in the locus of wealth, from monarchal to capitalistic, the money is continual and its source stable, since it always comes from the center of the state's power. In fact, this tribute to the wealth of the college explicitly links religion and spirituality (the church, hymns, the age of faith) with politics (kings and queens) and business (merchants and manufacturers) to suggest that they are all structures that buy their own power by funding educational institutions. Those institutions in turn become the foundations of culture as they inculcate the values necessary to preserve the power of church, state, and commerce. Dedicated to the maintenance and preservation of the power structures that fund and found it, education is further dedicated to the same principles of inclusion and exclusion that operate to produce *it* as a source of authority in culture.

From the outside, the speaker naturally feels frustration at her exclusion from the buildings that represent social power; yet her frustration and the marginality that produces it also give her a certain energy. As a wandering, even floating signifier of the repressed—the undesired, the unadmitted—she continually encounters forces that aim to contain her, to reduce her annoying pressure against their restrictions, but she still wanders. And that wandering protects her, at least temporarily, from the power of the institution to fossilize anyone, including a woman, who worships its power. Again, money and property are linked as sign systems within which the subject is positioned; these power structures are inescapable, and yet those who embrace the power of the codes absolutely risk the equally absolute closure, even death, of their signifying functions. We can contrast this situation at Oxbridge with the evening spent at Fernham, where questioning and frustration, attempts to revise the cultural predications of women, are the central activities.

The need for a certain kind of disruption, for the emergence of the repressed simply as a means of marking out the activity of repression, is noted once again during the luncheon at Oxbridge. The sight of the manx cat, an obvious sign of castration and thus of the cultural meaning of woman, evokes in the speaker a more specific sensation of historical rather than natural difference, the difference between this party and those that occurred before the war. In grounding that difference in her analyses of aesthetic and historical changes—the new poetry and the war—the speaker suggests that a certain social convention, luncheon party conversation, has remained consistent despite fundamental changes caused by the war in the material conditions of existence. The missing context or undertone to the luncheon conversation, figured by the poetry of Tennyson and Christina Rossetti, is thus a lost illusion. But the truth to be put in place of that illusion is never offered, except as a recognition of the gap between the convention's consistency and the specific historical rupture. And in marking out the repressed cultural incoherence that results from that gap, the speaker continues the activity that composes the first chapter of the narrative. The repetitive invocation of stable social structures foregrounds them as productions of culture that in turn produce their members. By representing the structures' hold on truth as a function of the repression of difference, change, and contradiction, the text initiates a questioning of cultural discourses that it will continue to elaborate even as it will refuse to systematize any conclusions.

The explicit questions raised by the comparison of Oxbridge and Fernham—"Why did men drink wine and women water? Why was one sex so prosperous and the other so poor? What effect has poverty on fiction? What conditions are necessary for the creation of works of art?" (*Room* 25)—culminate in a trip to the British Museum to discover the historical explanation of the difference between men's and women's lives. But the Museum threatens a closure similar to that experienced at Oxbridge: "London was like a machine," and "The British Museum was another department of the factory. The swing-doors swung open; and there one stood under the vast dome, as if one were a thought in the huge bald forehead which is so splendidly encircled by a band of famous names" (*Room* 26). That striking final image, suggesting again the power located in the culture's writing, defines the individual as a single thought produced by that writing's discursive machinery. In having been so appropriated, in having been made proper precisely through this appropriation, the subject is predicated by her language. The task of the individual subject questioning the forces that produce or "write" her is complicated by the fact that she can only question in the same terms by which she is inscribed. How much power does the single sentence have to undo the authority of the language that produces it? To what extent does this alienation, initiated by the mirror and continued by the entrance into language, and thus so proper to the subject, become the source of her own limited power?

The beginning of a response to those questions lies in the discoveries the speaker makes about how woman has been culturally predicated. First, she notes, thousands of books have been written on the topic of woman. Not surprisingly, though, women have not written these books. But an even more interesting disparity follows the one noted above: "Why does Samuel Butler say 'Wise men never say what they think of women'? Wise men never say anything else apparently. But, I continued, leaning back in my chair and looking at the vast dome in which I was a single but by now somewhat harrassed thought, what is unfortunate is that wise men never think the same thing about women" (*Room* 29). What the speaker discovers is that no apparent continuity underlies the male representations of woman: she is worshiped and attacked, revered and despised, all at the same time by historical contemporaries. The only consistency the speaker finds in these historical constructions of woman is that she is depicted inconsistently. Faced with these discontinuities, jotting madly in her notebook in search of some stability, the speaker begins "for brevity's sake" to mark the object of her search *W*. That single letter, familiar to the harried notetaker as a convenient shorthand, operates in this context as another kind of shorthand: the *W* aptly suggests that woman as cultural sign has no absolute signified. Its plurality of meanings is thus proper to it.

The pun in *W*/"double you" indicates the one coherence that may actually underlie woman as signifier: as the sign of the other, woman doubles you, the one who speaks, but this doubling is not a simple mirroring of the speaker. Rather, this double is the other who, in her status *as* other, frees the subject to signify himself as subject. It is interesting, too, that *W* is Woolf's initial, the mark by which she might identify herself in a kind of shorthand. Her disguised entrance into the text at this point suggests something that will become explicit in her writing later on—the role of the writer as one who speaks from her position of acknowledged otherness to the identity ascribed her by culture. But most significantly, the notion of any particular being proper to woman is undermined by the shorthand: woman as sign is the property of her other, but her other is actually less man than it is the patriarchal constructions of man. Those discourses predicate woman as a property whose properties are not naturally ascribed, but not haphazardly either: *woman* as signifier floats, not freely but directed by the requirements of the patriarchy, to mean whatever must be opposed to a particular meaning of *man*. Thus, the proper being of woman is relational. Logically, that relativity must extend to man as well, but since the relation is inscribed by patriarchal discourses, man comes to be seen as being itself in whatever terms being is currently defined, while woman comes to signify all that man cannot, all the otherness appropriate to himself that must be repressed to ensure his stability as a legitimate subject of being.

The cultural coherence of woman as signifier thus lies only in its representation of a shifting structure of otherness. But when the speaker begins to reconstruct the author of woman's signification, she imposes another sort of coherence. Her sketch of Professor von X expresses all the anger she has felt in response to her research: "I had been drawing a face, a figure . . . of Professor von X. engaged in writing his monumental work entitled *The Mental, Moral, and Physical Inferiority of the Female Sex*. He was not in my picture a man attractive to women. . . . His expression suggested that he was labouring under some emotion that made him jab his pen on the paper as if he were killing some noxious insect as he wrote" (*Room* 31). Despite the speaker's claim, the picture is indeed a conclusion, and for that reason we must distrust it. Attempting to end the questioning of the historical representations of woman, it replaces that process with a simple and reductive assertion: the men who represent woman, who take away her power to predicate herself, are ugly, red-faced cuckolds.

The speaker's appropriation of the discourses that define women, occurring in this aesthetic representation of the enemy, is at least an active response to the power of these enforced meanings and thus certainly preferable to passive acceptance. It is, however, still illegitimate: forcing one single, simple figure to represent the locus of the oppression of women reduces its complexity. In humanizing that oppression, this reduction further obscures the real source of oppression in the languages of culture. And this image makes the enemy coherent, while the primary discovery the speaker makes in her attention to history is that its accounts of woman have not been consistent: woman has rather been liable to significations of the utmost diversity. In opting for the simplistic coherence of her representation of the enemy, the speaker begins to participate in the culture's construction of the desirable, the good, as that which is stable, unchanging, in opposition to the undesirable nonbeing of mutability and process. She does not, of course, wish to represent man in this case as good, but she wishes to reduce the signifier *man* to an easily comprehensible singularity. For to give up man as the enemy, the source of the problems facing women, is to lose the simple and direct end or solution to these problems, which would be to expose him for the beast he is and take away his power.

In granting the signifier *man* an absolute referent, the speaker participates in an activity identical to that of the culture's reduction of woman to something natural, essential, and unchanging. However, it is precisely the detachment of these signifiers *man* and *woman* from their ostensibly natural objects that must occur if cultural conventions are to accommodate transvaluation. In fact, to force the source of oppression to be coherent and stable is to give up the one power the speaker already has: her ability to challenge the power of oppression by demonstrating that its apparent stability actually veils internal contradictions. To exploit the variousness of woman as signifier is to announce that woman is nothing *but* signifier, to display its lack of any essential referent. And it is here that involvement in, if not freedom from the determinations of the signifiers of sexual identity lies.

Unfortunately, though, in a negative transference, the speaker's revision of history maintains the terms of that history, changing the positions of the oppressed and the oppressor but preserving both the faith in and the desire for mastery over one's own meaning. The speaker ultimately rejects this attempt at mastery, but its occurrence is nevertheless an important indication of how fear and anger make one read. The speaker's understandable fury over the identities she is ascribed by culture acknowledges the power of those identities to determine her. But when she gives up her desire for authority as an end in itself, she makes a far more important discovery. She analyzes her representation of the professor to realize that she has projected her own anger into his image. The professor here functions as the speaker's double: if a woman's angry self-assertion provokes her impulse to reduce the other that threatens her capacity for freedom, perhaps we understand better how and why woman has been made to signify so reductively and so oppositionally. The speaker constructs an image of the professor in order to be able to minimize his power over her: her understanding of him is determined by her wish to represent herself as valuable, significant, powerful in herself. To see herself in that way, she imagines she must reduce the other's capacity to signify anything of value. She must, that is, make him out to be irrational, vindictive, stupid, so that she herself will be free to signify reason, justice, and intelligence. Her self-assertion, however, her assumption of freedom and individuality, occur in a form that repeats the threat the other poses to her.[24]

The speaker comes to a similar conclusion about her activity, but only after she rejects her own desire for mastery over the historically determined signifiers of sexual identity. Analyzing the "element of heat" in the books she has been reading, the speaker interprets it as anger, "But it was anger that had gone underground and mixed itself with all kinds of other emotions. To judge from its odd effects, it was anger disguised and complex, not anger simple and open. . . . What is the real nature of what I call for the moment their anger?" (*Room* 32–33). The speaker's own anger, so clearly a response to reductions of her potential value, is simple, open, and thus fairly easy to recognize, if not necessarily to overcome. But to what might the disguised and complex anger of the male discourses on woman be a response? And how does the speaker's open and simple anger help to demystify the element of heat in the writing about women?

Remarking on the obvious patriarchism of Western culture, the speaker wonders why men, inhabiting apparently enviable positions of power, at least in relation to women, should be angry. She concludes that anger is necessarily "the familiar, the attendant sprite on power" (*Room* 34): "Possibly when the professor insisted a little too emphatically upon the inferiority of women, he was concerned not with their inferiority, but with his own superiority" (*Room* 34–35). The element of heat in male writing on woman appears to be anxiety metamorphosed from its objectless state into active fear with a clear trajectory toward a named other: the woman whose difference from man threatens his stable necessity. But if this fear were to remain open and direct, the threat posed by woman would have to be acknowledged, and that acknowledgment would grant woman precisely the status that the patriarchy fears. Thus it is the denial of woman's threat that the patriarchy requires. The imaginary threat of difference posed by woman must be rejected or disguised: patriarchal anxiety about woman is repressed and displaced into angry assertions of her inferiority, just exactly as we have seen the speaker's anxiety about the power of the professors motivate her own hostile reduction of them. The speaker's direct and simple anger thus opens up by repeating the patriarchy's anxious desire to reduce the meaning of woman to something simple, controllable, if not altogether stable. The speaker's self-consciousness about her own anger allows her to read the professor's apparently contradictory hostility as a sign of negation and to arrive at a sophisticated understanding of the precariousness of authority itself.

Woman Is Not-All

When the speaker turns from particular statements about women to the historical texts that place women in their temporal contexts, she discovers another series of problems.[25] Analyzing a renaissance history book, for example, she finds that woman in fiction, burning "like [a beacon] in all the works of all the poets from the beginning of time" (*Room* 44–45), seems to have no basis in fact. "In fact, as Professor Trevelyan points out, she was locked up, beaten and flung about the room" (*Room* 45). Again, why the capacity of woman to signify in fiction so powerfully at the same time that she signifies in reality a creature of such apparently slight importance? Why the pervasiveness of women in poetry if history can account for the lives of real women only with respect to their oppression, their circumscription, their absence?

Neither the history books nor the speaker can provide any answers to this question, but the gap suggests again the limitation of history as explanation: "By no possible means could middle-class women with nothing but brains and character at their command have taken part in any one of the great movements which, brought together, constitute the historian's view of the past" (*Room* 47). As a *constitution* of the past, history is produced by the same principles of selection that determine other prevailing cultural institutions, like the family and the universities.

The contradiction between historical and fictional representations of woman, like the contradictions within history itself, allows the speaker to discover that the historical is always already fictional. But once again, she does not work to replace the lie with a truth: she is more interested in opening up history to significations of woman different from those already available as a way of supplementing the existing readings of history.[26] Derrida defines the crucial doubleness of the supplement in terms remarkably close to the speaker's construction of her own aim:

> For the concept of the supplement—which here determines that of the representative image—harbors within itself two significations whose cohabitation is as strange as it is necessary. The supplement adds itself, it is a surplus, a plenitude enriching another plenitude, the *fullest measure* of presence. . . . It is thus

> that art, *techné,* image, representation, convention, etc., come as supplements to nature.
>
> But the supplement supplements. It adds only to replace.[27]

And the speaker in *A Room of One's Own* wants to exploit all the dangerous and subversive implications of the supplement's doubleness:

> It would be ambitious beyond my daring, I thought, looking about the shelves for books that were not there, to suggest to the students of the famous colleges that they should rewrite history, though I own that it often seems a little queer as it is, unreal, lop-sided; but why should they not add a supplement to history? calling it, of course, by some inconspicuous name so that women might figure there without impropriety? (47)

Woolf's essay is just such a supplement, in part just because it calls itself by its inconspicuous name. The problem with *rewriting* history to include women is, as we have seen, that the new text runs the risk of trying to master those other histories, to overcome their inadequacies with its own full speech. To replace the lie with truth is to preserve one's faith in the subject-who-knows and to derive one's own status from one's relation to that subject. Better, this speaker suggests, to add to those old signifiers others which, not replacing the old, must nevertheless displace or decenter them.

A certain kind of writing thus becomes the goal of this text, a writing that cannot be quite so easily subsumed within or mastered by discursive conventions because it already *includes* those conventions as one of its objects of representation. If the aim of this writing is to undo a certain cultural rigidity, the apparent coherence of woman and the basis of that coherence in the nature of the sexes, then that goal cannot be achieved through the simple substitution of one formalism for another. This writing, supplementing the traditional signifiers of woman's representation, will occur in the exploitation of both language's and the subject's instability.

The speaker begins to define such writing when she describes the work of Mary Carmichael, a writer struggling to produce a version of the world not so firmly rooted in complacent assumptions of the subject's authority. Interestingly, the descriptions of this writing are marked by negation: "something was not quite in order," it is "interrupted," and the author seems to be "'unhanding' herself as they say in the old plays": "She is like a person striking a match that will not light, I thought. But why, I asked her as if she were present, are Jane Austen's sentences not the right shape for you? Must they all be scrapped because Emma and Mr. Woodhouse are dead? Alas, I sighed, that it should be so. For while Jane Austen breaks from melody to melody as Mozart from song to song, to read this writing was like being out at sea in an open boat" (*Room* 84).

The adjectives describing the writing focus on its disruptive activity, and the effect of these disruptions is the reader's discomfort, alienation, and anxiety. When the speaker says that Carmichael "unhands herself," she suggests the source of her uneasiness: the writer has lost control over her writing, things get away from her, but apparently because she has somehow gotten away from herself. In fact, the speaker cannot tell "whether [Carmichael] is being herself or someone else": the struggle here between the ego-as-representation and that which is in-Carmichael-more-than-Carmichael is apparently part of the representation itself. The writer has let herself go, or let go of herself, and the result is her strange and not particularly pleasant text.

But, the speaker insists, the writing's strangeness "does not lower one's vitality" (*Room* 85). Not that the writing itself is necessarily vital, but it initiates some interest, some productive confusion in the reader. In absenting herself from her writing, at least insofar as the authorial self conventionally operates as a force of control, Carmichael produces a text of tricks. She breaks sentences and sequences, she upsets expectations, she is missing as the reassuring center of her own discourse. And the situation she produces follows and repeats this series of ruptures: "Chloe liked Olivia" (*Room* 86). The speaker finds here an immense change, but not because the relation of woman to woman produces some truth about women. Rather, the relation breaks another sequence of conventional predication in which women tend to be represented in relation to men.

But the other does not emerge here to be finally granted her rightful place of subjectivity, complete and legitimized. In fact, the speaker suggests that there are serious problems in trying to talk about woman referentially, in trying to discover some truth to present. Female people, she implies, are elusive objects of representation, so used are they to accommodating their differential relation to woman as signifier, so used to living as a series of signifiers.[28] Women live within their difference from the inscribed woman and thus perhaps experience more directly than men their own otherness to their ego representations. So to speak referentially about women is impossible because in some sense they are not stable objects of representation. But to speak referentially is also to miss the point about the kind of writing the speaker finds in Carmichael's work: it does not refute previous accounts of woman, it does not imitate male assertions of self, it does something *other* than what might be expected. And to maintain that otherness as the object and technique of representation requires that the writer "[t]alk of something else, looking steadily out the window, and thus note, not with a pencil in the notebook, but in the shortest of shorthand, in words that are hardly syllabled yet, what happens when Olivia—this organism that has been under the shadow of the rock these million years—feels the light fall on it . . . " (*Room* 88). The shorthand the speaker refers to here, like the abbreviated notation *W* in her notebook, becomes an appropriation of the linguistic and literary conventions already available to the writer, a manipulation that, in deforming the signifiers that constitute our language, reveals both their power and their instability.

Thus, to write "like a woman," that phrase used sometimes disparagingly, sometimes encouragingly, but almost always reductively, does not mean anything very specific. It appears to mean only "to write differently": to disrupt the closure of existing conventions, to resist the seduction of the "I" as a subject who knows, to acknowledge one's desire. In short, to record or enact the operations of mind that are conventionally put out of play in order that writing should maintain its hold on truth. Those operations, though not by any means prelinguistic or nonlinguistic, exist in "the pressure of dumbness, the accumulation of unrecorded life" (*Room* 93): in the language of the unconscious, perhaps, whose system of representation must be mirrored by the writer's. These operations are manifested in the impulses to break the expected sequences, to transgress and to supplement, to tamper with the institutions of power as they conventionally predicate the subject: not to assert that what is repressed is the truth, but only to point to repression as what makes truth possible as the other of falseness.

These impulses lead not to the establishment of another enclosure, but to continued writing, further supplementation of signifiers. The effect of Carmichael's writing, the speaker says,

> was somehow baffling. . . . For whenever I was about to feel the usual things in the usual places, about love, about death, the annoying creature twitched me away, as if the important point were just a little further on. And thus she made it impossible for me to roll out my sonorous phrases about "elemental feelings," the "common stuff of humanity," "depths of the human heart," and all those other phrases which support us in our belief that, however clever we may be on top, we are very serious and profound and humane underneath. She made me feel, on the contrary, that instead of being serious and profound and humane, one might be—and the thought was far less seductive—merely lazy minded and conventional into the bargain. (*Room* 95)

Carmichael's displacement of the authorial self as the center of the text and her replacement of that center with an activity of language effects a similar displacement in the reader. The comforting and self-congratulatory implications of humanism—the ultimately narcissistic faith in the essentiality of humanness as we conventionally understand it—are not replaced with explicitly antihumanistic sentiments. In fact, they are not replaced with anything except a continued "twitching away" from the expected. In the process, the faith in our profound humanity gives way to confusion and then to a partial recognition of the motives of humanism: it lets us be lazy and conventional and yet think quite well of ourselves.

And the high-sounding moralism of that humanism is revealed to be a fundamentally conservative structure, one that ensures the preservation of its implicit power structure in the guise of liberal altruism. In deforming the mode of language that underlies and thus propagates such conservativism, Carmichael's writing reveals as well its motives: "[her writing] ranged, too, very subtly and curiously, among almost unknown or unrecorded things; it lighted on small things and showed that perhaps they were not small after all. It brought buried things to light and made one wonder what need there had been to bury them" (*Room* 96). That last consideration need not be read as merely rhetorical: it invites serious thought about the historical forces that prompt repression, the objects of which are not always the same. Because repression in Carmichael's writing does not end—is not permanently lifted to reveal truths—its operations are simply revealed to be the forces which, in burying certain things, allow others to rise and congeal into the solid and comforting predications of convention.

In writing this way, Carmichael "mastered the first great lesson; she wrote as a woman, but as a woman who has forgotten that she is a woman, so that her pages were full of that curious sexual quality which comes only when sex is unconscious of itself" (*Room* 96). This troubling passage may raise more questions than we could hope to resolve. Who is the woman who has forgotten that she is a woman, and what sort of mastery has she achieved? To forget that one is a woman might mean to forget the identity one has been ascribed by culture, but that does not seem to be forgettable, unless one could actively encourage the ego-as-representation to encounter that in the self that exceeds the representation of the self. One's writing, then, would have to be at least in part the writing of the unconscious, the return of the repressed, and perhaps that would account for the "curious sexual quality which comes only when sex is unconscious of itself." That sexual quality might mean libido, the primal energy that Freud said is characteristic of all individuals before and in spite of sexual differentiation but most available when the rigidity of that differentiation ceases so actively to sublimate it—in dreams or psychosis, for example. And perhaps then the phrase "when sex is unconscious of itself" alludes to the sexuality *of* the unconscious. In this sense, "unconscious of itself" would not mean unaware of itself. Rather, parodically, invertedly, the activity of knowing that is usually ascribed to the conscious mind is here attributed to the unconscious, which "knows" at least a certain element of sexuality. And that sexuality, commonly repressed and redirected into the culturally appropriate channels of masculinity and femininity, should somehow emerge in and as its capacity to undermine or complicate the roles—roles of man, woman, and subject—that its repression makes possible. This would indeed seem to be a writing of doubling, conflict, rupture, and estrangement.

And this writing returns us to the cipher of androgyny, a term that locates and gives voice to all the forces of the writing mentioned above. The androgynous mind is precisely what the contemporary male narcissist, Mr. B, lacks: "When one takes a sentence of Mr. B into the mind it falls plump to the ground—dead"; the writing of Coleridge, on the other hand, when taken into the mind, "explodes and gives birth to all kinds of other ideas, and that is the only sort of writing of which one can say that it has the secret of perpetual life" (*Room* 105). Mr. B's sentence is sterile; its unrelenting "I" requires a singleness of vision and of voice that, in repressing all that counters it, kills its own vitality by denying its relation to anything else. It is a writing that fails to have intercourse, that onanistically celebrates only the illusion of the self and that paradoxically speaks of the greatest anxiety. The upright desiring "I," in the course of such self-love, ignores the others that, in countering it, inspire its activity. It can produce no offspring but its own limp sterility. Writing that has the "secret of perpetual life," however, inseminates by disseminating: Coleridge's sentence, giving "birth to all kinds of other ideas," enters the mind of the reader to produce an active engagement with itself. It produces ideas not necessarily contained within itself but which, by association of some kind, are born of its predication. The language is procreative; it reproduces not just itself again, or a repetition of the activity that produced it, but other language, even language that is other to itself. And the mind that produced such a sentence must have performed a self-fertilizing activity similar to the one above: by discovering and acknowledging the forces within itself that do not belong to the "I," that surround it and converge on it in the language of unconsciousness. In the vernacular, the mind that "fucks with" itself produces not further versions of the complacent "I," but rather fundamental confusions about what the mind, and the language that produces it, might be. And where can those confusions go but back into language—into texts that, reproducing the processes of psychic estrangement that produce them, enter the mind of a reader to fuck with his—or her—"I"?

Chapter 6

An Ending That Fails to Conclude

This book traces what Kristeva has called "the implacable violence . . . which constitutes any symbolic contract."[1] Indeed, the trope of dead fathers is about the persistence of violence in disguised forms, a violence that is at the root of both the subject and the law. From the very beginning, the dead father is a screen. In the oedipal complex, the father who is already dead, beyond both (his) desire and (my) revenge, arises as a fantasy: through this fantasy, the child explains to himself or herself the loss of the mother, the death of the originally unified self, though such unity, of course, never existed. The myth of the dead father, appearing to explain death, in fact really *screens* a prior death, loss, violation. This myth and the subsequent transference that arises from it are mechanisms for protecting the subject against its own rage, mechanisms that work by enabling the subject to identify with that rage itself as a *paternal* legacy.

The narratives I have considered give us access to some of the modern disguises of this rage. In *Heart of Darkness*, for example, Marlow responds to the explicit material violence perpetrated against others in the African jungle by first repudiating it and then replacing it with his own act of violation: he refuses nature—the call of the jungle wild—and chooses instead his deliberate belief. But in this existentialist alternative to cultural horror—Kurtz, the traders, etc.—Marlow's admission of violence is purely imaginative, purely negative, and therefore still repressive. The Africans remain mythic so Marlow can distinguish himself from them in conventional terms. Marlow's story continues to identify with and thus to preserve the rage of the oedipal son who protects the father's authority in order to enjoy it for himself at a later date: he alone bears the knowledge of the horror.

But by setting *Heart of Darkness* in the context of Western imperialism, Conrad demonstrates that Marlow's existential struggle has stakes that are more than metaphorical. The modern nation's struggle for mastery produced a violence against colonized subjects to which it was as blind as it was unrelenting. The scramble for a place in the new world of international markets and emerging nationalisms was accomplished behind the screen of deliberate belief and earned authority. Thus, the modern drive toward a new world contained, in transferential forms, the violence of a patriarchal past that Marlow could neither escape nor fully understand; indeed, his resistance to such understanding makes possible his exploitation of that same past for his own private purposes.

James, turning from the male to the female centers of consciousness in Kate and then Milly, adds to Conrad's representation of transferential repetition the knowledge that the oedipal dynamic underlying male subjectivity can also constitute female desire. This novel thus anticipates Lacan's notion that masculine and feminine identities are structural, not biological matters.[2] This substitution of woman for man further introduces the issue of gender into these considerations of authority, originality, and repetition.[3] In *The Wings of the Dove,* however, male subjective privilege is undermined by the fact that women receive the legacy of the fathers, with the result that women are as duped by the desire for mastery as men have traditionally been.

The violence that contaminates the interpersonal relations of the characters in this novel is not merely psychological: it extends to and implicates the modern industrial economy. The source of Milly's and Maud's great wealth is, of course, business, capitalism: Milly's New York money and Maud's husband's fortune (Kate calls her aunt "Britannia of the Market Place" [James, *Wings* 37]). In fact, money is so central to the conflicts in the novel that the aggression that arises in the characters' relations might seem contingent, as if the problem were *only* money and not something else. Money, that is, has become in the modern world another screen for the will to power that cannot be admitted to but that persists in continually new disguises. By revealing the function of business to be, among other things, such a disguise, James adds a dimension to the analysis of capitalism that Marx himself left out.

In *The Sun Also Rises,* the modern disguise for human violence occurs in the explicit but coded contest of the bullfight. The ritual's charm seems to be that it gives us contact with a certain real primitive aggression that has been driven out of or repressed by modern society. In truth, however, such violence is quite persistent in the modern age, as is evident in Jake's mutilation, the novel's most obvious reminder of the trauma of World War I. The bullfight, then, exists not to give us *access* to a lost natural drive but to hide the terrifying forms the drive continues to take, not just in modern technological warfare, but in business enterprises, sexual relations, and anti-Semitism, among other things.

The novel makes the further step of implicating gender itself as one of the transferential strategies for coping with the implacable violence of the subject. Jake manages his physical mutilation—his bodily "feminization"—through his cathexis onto the bullfight, using this displaced violence in a strategy of mastery that repeats that of the castration complex; the renunciation of immediate (but impossible) pleasure sustains the illusion of such pleasure's reality and promises its eventual satisfaction for those who imitate the subject-who-possesses. Despite its pretense that these characters continually struggle with the existential anxiety of their freedom, then, the narrative reveals their commitment to cultural and personal repetition compulsions. Their striving for freedom manifests a modern fantasy of control preserved by those who cannot bear their weakness.

In *A Room of One's Own,* gender takes on a different status from its reified representation in Hemingway's novel. For Woolf, gender marks a fissure in cultural closure: it is an effort to stitch up the gap of difference that simultaneously reveals that lack. As Dennis A. Foster has remarked, playing on the title of Judith Butler's recent work, *Gender Trouble,* gender in fact is *not* the trouble itself but rather one cultural *response* to trouble, a reaction formation attempting to manage the trouble of the Real.[4] Indeed, gender performs some of the most fundamental dividing and organizing work in culture and, as such, seems to be the indispensable ground for many of the other structuring binaries that subtend identity. Woolf alone among the writers I discuss considers the function of gender directly, suggesting how motivated we have been to resist seeing its place in the constitution of culture. As Butler has claimed in her discussion of drag as gender parody, *"In imitating gender, drag implicitly reveals the imitative structure of gender itself—as well as its contingency"* (137; Butler's emphasis). Drag makes explicit that gender is constituted of and by performative acts, gestures, and costumes that can be enacted and assumed by anyone, regardless of biological sex. It therefore exposes the *lack* of any essential foundation to particular gender identities. I would argue along these lines that Woolf's writing in *A Room of One's Own* constitutes a similar kind of imitative work, not of gender itself but of the discourses that, claiming merely to describe it, actually participate in its construction.

But to announce gender's artificiality and contingency is certainly not to escape from its determinations. Gender is not, after all, merely an external imposition on an otherwise coherent but freer subjectivity. It is precisely one of the strategies of subjectivization, one of the means by which subjects are produced through their entrance into language and the other manifestations of the symbolic. Despite Butler's assertion that gender parody "suggests [gender's] openness to resignification and recontextualization," then, *we are always already gendered,* even as we express the wish to resignify ourselves and thereby alter our gender commitments.

As a discourse not bound to truth written by a subject without mastery, Woolf's essay recognizes the difficulty of such resignifying efforts. It also fails to arrive at a conclusion, except for the nonending of androgyny. That self-contradictory term admits the fissures—psychic, sexual, social—that constitute the human subject at the same time that it disguises such traumas with its promise of neat, if metaphoric, closure. *A Room of One's Own* reveals those two operations of exposure and concealment to be at the root of some of Western culture's most crucial *points de capiton:* woman, history, truth, the subject.

But the text does more than admit the undecidability of important words in the language. If Woolf seems to have become the heroine of my narrative of modernism, it is because in her essay, the speaker not only denies the existence of a subject-who-knows, but she also mocks her own desire to discover (and become) one. In so doing, she avoids both positive and negative transferences—faith and doubt—onto cultural authority figures. Indeed, her resistance to both textual and subjective closure—unity, cohesion, integrity—enacts a concomitant resistance to the seductions of authority itself. Such resistance permits the subject to *manage* violence rather than to project it outward, to accept it as the subject's property. The speaker thus admits to a desire for what she knows to be impossible. This admission does not put an end to desire, but contextualizes it in such a way as to make possible a recognition of its simultaneous essentiality and artificiality: it may be in the nature of consciousness to desire in response to its constitutive lack, but *what* it desires is nonetheless interpretable as a symptom of a fantasy.

Woolf's *A Room of One's Own* embraces what the other narratives I have considered represent but also resist: the knowledge of violence at the subject's heart, figured in androgyny's disunity. This is precisely the violence that Kristeva, Lacan, and Žižek insist must be accepted if one is to live with it rather than unconsciously reenact it. In the figure of the androgynous self, Woolf presents an image of subjectivity that permits us to think past the repetition of transference. But this figure of androgyny is not about fullness, completion, "being all"; in fact, it is precisely a figure of castration—of limitation, lack, inconclusiveness—the acceptance of which is crucial to the management of violence that often evades us in Western culture.

At the conclusion of *The Sublime Object of Ideology*, Žižek describes "subjective destitution," the last stage of the psychoanalytic process and something that sounds like this acceptance:

> What is at stake in this "destitution" is precisely the fact that *the subject no longer presupposes himself as subject*. . . . In other words, he assumes not the existence but the *nonexistence* of the big Other; he accepts the Real in its utter, meaningless idiocy; he keeps open the gap between the Real and its symbolization. The price to be paid for this is that by the same act he also *annuls himself as subject*.[5]

These are almost the book's last words, and their abstractness is no doubt intentionally provocative. What can it mean to stop presupposing oneself as subject, to annul oneself as a subject? The fact is, the grammatical subject of Žižek's first italicized construction is the word *subject: "the subject no longer presupposes himself as subject."* Apparently, then, if such a nullification of subjectivity were to take place, it would paradoxically but crucially be at one's bidding: the subject does the work of his or her own annihilation, which leaves out the likelihood that Žižek is describing psychosis here. Indeed, the double appearance of the word *subject* in the clause suggests that this condition, in addition to being chosen, worked for, also consists in seeing oneself, acting (as) oneself, double, in two places at one time. One identifies (with) oneself, that is, as both subject (agent) and object (effect) simultaneously.

The achievement of subjective destitution, coterminous with the dissolution of the transference, results from the process of "going through the fantasy." Fantasy, whether personal or ideological, we remember, has been defined as the illusion that structures reality by masking the traumatic Real. According to Žižek, in the fantasy we discover not how to fulfill our desire, but rather how our desires have been constituted in the first place: *"through fantasy,"* Žižek says, we have learned *"'how to desire,'"* (*Sublime Object* 118; Žižek's emphasis), and, he continues, the particular forms taken by our desires have actually functioned to disguise the arbitrariness of the symbolic: "the desire structured through fantasy is a defence against the desire of the Other," against, that is, the knowledge of the lack in the Other, of the "hole in the symbolic" that gives evidence of the Real.

What Žižek helps us to see here is that the end of analysis involves a kind of return to origins, not a reexperience of birth trauma, but an acknowledgment of how one's entrance into the symbolic occurred. Beyond or underlying one's interpretable symptoms lies the fantasy, a scene that stages one's desire and reveals the nonsense core initiating its structuring. The fantasy "block[s] the further movement of interpretation" (Žižek, *Sublime Object* 74) because it is the arbitrary point of the subject's entrance into the symbolic. In "going through the fantasy," Žižek says, "we experience how this fantasy object . . . only materializes the void of our desire" (*Sublime Object* 65): "we must accomplish the crucial step of going through the fantasy, of obtaining distance from it, of experiencing how the fantasy-formation just masks, fills out a certain void, lack, empty place in the Other" (*Sublime Object* 74). In Lacan's words, "What is essential is that [the analysand] should see, beyond this signification [the interpretation of symptoms], to what signifier—to what irreducible, traumatic, non-meaning—he is, as a subject, subjected" (*Four Fundamental Concepts* 250–51). The fantasy records the point at which one's desire in the Real converged with the symbolic and thus began to take "interpretable," i.e., symptomatic, form.

It is still difficult to imagine in practical terms, however, what "subjective destitution" would consist in, since it is an imagining that "practical terms" exist precisely to make difficult. Glossed as I have suggested, though, the notion may describe something close to what Woolf's speaker announces herself as doing in *A Room of One's Own* when she sits on the banks of a river and wonders what words mean. But what Žižek defines and Woolf performs must be more than an intellectual acknowledgment that one is constructed, produced, interpellated. These theoretical terms themselves frequently enact the "admission as repression" that characterizes cynicism in Žižek's account of "cynicism as ideology." "Cynical reason is no longer naive, but is a paradox of an enlightened false consciousness: one knows the falsehood very well, one is well aware of a particular interest hidden behind an ideological universality, but still one does not renounce it" (*Sublime Object* 29). We know very well, that is, that we are not unique individuals free to choose our own meaning and values from a wide variety of different options, but still we continue to *behave* as if we believed we were free, and in that behavior, we can locate our actual but unadmitted belief in freedom.

The difficulty of saying exactly how subjective destitution might manifest if it is not such cynicism derives from the importance a belief in the subject position has had in the production of our world. Žižek does not claim that we can or should give up that position, but he suggests that our practical behavior might somehow include the knowledge of what makes that position possible, of what cultural and personal interests it serves, what truths it denies. I suspect that such a transformation of one's subjectivity involves something hard to name and harder to sustain: an unglamorous and unnoble recognition of the self's mediocrity and lack of specialness, a condition that we are used to recognizing in others and generally measure ourselves, happily or not, against; if not a giving up of the striving for excellence, then at least a recognition that such striving is a banal and deluded desire for impossible mastery rather than the submission to a legitimate and reasonable task. Again, this is not to suggest that the end of psychoanalysis or ideological criticism is also the end of desire: such a goal would be consistent with (and thus as deluded as) the belief in some unfragmented wholeness, beyond the loss, separation, and sacrifice of Kristeva's "symbolic contract." However, to recognize that desire is never to be fulfilled might give one a different relation to it than the generally shared fantasy that sometime, in some way, one might get what one *really* wants. Rather than the source of life's glamour and meaning, desire is the awkward, inevitable side effect of the peculiarly human trauma of language—loss, lack, substitution. To live with this knowledge as something other than a cynical admission would be to lose the sustaining illusion of a future wholeness, but it might also enable one to move outside of the endless repetition of transference and the master/servant relation, a goal that so many of the texts of modernism fearfully record and yet fail to achieve.

Notes

Chapter 1

Epigraphs from Donald Barthelme, *The Dead Father* (New York: Penguin, 1975), 3; Jacques-Alain Miller, "The Analytic Experience: Means, Ends, and Results," in *Lacan and the Subject of Language*," ed. Ellie Ragland Sullivan and Mark Brache (New York: Routledge, 1991), 86. Future references to these works will be included in the text.

1. Vincent Pecora discusses a slightly different version of the double bind of resistance in modernist narrative in *Self and Form in Modern Narrative* (Baltimore: Johns Hopkins University Press, 1989). I consider Pecora's work more fully in note 35 of this chapter. Future references to this work will appear in the text.
2. Fredric Jameson, *The Political Unconscious: Narrative as a Socially Symbolic Act* (Ithaca: Cornell University Press, 1981), 9. Future references to this work will appear in the text.
3. Shoshana Felman, *Writing and Madness (Literature/Philosophy/Psychoanalysis)*, trans. Martha Noel Evans and the author with the assistance of Brian Massumi (Ithaca: Cornell University Press, 1985), 148. Future references to this work will appear in the text.
4. See also Bette London, *The Appropriated Voice: Narrative Authority in Conrad, Forster, and Woolf* (Ann Arbor: University of Michigan Press, 1990), for a discussion of how Jameson's representation of modernism participates in the reading effect, "uncannily" "reproduc[ing] critical orthodoxies," particularly those of Albert J. Guerard (3).
5. Slavoj Žižek, *The Sublime Object of Ideology* (London: Verso, 1989). Future references to this work will appear in the text.
6. Paul de Man, "Literary History and Literary Modernity," *Blindness and Insight: Essays in the Rhetoric of Contemporary Criticism* (New York: Oxford University Press, 1971). Future references to this work will appear in the text.

   In *The Myth of the Modern: A Study in British Literature and Criticism after 1850* (New Haven: Yale University Press, 1987), Perry Meisel's consideration of modernism is also structured around precisely this double bind. He distinguishes between "strong" and "weak" modernist texts, in clearly Bloomian language, on the basis of their accepting or repressing their own belatedness. In the following passage, though, his terms are more explicitly de Manian: "The will to modernity that we commonly equate with the structure of modernism as a whole is largely a defensive response to the increasingly intolerable burdens of coming late in a tradition" (2).

7. This claim may be similar to Žižek's that *"it is language which is, in an unheard-of sense, a 'Stalinist phenomenon.'* The Stalinist ritual, the empty flattery which 'holds together' the community, the neutral voice, totally freed of all 'psychological' remnants, which pronounces the 'confessions' in the staged political processes—they realize, in the purest form to date, a dimension which is probably essential to language as such" (Žižek, *Sublime Object* 212; Žižek's emphasis).
8. London also discusses the problem of authority in modernism; see in particular chapter 1 in *The Appropriated Voice*.
9. Harold Bloom, *The Anxiety of Influence: A Theory of Poetry* (London: Oxford University Press, 1973), 5. Future references to this work will appear in the text.
10. Sigmund Freud, *Introductory Lectures on Psycho-Analysis, The Standard Edition of the Complete Psychological Works of Sigmund Freud* (London: Hogarth, 1953), 16:443–44. Future references to this work will appear in the text.
11. Miller describes transference with a similar formulation: "For Freud, analysis was interpretation, serious, intellectual work; and the emergence of the affective component of the experience was for him at first not a means to cure, but an obstacle, and he had to turn the obstacle into a means" (91).
12. Freud, "Observations on Transference Love," *Standard Edition* 12:168. Miller notes too that there is a sense in which "all neuroses are transference neuroses—i.e., are established in relation to an other, a transferential other" (90). This is an implication of transference theory I will develop further a bit later on.
13. As Jacques Lacan says, "[T]he positive transference is when you have a soft spot for the individual concerned, . . . and the negative transference is when you have to keep your eye on him." *The Four Fundamental Concepts of Psycho-Analysis*, ed. Jacques-Alain Miller, trans. Alan Sheridan (New York: Norton, 1981), 124. Future references to this work will appear in the text.
14. "[W]e would rather love than know, and that is the value of transference as obstacle: love, instead of knowledge. . . . There is no desire to know. It is love, not the desire to know, that is directed toward knowledge" (91).
15. Freud, *Totem and Taboo: Some Points of Agreement between the Mental Lives of Savages and Neurotics, Standard Edition* 13:141–42. Future references to this work will appear in the text.
16. Freud, *Moses and Monotheism, Standard Edition* 23:119. Future references to this work will appear in the text.
17. This may be an example of what Žižek calls "choosing what is given," something I'll talk more about later (*Sublime Object* 220).

    Lacan also comments that Freud "[linked] the appearance of the signifier of the Father, as author of the Law, with death, even to the murder of the Father—thus showing that if this murder is the fruitful moment of debt through which the subject binds himself for life to the Law, the symbolic Father is, in so far as he signifies this Law, the dead Father." "On the Possible Treatment of Psychosis," in *Ecrits: A Selection*, trans. Alan Sheridan (New York: Norton, 1977), 199.
18. We should keep in mind here that fathers are, after all, only metaphors for origins, metaphors that function simultaneously to displace and repress real origins: the mothers who must be forgotten or otherwise repudiated so that separation, language, and all other kinds of symbolic substitution can become possible.

19. In chapter 2, regarding *Heart of Darkness,* I will discuss this horror more specifically as the source of Kurtz's self-destruction.
20. The Christian myth is another of these symptomatic constructions that give evidence of a trauma in their disguise of it, as Freud points out in *Moses and Monotheism* (see in particular 86–88). In this case, the myth presents a son who is killed with his father's knowledge, who sacrifices himself but in doing so becomes, like the original dead father, dead but not dead, human and immaterial, the traumatic source of the Law that carries his name. I am indebted to Donald Schwartz for reminding me of the relevance of Christianity to this discussion.
21. Freud, *Civilization and Its Discontents, Standard Edition* 21:129.
22. "The real is beyond the *automaton* ["the network of signifiers" (52)], the return, the coming-back, the insistence of the signs, by which we see ourselves governed by the pleasure principle. The real is that which always lies behind the automaton . . . " (*Four Fundamental Concepts* 53–54).
23. Žižek, however, claims that there is no real *Aufhebung* in Hegel either:

    [T]he "synthesis" is not any kind of return to the thesis, some kind of healing of the wound made by the anti-thesis—*the "synthesis" is exactly the same as the anti-thesis;* the only difference lies in a certain change of perspective, in a certain turn through which what was a moment ago experienced as an obstacle, as an impediment, proves itself to be a positive condition. . . .

    This is also, in a nutshell, the logic of the "negation of the negation" . . . , [which] does not entail any kind of return to positive identity, any kind of abolition . . . of the disruptive force of negativity. . . . (*Sublime Object* 176; Žižek's emphasis)

    See also John Smith's "U-Topian Hegel: Dialectic and Its Other in Poststructuralism," *German Quarterly* 60 (1987). Smith analyzes how poststructuralist theory has produced a particular and limited interpretation of Hegel.
24. J. Laplanche and J.-B. Pontalis, *The Language of Psychoanalysis,* trans. Donald Nicholson-Smith (New York: Norton, 1973), 136.
25. "As soon as the subject who is supposed to know exists somewhere . . . there is transference" (Lacan, *Four Fundamental Concepts* 232).
26. See Žižek on Hegel's theory of repetition in history (*Sublime Object* 60–61). Hegel realized, Žižek argues, that "so-called historical necessity itself *is constituted through misrecognition,* through the initial failure of 'opinion' to recognize its true character. . . . " (61; Žižek's emphasis).
27. Georg Lukács, "The Ideology of Modernism," in *Marxism and Human Liberation,* ed. E. San Juan, Jr., trans. John and Nekke Mander (New York: Delta, 1973).
28. Lillian S. Robinson and Lise Vogel, "Modernism and History," *NLH* 3 (1971): 198; their emphasis.
29. I should be clear here, though, that Jameson's critical project in *The Political Unconscious* involves characterizing modernism as precisely *double:* it is simultaneously complicit in the ideological naturalization of cultural conditions and *also* capable of negatively articulating "Utopian" possibilities of a world beyond the one(s) realistically depicted in the narratives. Pecora offers a persuasive critique of Jameson's theoretical assumptions; see in particular chapter 3 of his *Self and Form in Modern Narrative.*

30. Terry Eagleton, *Literary Theory: An Introduction* (Minneapolis: University of Minnesota Press, 1983), 139. Future references to this work appear in the text.
31. In Roland Barthes's words, "It is when History is denied that it is most unmistakably at work. . . . " *Writing Degree Zero,* trans. Annette Lavers and Colin Smith (New York: Hill and Wang, 1967), 2.

    For further observations about the limits of Lukács's critique of modernism, see Rosalind Coward and John Ellis, *Language and Materialism: Developments in Semiology and the Theory of the Subject* (London: Routledge and Kegan Paul, 1971), who discuss the failure of this kind of Marxism to account in any rigorous fashion for the materiality of language or the ideological nature of the subject (34–44, 61). See also Makiko Minow-Pinkney, *Virginia Woolf and the Problem of the Subject* (New Brunswick, N. J.: Rutgers University Press, 1987), 12–14.
32. For a thorough account of the ways, for example, criticism has tended to reduce contradiction and ambivalence to the aesthetically more manageable and satisfying "paradox," see chapter 1 of Astradur Eysteinsson's *The Concept of Modernism* (Ithaca: Cornell University Press, 1990).
33. See in particular the final chapter of *Sublime Object* (201–31).
34. See Eysteinsson on the "Crisis of the Subject" in *The Concept of Modernism* (26–30).
35. Pecora also addresses the doubleness of modernism's relation to its sociohistorical context. However, his formulation poses some problems for me. In essence, Pecora understands the conflict of modernism as a binary, the opposition between its *resistance* and *capitulation* to ideology. But for Pecora, modernist resistance is always inadequate to provoke the kind of social transvaluation a progressive critic seeks because the important mode and object of representation, the form of the bourgeois self in literary and philosophical reflection, has been in these texts so thoroughly appropriated and therefore deformed by capitalism as to be useless for critical purposes. In modernism, says Pecora, "the ironic, distanced subjectivity upon which the earlier realist novel depended as its critical and progressive 'idea' is deconstructed and usurped as *an instrumentalized function of the narrative structure*" (89–90; Pecora's emphasis).

    I have no quarrel with Pecora's evaluation of the limits of irony in modernism; but I think his desire for a "way out" of the ideological determinism of capitalism is symptomatic of what Žižek calls the desire for harmony characteristic of much leftist literary criticism. Pecora seems to want to acknowledge the constructedness and artificiality of the subject of modernism and simultaneously to preserve its form as the only possible means of critique; to say, in short, something like "I know the subject isn't real, but for practical critical purposes we will speak as if it were." But of course, he isn't himself satisfied with the implications of such a self-delusion. In my own conclusion, I will try to articulate what kind of analytic project might be undertaken by the subject-under-erasure that Pecora's critical vocabulary provides no name for, but that Lacan calls "subjective destitution." In the meantime, I will simply anticipate that discussion by mentioning here that the fully conscious agency Pecora wishes to direct both literary and critical authorship overlooks the power of transference in frustrating individual and institutional efforts to resist authority.

36. In linguistic terms, this structure derives from the repression of what Derrida calls *differance,* the wandering, straying, sliding of signifiers not held in place by any transcendental signified. It is Derrida's supposed denial of any such nodal point as the *point de capiton* that divides Derrida from Lacan.
37. If we understand these nodal points to be "pure signifiers" without signifieds, "word[s] to which 'things' themselves refer to recognize themselves in their unity" (Žižek, *Sublime Object* 95–96), we may also distinguish here a version of Jean Baudrillard's hyperreal, "the generation by models of a real without origin or reality: a hyperreal." *Simulations,* trans. Paul Foss, Paul Patton, and Philip Beitchman (New York: Semiotext(e), 1983), 2. Baudrillard characterizes this phenomenon as peculiarly postmodern, but Žižek seems to attribute it to the operations of language itself.
38. G. W. F. Hegel, *Phenomenology of Spirit,* trans. A. V. Miller (Oxford: Oxford University Press, 1977).
39. Nietzsche, however, will revise the status of stoicism in his furious critique of Judeo-Christian slave morality in *Genealogy of Morals,* trans. Francis Golffing (New York: Doubleday, 1956).
40. Walter Benjamin discusses this topic in "The Author as Producer," in *Reflections,* ed. Peter Demetz, trans. Edmund Jephcott (New York: Harcourt, 1978).
41. Žižek explains why it is never enough to "demonstrate" that the object of racist or sexist fantasy is not what the fantasy claims. If such a stereotype can be overcome by logic, Žižek claims, then the racist or sexist ideology has not fully grasped us: "An ideology really succeeds when even the facts which at first sight contradict it start to function as arguments in its favour" (*Sublime Object* 49).
42. See Lacan's discussion of the difference between doubt (always expressing a desire for certainty) and skepticism ("holding the subjective position that *one can know nothing*") (*Four Fundamental Concepts* 223–24; Lacan's emphasis).
43. We see this paradoxical dynamic at work in the literary text's relation to its objects of representation. Thus, an effort to escape the authority of existing systems can only occur as an act of imitative supplementation, as Jacques Derrida defines the latter term. "[T]he concept of the supplement," he says, "harbors within itself two significations whose cohabitation is as strange as it is necessary. The supplement adds itself, it is a surplus, a plenitude enriching another plenitude. . . . But the supplement supplements. It adds only to replace." *Of Grammatology,* trans. Gayatri Chakravorty Spivak (Baltimore: Johns Hopkins University Press, 1974), 144–45. As an inadvertent supplement, an unconscious displacement of the imitated "original," the text cannot help but suggest the inessentiality of what it reproduces. That is, as a kind of transference effect, the text reveals the original of its imitation to be simply an earlier transference.

    Kristeva makes a similar point when, regarding feminism, she says "the very logic of counter-power and of counter-society necessarily generates, by its very structure, its essence as a simularcrum of the combatted society or of power." "Women's Time," in *The Kristeva Reader,* trans. Alice Jardine and Harry Blake, ed. Toril Moi (New York: Columbia University Press, 1986), 203. I will discuss this issue, and this essay, more fully in chapter 5.

44. Slavoj Žižek, *Looking Awry: An Introduction to Jacques Lacan through Popular Culture* (Cambridge: MIT Press, 1991), 151. Future references to this work will appear in the text.

Chapter 2

Epigraph from G. W. F. Hegel, *The Philosophy of History,* trans. J. Sibree (New York: Dover, 1956), 91. The citation from Leopold appears in Joseph Conrad, *Heart of Darkness,* ed. Robert Kimbrough (New York: Norton Critical Edition, 1988), 79. Future references to these works will appear in the text.

1. But see note 23 in chapter 1 for an account of Žižek's counterintuitive reading of Hegel's dialectic as a nontotalizing discourse.
2. Edward Said makes this point in his analysis of the novel: "The trouble with unrestrained and militant egoism as Conrad saw it was that it becomes an imperialism of ideas, which easily converts itself into the imperialism of nations." *Joseph Conrad and the Fictions of Autobiography* (Cambridge: Harvard University Press, 1966), 140. Future references to this work will appear in the text.
3. See for example Jean Paul Sartre, *Being and Nothingness: An Essay on Phenomenological Ontology,* trans. Hazel E. Barnes (New York: Philosophical Library, 1956):

   > To say that the for-itself has to be what it is, to say that it is what it is not while not being what it is, to say that in it existence precedes and conditions essence . . . —all this is to say one and the same thing: to be aware that man is free. Indeed by the sole fact that I am conscious of the causes which inspire my action, these causes are already transcendent objects for my consciousness. . . . I am condemned to exist forever beyond my essence, beyond the causes and motives of my act. I am condemned to be free. This means that no limits to my freedom can be found except freedom itself or, if you prefer, that we are not free to cease being free. (439)

4. Benita Parry makes a similar argument about the history of Conrad criticism, noting that "the predominant trend has been away from discussing what has been termed the 'public dimensions' and towards analysing the novels as either ontological meditations and psychological explorations, or as symbolic representations of 'transhistorical' realities." *Conrad and Imperialism: Ideological Boundaries and Visionary Frontiers* (London: Macmillan, 1983), 6. For a recent example of this dominant tendency, see Michael Levinson, "The Value of Facts in the *Heart of Darkness,*" *Nineteenth Century Fiction* 40 (1985):

   > Through its own strenuous logic *Heart of Darkness* pursues the representation of bureaucracy until it becomes the representation of a monstrous passion; and fully to appreciate the tale as a psychological fiction is to appreciate the way it must excavate a place for the mind. Here is Conrad's promised *apres:* the psyche is a sequel to society.
   >
   > What is more, it is an alternative to society. (274)

   While I would agree with Levinson that the novel is, among other things, "a psychological fiction," I want to emphasize in my own analysis both the relation of the psychological to the social (as something other than alternative) *and* the motives for suggesting that psyche actually could function as alternative to an inadequate or unpleasant social situation.

See also Perry Meisel's *The Myth of the Modern: A Study in British Literature and Criticism after 1850* (New Haven: Yale University Press, 1987) for an interesting example of a deconstructive turn on this particular mode of reading. Meisel reads the text as offering "a pedagogy of reading" that demonstrates repeatedly how language is divided against itself (236): "Every discovery of a center or an origin is subject to a decentering, or, to put it another way, every disclosure of a ground is subject to the recession of that ground" (239). What Meisel does here is shift the terms of the work from the social (as represented in the historically specific account of colonial activity in Africa) to the linguistic or semiotic: the novel tells the story of language, not history. I do not, of course, disagree with Meisel's reading, but I would like to explore the connections between language and ideology that Meisel leaves out.

5. See for example J. Hillis Miller, *Poets of Reality* (New York: Atheneum, 1974) and Ian Watt, *Conrad in the Nineteenth Century* (Berkeley: University of California Press, 1979). For a discussion of Marlow's education, see Murray Krieger, *The Tragic Vision: Variations on a Theme in Literary Interpretation* (Chicago: University of Chicago Press, 1960), 154–65; Daniel Schwarz, *Conrad:* Almayer's Folly *to* Under Western Eyes (Ithaca: Cornell University Press, 1980), 63–75; and Fred Milne, "Marlow's Lie and the Intended: Civilization as the Lie in *Heart of Darkness*," *Arizona Quarterly* 44 (1988), 108 and 111. For a contrasting interpretation of Marlow's education, whose terms of value do not differ from those noted, see Eloise Knapp Hay, *The Political Novels of Joseph Conrad: A Critical Study* (Chicago: University of Chicago Press, 1963), 109–58.
6. Garrett Stewart, "Lying as Dying in *Heart of Darkness*," *PMLA* 95 (1980): 319. See also Marianna Torgovnick, *Gone Primitive: Savage Intellects, Modern Lives* (Chicago: University of Chicago Press, 1990) for a consideration of both Marlow's and Conrad's construction of the primitive in this work.
7. See chapter 4 for another discussion of existentialism's foundation in the ideologies of Western Romanticism. See also Jacques Derrida, *Writing and Difference*, trans. Alan Bass (Chicago: University of Chicago Press, 1978), 308 n. 4; and Jacques Lacan, "The Mirror Stage," in *Ecrits: A Selection*, trans. Alan Sheridan (New York: Norton, 1977), 6.

Fredric Jameson calls existentialism "one of the great containment strategies of the day, . . . the pretext for the production of a new metaphysic—a new myth about the 'meaning' of life and the absurdity of human existence in the face of a malevolent Nature." *The Political Unconscious: Narrative as a Socially Symbolic Act* (Ithaca: Cornell University Press, 1981), 216. I think it might also be relevant to characterize existentialism as another of the reaction formations of culture, working in ways similar to those of Romanticism to cope with the threat of the Real.

8. Said suggests the same thing when he calls the form of the novel a totalizing discourse:

> *Heart of Darkness* works so effectively precisely because its politics and aesthetics, so to speak, are imperialist; and that, by the time that Conrad wrote, seemed an attitude that was inevitable and for which there could be no alterna-

> tive. . . . Except . . . that Conrad is self-conscious about setting and situating the narrative in a narrative moment, thus allowing us to realize after all that far from swallowing up its own history, imperialism has in fact been placed and located by history, one that lies outside the tightly inclusive ring on the deck of the yawl Nelly. ("Intellectuals in the Post-Colonial World," *Salmagundi* 70–71 [1986]: 48)

See also Patrick Brantlinger, "*Heart of Darkness:* Anti-Imperialism, Racism, or Impressionism?" *Criticism* 27 (1985): 364–65.

9. See also Bette London, *The Appropriated Voice: Narrative Authority in Conrad, Forster, and Woolf* (Ann Arbor: University of Michigan Press, 1990) on the appropriation of authority in Conrad.
10. I am grateful to Donald Schwartz for pointing out to me the significance of this metaphor.
11. Once again, Jean Baudrillard's notion of the hyperreal seems appropriate here. Speaking specifically of the Borges tale about a map so accurate that it covers the territory it represents, Baudrillard says "Henceforth, it is the map that precedes the territory . . . it is the map that engenders the territory. . . . " *Simulations,* trans. Paul Foss, Paul Patton, and Philip Beitchman (New York: Semiotext(e), 1983), 2.
12. Said comments on this passage, noting that "The cosmopolitanism of geography was . . . its universal importance to the whole of the West, whose relationship to the rest of the world was one of frank covetousness. Yet geographical appetite could also take on the moral neutrality of an epistemological impulse to find out, to settle upon, to uncover. . . . " *Orientalism* (New York: Vintage, 1979), 216.
13. The very etymology of the term *perception* suggests its complexity and originary self-contradiction. The Latin *percipere* means "to seize wholly, to see all the way through." The coordinate juxtaposition of those two phrases would have us believe that they are synonymous. In fact, they are logically exclusive. *To see* is ostensibly a passive act, one that preserves the difference between subject and object. *Seizure,* on the other hand, dissolves the difference between actor and acted-upon, making the latter the property of the former. If "to see all the way through" requires a prior seizing, then perception, as we commonly understand the act, can never occur. We wish to use the word to refer to an act of unmediated sensory experience; it is the word itself, however, that offers us the illusion of such a possibility. Jacques Derrida comments on Ythe relation of perception to the metaphysics of presence:

> As to perception, I should say that once I recognized it as a necessary conservation. I was extremely conservative. Now I don't know what perception is and I don't believe that anything like perception exists. Perception is precisely a concept, a concept of an intuition or of a given originating from the thing itself, present itself in its meaning, independently from language, from the system of reference. And I believe that perception is interdependent with the concept of origin and center and consequently whatever strikes at the metaphysics of which I have spoken strikes also at the very concept of perception. ("Structure, Sign, and Play in the Discourse of the Human Sciences," in *The Structuralist Controversy: The Languages of Criticism and the Sciences of Man,* ed. Richard Macksey and Eugenio Donato [Baltimore: Johns Hopkins University Press, 1970], 271)

In fact, *Heart of Darkness* makes this clear early in the narrative, before Marlow begins his tale. The unnamed frame narrator, who appears to be merely establishing the context and location of Marlow's story, five times in two pages uses a variation on the combination of the words *gloom* and *brooding* in his description of the setting (Conrad 7–9), as if to make clear that it is impossible to speak of the natural world without transforming it through the language that both manifests and institutes our interpretive categories and habits.

Jameson also makes an interesting argument in this regard: "If the multiple narrative shifts in Conrad are to be seen as textbook exercises in point of view, then we must add something which changes everything: they are point of view conceived as being inseparable from speech, from the materiality of language" (*The Political Unconscious* 224). Bruce Johnson, on the other hand, discussing Conrad's impressionism and Watt's characterization of the writer's style of "delayed decoding," remarks that almost all the instances of delayed decoding "imply not so much an initial misunderstanding that will subsequently 'clear up' as they do an initial unguarded perception whose meaning may be far more revealing to the reader than the subsequent 'decoding.'" "Conrad's Impressionism and Watt's 'Delayed Decoding,'" in *Conrad Revisited: Essays for the Eighties,* ed. Ross C. Murfin (Tuscaloosa: University of Alabama Press, 1985), 57. The problem with this view, however, is that it leaves out of account the always already ideological nature of any perception.

14. Schopenhauer's influence on Marlow's representation of the jungle is clear here. Said notes the philosopher's more general importance to Conrad, referring specifically to the writer's fascination with the knitting machine as a metaphor for existence:

> [T]he knitting machine itself was Conrad's version of what Schopenhauer had uncompromisingly distinguished as the *principium individuationis,* the principle of differentiation that is man's—and not the universe's—power. Without thought, Schopenhauer had said, man is in almost mystic and passive community with shadowy truth. In that state man is at one with the unextended, unimagined, and formless will to live. Yet as soon as man begins to use his intellect, he asserts his ego and becomes objectified will. The highest form of objectified will is civilized man; the most typical faculty of his mind is the power of intellectual differentiation (the *principium*); and the highest level of differentiation is the ability to say "the world is my idea." (*Joseph Conrad* 139)

15. Chinua Achebe's attack on the novel for its complicity in Western racist misrepresentations of Africa and Africans is eloquent and in many ways persuasive. However, the conclusions Achebe draws about Conrad's racism are somewhat troubling and, I think, self-defeating. Achebe would have the novel removed from college curricula and repudiated by those whose job it has traditionally been to define and protect the canon of great works. "The question," Achebe insists, "is whether a novel which celebrates [the] dehumanization [of Africans], which depersonalizes a portion of the human race, can be called a great work of art. My answer is: No, it cannot." "An Image of Africa," *Massachusetts Review* 18 (1977): 788. The problem with Achebe's assessment of the novel lies in part in its insistence on preserving the category of great works even as it wishes to remove this novel from such a privileged position. On the one hand, the category itself perpetuates the

notion that there are actually objectively great works outside the determination of some limited social and/or academic power structure's decision to see them so. On the other hand, Achebe's desire to eliminate the novel from those we read and teach eliminates as well, I believe, one of the best opportunities available for teaching ourselves about not just the crimes of Western imperialism in non-European nations but also the more subtle and pervasive interpretive habits that make imperialism possible and that continue to influence too many Western behaviors today.

16. However, Marlow's conception of the essential criminality of the human betrays a debt to another text as well, Nietzsche's *The Birth of Tragedy*, trans. Francis Golffing (New York: Doubleday, 1956). Consider for a moment the parallels between Marlow's representation of the source of humanness in the violation of nature's order and Nietzsche's account of "an ancient popular belief . . . that a wise magus must be incestuously begotten" (61). Using Oedipus as an example of this belief, Nietzsche concludes,

> [W]herever soothsaying and magical powers have broken the spell of present and future, the rigid law of individuation, the magic circle of nature, extreme unnaturalness—in this case incest—is the necessary antecedent; for how should man force nature to yield up her secrets but by successfully resisting her, that is to say, by unnatural acts? This is the recognition I find expressed in the terrible triad of Oedipean fates: the same man who solved the riddle of nature (the ambiguous Sphinx) must also . . . break the consecrated tables of the natural order. It is as though the myth whispered to us that wisdom, and especially Dionysiac wisdom, is an unnatural crime, and that whoever, in pride of knowledge, hurls nature into the abyss of destruction, must himself experience nature's disintegration. (61)

Nietzsche implies here that the wisdom Oedipus used to solve the riddle of the sphinx is the result of his incest. However, Nietzsche offers a genealogy of wisdom that inverts the two events—knowledge and incest—naming as cause, "necessary antecedent," what actually follows in time. To call the crime of incest unnatural is also a paradoxical inversion of genealogy, "parent" and "child": incest is not naturally abhorrent to living organisms and, in fact, establishes artificially the difference between an inside and an outside. Indeed, the taboo itself constitutes the unnatural act that, according to Freud's myth of the primal family, actually brings culture into being as its self-conscious opposition to nature and natural inclination. It would seem clear, then, that the nature that Dionysiac wisdom violates must already be *unnatural* in its difference from the ostensibly original Dionysiac unity.

Nietzsche's analysis of the myth holds up the dichotomy of natural and unnatural at its center, suggesting that this binary parallels that of the Dionysiac and Apollonian. But despite the apparent priority granted the Dionysiac, Nietzsche continually represents the two opposing impulses as mutually constitutive. He undermines the very notion of an origin when he speaks of a genealogy of Dionysos and yet accounts for the appearance of the Dionysiac only in relation to the Apollonian dream similitude (24–25).

Nietzsche's apparent commitment to the traditional Romantic oppositions of culture/nature, self/other, history/ideal is therefore quite clearly at odds with his rhetorical strategies, all of which involve his confusion of such hierarchies. What Nietzsche reveals in *The Birth of Tragedy* is that the representation of the natural dichotomy of Dionysiac and Apollonian forces actually brings the binary *as* binary into being. In demonstrating that the notions of father, birth, and genesis are themselves produced by the repression of the psychic structure of difference and manifested in the will to power, the will to truth, Nietzsche further suggests that all that is not human has been constituted in the signifying response to otherwise meaningless pressures and requirements of the natural material world. This notion is akin to Žižek's argument that the Real is *not,* though it produces effects within the symbolic. This reading also suggests that the Nietzschean construction of the will to power is itself a transformation of the Hegelian aggression at the root of human consciousness, another acknowledgment that the symbolic itself grows up as a response to the traumatic lack of a stable ground to human community.

17. Kurtz's casual certainty here that trade, the movement of commodities, can coexist with the idealism of humanising the natives shares much with Marlow's earlier repression of idealism itself as one of the commodities Romantic philosophy and imperialism make possible.
18. See Johanna M. Smith, "'Too Beautiful Altogether': Patriarchal Ideology in *Heart of Darkness,*" in *Heart of Darkness,* ed. Ross C. Murfin (New York: St. Martin's, 1989), for an excellent analysis of the relationship between patriarchal and imperialist ideologies.
19. See Derrida, *Of Grammatology,* trans. Gayatri Chakravorty Spivak (Baltimore: Johns Hopkins University Press, 1974), 145.

Chapter 3

Epigraph from a letter Henry wrote to William James in 1892 referring to his friendship with Paul Bourget. Cited in Leon Edel, *The Life of Henry James,* 5 vols. (Middlesex, England: Penguin, 1977), 2:49. Future references to this work will appear in the text.

1. Henry James, *The Wings of the Dove* (New York: Norton, 1978), 56. Future references to this work will appear in the text.
2. Michael Moon reads this passage significantly differently, claiming that Densher terrorizes Kate with his looks: "In the context of the novel, what power Merton has lies in his desirous looks, and it is Kate who is represented as being deeply dependent on these, not Merton on her. . . . " "Sexuality and Visual Terrorism in *The Wings of the Dove,*" *Criticism* 28 (1986): 431. In his analysis, Moon claims to consider "the gaze" as Lacan defines it, but Moon seems to me to oversimplify the power of the gaze. As Lacan articulates it, the gaze is not powerful in itself; it is powerful because the one being looked at invests the looker with the imaginary power of the subject-supposed-to-know, the incarnation of the Law of the Symbolic. In the passage both Moon and I refer to, however, Kate knows more than Densher, and Densher's look thus validates Kate's privileged vision. Kate, that is, may depend on Densher's looks, but only because they assist in her self-construction as the one in possession of the seductive secret. See in particular Lacan's discussion of the *ocelli* in *The Four Fundamental Concepts of Psycho-Analysis,* ed. Jacques-Alain Miller, trans. Alan Sheridan (New York: Norton, 1981), 73; and his

distinction between the gaze and normal vision (78) when he reminds us that analysis is not carried out face-to-face. Future references to this work will appear in the text.

3. In "The Beast in the Jungle," the secret May Bartram and John Marcher share functions similarly as the basis of their private community; the consequences of building the private world on a shared secret are in this work as tragic as in *The Wings of the Dove*.
4. John Carlos Rowe, *Henry Adams and Henry James: The Emergence of a Modern Consciousness* (Ithaca: Cornell University Press, 1976), 182–83. Future references to this work will appear in the text.
5. Susan L. Mizruchi also notes that Croy's "fallibility allows for [Kate's] assumption of narrative power." *The Power of Historical Knowledge: Narrating the Past in Hawthorne, James, and Dreiser* (Princeton: Princeton University Press, 1988), 187. Future references to this work will appear in the text.
6. In fact, Slavoj Žižek defines modernism as precisely constituted by this knowledge: "The lesson of modernism is that the structure, the intersubjective machine, works as well if the Thing is lacking, if the machine revolves around an emptiness" as it would if the Thing were present. *Looking Awry: An Introduction to Jacques Lacan through Popular Culture* (Cambridge: MIT Press, 1991), 143. Future references to this work will appear in the text.
7. In his reading of "The Figure in the Carpet," Dennis A. Foster has suggested the secret's capacity to invest its bearer with authorial control. Foster argues that the tale's plot demonstrates

    > not a definition of the figure but a pattern of effects that arise from the desire to know about the figure. More specifically, each character who knows about the figure . . . uses this knowledge to evoke a response from someone who stands in a relation of rivalry or opposition to him. . . . Each works under the assumption that the figure can be discovered and articulated, even though each of its literary manifestations—Vereker's works, Corvick's manuscript, and Gwendolen's *Overmastered*—fails to reveal it. Yet something is passed from one character to another, the critic's account of which is yet another vessel of the figure. The figure propagates itself without the enlightenment of those touched by it. (*Confession and Complicity in Narrative* [London: Cambridge University Press, 1987], 44)

    When the tale's narrator recognizes that he can make his own bondage to the unresolved secret the means of effecting a similar bondage in another, he exploits, consciously or not, the power the mystery has possessed all along: to invest its bearer with authority over another. But that mastery derives only from the master's willingness to remain in ignorance of the mystery, to work in service to its power.

    See also Dorothea Krook's summary of *The Sacred Fount* in *The Ordeal of Consciousness in Henry James* (London: Cambridge University Press, 1962), 167–73, for a discussion of the epistemological theme in James.
8. Henry James, "The Tempest," in *Selected Literary Criticism*, ed. Morris Shapira (Westport, Conn.: Greenwood Press, 1978). Future references to this work will appear in the text.

9. Shakespeare is a bit like Lionel Croy here; each is saved from vulgarity only by his dimness.
10. This fact is made clearer by the allusion, in the passage's final line, to the reader's playing Romeo to Shakespeare's tantalizing Juliet.
11. See Roland Barthes, "The Death of the Author," in *Image-Music-Text,* trans. Stephen Heath (New York: Hill and Wang, 1977). In this essay, Barthes claims that "the Author, when believed in, is always conceived of as the past of his own book: book and author stand automatically on a single line divided into a before and an after. The Author is thought to nourish the book, which is to say that he exists before it, thinks, suffers, lives for it, is in the same relation of antecedence to his work as a father to his child" (145). This is the model of reading and criticism that James seems to be consciously committed to in his analysis of *The Tempest*. However, what his discussion of Shakespeare actually demonstrates is something different; as Barthes remarks at the conclusion of his essay, "the birth of the reader must be at the cost of the death of the Author" (148). James talks as if the absence of the author were an affront to him as reader, but, as I hope to demonstrate, he depends on that absence for his own readerly, and writerly, identity.
12. James refers to the witnesses to Shakespeare's suicidal leap (by which I take him to mean the unilluminating facts of the writer's life) as only "a dozen or two dim, scarce articulate ghosts" ("The Tempest" 309). This strikes me as one of the essay's several important references to *Hamlet,* a play whose relevance to the oedipal drama is obvious. Like the dead king-father of Hamlet, the presence of those ghostly facts betokens a crime of some sort (or in this case at least a violation of logic), as if Shakespeare had left behind him a clue to suggest our own task of redemption and retaliation. But if the clue those facts offer functions as the ghost did for Hamlet, we experience the same double bind that paralyzed that other dutiful son. As rightful heir to the kingly father, Hamlet had to fulfill the father's command: to displace the false king and become king himself. Hamlet's duty to become sovereign was not a duty to himself, but one prescribed for him by the one without any predecessor, the dead father. But his task must have been complicated by its uncanny nature: the dim ghost of the dead father demanded, as fulfillment of its desire, precisely the act that the son would recognize as his own repressed and taboo impulse, a symbolic patricide. No wonder Hamlet distrusts his animosity to Claudius, fearing the ghost's provocations to be the workings of his own inflamed and illicit desire, the devil that "hath power / T'assume a pleasing shape." William Shakespeare, *Hamlet, The Riverside Shakespeare* (Boston: Houghton Mifflin, 1974), III, ii, 599–600.
13. It may be relevant to note here that the name of the new king who follows Elizabeth is also James.
14. But Hamlet killed Polonius unintentionally: he mistook the curious fool for Claudius, the incestuous stepfather who became king by killing the rightful king and father. The consequences of Hamlet's mistake are multiple: ultimately, his error kills him, but not before effecting a fairly magnificent transformation in the status of Polonius. In being killed for a king, even a spurious one, Polonius exchanges his rightful identity—pompous and nosy busybody—for a new and significant function: through Hamlet's mistake, Polonius becomes a dead father who,

like Hamlet's dead father, compels his son Laertes to sacrifice himself to the cause of his father's vengeance.

I am grateful to John Carlos Rowe for pointing out to me in conversation another important ramification of James's discussion in "The Tempest." Hamlet must murder a surrogate father in order to satisfy his oedipal needs, whether that surrogate be Claudius or Polonius. As Hamlet is deprived of the actual father—always only a ghostly presence—his situation mirrors the relation of the writer as ephebe to the literary father.

15. See Shoshana Felman's "Henry James: Madness and the Risks of Practice (Turning the Screw of Interpretation)," in *Writing and Madness (Literature/Philosophy/Psychoanalysis),* trans. Martha Noel Evans and the author with the assistance of Brian Massumi (Ithaca: Cornell University Press, 1985) for a discussion of how "James's very mastery consists in the denial and in the deconstruction of his own mastery" (245).
16. Jacques Lacan, "Subversion of the Subject and the Dialectic of Desire in the Freudian Unconscious," in *Ecrits: A Selection,* trans. Alan Sheridan (New York: Norton, 1977), 323–24.
17. James's attitude toward the biographies of artists suggests his understanding of this chain and the authority it confers. In reference to George Sand, Leon Edel tells us that

> James suggested that perhaps the artist, the subject, should organize the game of biography on his own terms, rather than leave it to the biographer. . . . The thing was indeed to burn papers, keep secrets, challenge the biographer to dig harder for his facts, demand a genuine effort of inquiry and research. . . . "Then," wrote James, "the cunning of the enquirer, envenomed with resistance, will exceed in subtlety and ferocity anything we today conceive, and the pale forewarned victim, with every track covered, every paper burnt and every letter unanswered, will, in the tower of art, the unvulnerable granite, stand, without a sally, the siege of all the years." (5:144)

James, of course, followed his own advice, which appears in fact to have been extrapolated from the model Shakespeare provided; again, it is as if James's "human curiosity" about Shakespeare had been metamorphosed into an "aesthetic passion" to be for another what Shakespeare was for James.

18. Henry James, "Preface to *The Wings of the Dove,*" in *The Art of the Novel: Critical Prefaces,* ed. R. P. Blackmur (London: Scribner's, 1934), 295. Future references to this work will appear in the text.
19. Friedrich Nietzsche, *Beyond Good and Evil: Prelude to a Philosophy of the Future,* trans. Walter Kaufmann (New York: Vintage, 1966), 43. Future references to this work will appear in the text.
20. The fact is, though, that not everyone agrees on the identity of Milly's killer. See Caroline G. Mercer and Sarah D. Wangensteen for a review of the various diseases Milly may have had and for their own argument in favor of chlorosis. "'Consumption, heart-disease, or whatever': Chlorosis, a Heroine's Illness in *The Wings of the Dove,*" in *Journal of the History of Medicine and Allied Sciences* 40 (1985).
21. Jean Strouse, *Alice James: A Biography* (New York: Bantam, 1982), xii. Future references to this work will appear in the text.

22. Strouse provides an illuminating account of the way illness functioned generally in the James family dynamic, noting—as Edel does—that Henry and William tended to take turns being sick and frequently suffered from illnesses that were at least partly psychosomatic. Strouse even goes so far as to claim that, for the Jameses, "Suffering . . . paid for someone else's well-being, and being well might cost someone else pain" (121). As a result of this family version of the sacred-fount theme, Alice would have been encouraged to make her illnesses the opportunity to display a certain strength of character and familial devotion, bravely suffering herself that others might be spared (133).
23. Jacqueline Rose claims that Strouse oversimplifies the causes of Alice James's illnesses:

> In Alice James's case, what is most striking is the relentless activity of the symptoms and of Alice's relationship to them—one which if it is not covered adequately by the category of the victim is no more satisfactorily met by the idea, expressed for example by her biographer Jean Strouse, that this illness was Alice's design and purpose in seeking compensation and attention from a restricted and restricting social world. ("Jeffrey Masson and Alice James," *Oxford Literary Review* 8 [1986], 187)

Although I think Rose is incorrect about Strouse, who does not seem to me to make such a totalizing claim, Rose's argument about the complicated relation of hysteria and representation, particularly in the James family, is a persuasive one.
24. A number of critics have discussed how Milly's illness contributes to her sense of both identity and control in her life. See in particular Mizruchi; Elizabeth Allen, *A Woman's Place in the Novels of Henry James* (New York: St. Martin's, 1984); and Virginia Fowler, *Henry James's American Girl: The Embroidery on the Canvas* (Madison: University of Wisconsin Press, 1984).
25. In a letter to his son Bob, Henry James Sr. remarked of Alice "She has perfectly understood for a long time past that her frightful nervousness was a part of our troubles as a race, struggling to get free: that there is nothing in it peculiar to herself, and she never regards it as having the least sinister bearing upon her immortal interests" (Strouse 204). Milly too appears to see her own potential sickness as something binding her, both positively and negatively, to her otherwise absent family.
26. Such ambivalence, according to Freud, is at the foundation of the illness called melancholia:

> It is on the one hand, like mourning, a reaction to the real loss of a loved object; but over and above this, it is marked by a determinant which is absent in normal mourning or which, if it is present, transforms the latter into pathological mourning. The loss of a love-object is an excellent opportunity for the ambivalence in love-relationships to make itself effective and come into the open. . . . [T]he conflict due to ambivalence gives a pathological cast to mourning and forces it to express itself in the form of self-reproaches to the effect that the mourner himself is to blame for the loss of the loved object, i.e. that he has willed it. . . . The self-tormenting in melancholia, which is without doubt enjoyable, signifies, just like the corresponding phenomenon in obsessional neurosis, a satisfaction of trends of sadism and hate which relate to an object, and which

> have been turned round upon the subject's own self in the ways we have been discussing. In both disorders the patients usually still succeed, by the circuitous path of selfpunishment, in taking revenge on the original object and in tormenting their loved one through their illness, having resorted to it in order to avoid the need to express their hostility to him openly. ("Mourning and Melancholia," *The Standard Edition of the Complete Psychological Works of Sigmund Freud* [London: Hogarth, 1957], 14:250–51; future references to this work will appear in the text.)

Strouse also notes with regard to "Mourning and Melancholia" that Freud "might have been describing Alice James" during her illness of 1878 (203).

27. See Daniel Mark Fogel, *Henry James and the Structure of the Romantic Imagination* (Baton Rouge: Louisiana State University Press, 1981), for an account of the many references in the novel to *The Tempest*.

28. The following passage makes Milly's control explicit: "Exactly this—the handsome girl's compassionate manner, her friendly descent from her own strength—was what [Milly] had then foretold. She took Kate up as if positively for the deeper taste of it" (*Wings* 141–42). Milly's propensity for "tasting" triumphs in her relation to Kate should remind us again of the melancholiac:

> We have elsewhere shown that identification is a preliminary stage of object-choice, that it is the first way—and one that is expressed in an ambivalent fashion—in which the ego picks out an object. The ego wants to incorporate this object into itself, and in accordance with the oral or cannibalistic phase of libidinal development in which it is, it wants to do so by devouring it. Abraham is undoubtedly right in attributing to this connection the refusal of nourishment met with in severe forms of melancholia. (*Standard Edition* 14:249–50)

It is following this event in Milly's relationship to Kate—her incorporating, that is, both Kate's example of authority and Kate as an object of her own authority—that Milly misses the dinner party held by Maud in her honor, as she again in Venice misses her own dinner party.

29. By including the *history* of her desire to be taken seriously, James's representation of Milly exposes the activity, the will to power, underlying the girl's passivity. In this connection, Žižek's comments about the "beautiful soul" seem relevant. Žižek says Hegel "undermine[s] the position of the 'beautiful soul,' of this gentle, fragile, sensitive form of subjectivity which, from its safe position as innocent observer, deplores the wicked ways of the world," by exposing the "activity implied by this position of inactivity—in the way the 'beautiful soul' structures the 'objective' social world in advance so that it is able to assume, to play in it the role of the fragile, innocent and passive victim." *The Sublime Object of Ideology* (London: Verso, 1989), 215. In exemplifying the beautiful soul through the figure of the suffering mother exploited by all other members of her family, Žižek further demonstrates how women are prepared by the social roles available to them to accept the disguised power of the self-sacrifice.

30. As Fowler notes, Milly uses "her suspected illness to give her special status with Kate" (96). Indeed, Milly's reserve with Kate is represented here as a direct response to Kate's perverse otherness. At the moment when Milly is most conscious of her own secretiveness, she is reminded again of Kate's, and Kate does not intend to match Milly's confidence with her own. Indeed, Kate is not even conscious that

Milly knows what she withholds. Milly's elaboration of her mystery thus becomes retaliation: for Kate's silence, and for her failure to take Milly's mystery seriously enough. From now on, Kate will know only that Milly sees the doctor, that a secret relation (something like her own) has been initiated.

31. Strouse comments on Alice James's response to the discovery of the breast cancer that would ultimately kill her: like Milly, Alice celebrated the certainty of an organic illness because, unlike her other illnesses, it set her "within the very heart of the sustaining concrete" (333).

32. Rowe comments explicitly on Milly's authorial function in the novel:

> Milly Theale ultimately brings the characters of the novel to a consciousness of one another, forcing them to recognize the distance that separates their respective desires. The effect of Milly's sacrifice on Lancaster Gate is by no means redemptive, but is rather a revelation of the hollowness at the heart of such social games. . . . Milly's death does not promise an ultimate reconciliation of differences, but simply makes those differences manifest, revealing the impossibility of Kate's and Merton's "temple of love," the emptiness of Maud Lowder's historical "collection," and the deathliness of Lord Mark's Bronzino portrait. (174)

33. Laurence Bedwell Holland's analysis of Milly departs significantly from the general views of her as a victim, so his reading is worth examining at some length. The novel, he suggests, represents Milly's "initiation into English society," providing an account of her education and of her increasing self-consciousness:

> Milly's American manner, like James's, is adopted in the process of coming to understand society and its sharp divisions and . . . to bridge the intervals which separate her from it or from the groups and individuals in it whom she encounters. In the process, her manner has the effect of enabling Milly to play a role in her world and to share in altering and shaping it. Vulnerable in her illness but powerful with her money, she begins with her manner to take precedence over Aunt Maud and to become the governing center for the schemes and aspirations of the world which begins to form around her under the impact of her power and presence. (*The Expense of Vision: Essays on the Craft of Henry James* [Princeton: Princeton University Press, 1964], 300–301)

In attributing to Milly power and presence, in suggesting the role she plays in altering and shaping her world, Holland acknowledges Milly's effect on her friends and even her possession of a sort of authorial intention toward them. But he nevertheless continues to define Milly's intention as a beneficent and self-sacrificing one. Even if Milly's final bequest to Densher ultimately destroys his affair with Kate, Milly's desire has been generous, only a wish to forgive her friends' betrayal of her: "She joined in her friends' commerce, completed their transaction, redeemed their enterprise by transforming it into a gift, making her loving surrender to her tragic fortune . . . " (319).

34. See especially the very persuasive readings of Mizruchi and Allen. Marcia Ian also discusses "the mythopoeic pressure exerted on us" by James's representation of Milly and the "need . . . to resist sacramentalizing Milly's conflation of life, death, and selflessness. . . . " "The Elaboration of Privacy in *The Wings of the Dove*," *ELH* 51 (1985): 127. George McFadden wonders whether "James in the Preface was not one of the first converts to Millyolatry . . . " and remarks on Milly's complicity in

her own entrapment by others. "Henry James's Remorse for *The Wings of the Dove*," *Henry James Review* 9 (1988): 122. McFadden also notes that, "ill as she is, Milly chooses to be, and steadily becomes, an effective and at last a successful rival to Kate for Densher . . . " (125).

Dorothea Krook suggests that the novel's tragic theme "is the impact of the worldly world upon the unworldly—its power to undermine, reduce and (in this instance) finally to destroy those who cannot accommodate themselves to its values" (200). But Krook is clear that such a theme requires a representation of the victim's partial responsibility for her fate. In this case, Milly's faults are the same as her virtues: "innocence, ignorance and good faith," "generosity and tenderness" (200), traits that make it impossible for Milly to adjust to the world in which she finds herself.

Fowler elaborates some of the implications of Krook's analysis to suggest that Milly's "fatal illness might be viewed as a symbol or metaphor for an inner deficiency created by her situation as an American woman" (85). Where Krook sees Milly's goodness as rendering her unfit for the world, Fowler believes James is demonstrating "how crippling the American girl's psychology can be" (85). Fowler goes further than most critics, recognizing that "Milly's tendency to seek an identity in her fatal illness works both to justify her non-participation in life and provide her with a *modus vivendi*" (97). But Fowler still identifies Milly as passive, indeed as increasingly passive as the novel progresses, whereas I think her withdrawal is far more aggressive than may have been acknowledged.

35. In chapter 4, I will discuss a similar assumption about stories and storytelling made by Jake Barnes (and Hemingway).
36. Regarding this issue, Sallie Sears notes that characters in the novel think they can have everything they want, "Yet in each case circumstances decree that the choice of one . . . precludes the other." *The Negative Imagination: Form and Perspective in the Novels of Henry James* (Ithaca: Cornell University Press, 1968), 62.
37. Holland notes another significance of Milly's new identity as a dove. "One of the novel's main movements," he claims, is its depiction of Milly's

> anguished withdrawal from life into death, a movement that is confirmed and deepened by one of the evocations of the novel's title, Psalm 55. There, in fear and trembling at "the oppression of the wicked," a voice cries out: "O that I had wings like a dove! / Then would I fly away and be at rest. / Lo, then would haste me to a shelter / From the stormy wind and tempest." The voice then asks the psalmist's God to "Destroy, O Lord, and divide their tongue. . . . For it was not an enemy that reproached me— / . . . . But it was thou, a man mine equal, /My companion, and my familiar friend. / We took sweet counsel together, / We walked in the house of God with the throng. / Let death come suddenly upon them, let them go down alive into the pit: / For wickedness is in their dwelling, in the midst of them." (303)

Although Holland quotes much of the Psalm, he does not discuss the lines at odds with his description of Milly's anguished withdrawal. The plea of the Psalm, after all, is not just for escape, for transcendence of the world's corruption; it is also a prayer for God to wreak vengeance on those who have betrayed the speaker. If Milly finds in her new title the inspiration that will direct her future behavior toward others, that inspiration might also entail the awareness that self-sacrifice can become her greatest act of vengeance.

38. But see Eve Kosofsky Sedgwick for a compelling reading of the story that locates Marcher's desire and fear elsewhere. According to Sedgwick, the notion that Marcher "should have" desired May "denies the very possibility of difference in desires, in objects" and is a manifestation of the homophobia the story both records and derives from. "The Beast in the Closet: James and the Writing of Homosexual Panic," in *Sex, Politics, and Science in the Nineteenth-Century Novel,* ed. Ruth Bernard Yeazel (Baltimore: Johns Hopkins University Press, 1986), 164. Sedgwick also offers an interesting account of May's power in the relationship; see in particular 175–80.

Chapter 4

Epigraph from Laurence Sterne, *The Life and Opinions of Tristram Shandy, Gentleman,* ed. James Aiken Work (Indianapolis: Bobbs-Merrill, 1940), 647.

1. See Stephen Cooper, *The Politics of Ernest Hemingway* (Ann Arbor: University Microfilms, 1987), who comments at length on the novel's treatment of postwar disillusionment, particularly as it demonstrates the detachment of many young survivors from "political processes and institutions of their world" (26). See also Linda Wagner-Martin, "Introduction," *New Essays on* The Sun Also Rises, ed. Linda Wagner-Martin (Cambridge: Cambridge University Press, 1987): "If the mood of postwar America was disillusion and frustration, then Jake's physical incapacity is a striking image of many kinds of disability. The loss of promise after World War I was one of the chief reasons for the expatriation of America's writers and artists" (5). Future references to this work will appear in the text.
2. Leon F. Seltzer, "The Opportunity of Impotence: Count Mippipopolous in *The Sun Also Rises,*" *Renascence* 31 (1978): 13–14. Future references to this work will appear in the text.
3. As C. Hugh Holman puts it, "Hemingway's Vanity Fair is an Existential one. Men live in this hollow world, not because they defy God as the citizens of Bunyan's city of Vanity do, nor because they are willfully and cynically selfish as the citizens of Thackeray's Vanity Fair are, but because they are in a jungle where God is a word in a forgotten language and only in the self is value to be found." "Hemingway and Vanity Fair," in *Ernest Hemingway: Six Decades of Criticism,* ed. Linda Wagner-Martin (East Lansing: Michigan State University Press, 1987), 145. Future references to this work will appear in the text. See also Jackson J. Benson, *Hemingway: The Writer's Art of Self-Defense* (Minneapolis: University of Minnesota Press, 1969), who argues that the novel defines the meaning of manhood as "the strength to see [oneself] clearly and the strength to bind [oneself] to an ideal worth living by" (36). Carlos Baker defines the "moral norm of the book" as "a healthy and almost boyish innocence of spirit . . . carried by Jake Barnes, Bill Gorton, and Pedro Romero." *Hemingway: The Writer as Artist* (Princeton: Princeton University Press, 1963), 82. That moral norm is most clearly represented by the bullfighter, "a force of antithesis, manly, courageous, of complete integrity and self-possession" (86). The terms of value in these readings all significantly emphasize the individual's authentic psychic autonomy: he is self-conscious, courageous, and self-possessed.

According to these critics, man has the capacity to own himself; like the frontiersman, a figure that is itself almost an existential platitude, modern man must detach himself from the false and effeminizing conventions of his culture to discover his true independence. Even the most recent criticism of the novel remains informed by existential values and assumptions. See for example Nancy Comley, "Hemingway: The Economics of Survival," *Novel* 12 (1979); Patrick D. Morrow, "The Bought Generation: Another Look at *The Sun Also Rises*," *Genre* 13 (1980); Warren Wedin, "Trout Fishing and Self-Betrayal in *The Sun Also Rises*," *Arizona Quarterly* 37 (1981); and Sibbie O'Sullivan, "Love and Friendship/Man and Woman in *The Sun Also Rises*," *Arizona Quarterly* 44 (1988).

4. Herein lies the difference between the existential and psychoanalytic meanings of *contingency*. In psychoanalysis, recognizing one's contingency does *not* become the source of one's freedom and responsibility to *invent* oneself; rather, it founds the recognition that one has always already *lost* such autonomy to the Other, forces alien to and yet constitutive of the subject, the "in you more than you."
5. Jacques Derrida, "Cogito and the History of Madness," *Writing and Difference*, trans. Alan Bass (Chicago: University of Chicago Press, 1978), 308 n. 4. Future references to this work will appear in the text.
6. Jacques Lacan, "The Mirror Stage as Formative of the Function of the I," *Ecrits: A Selection*, trans. Alan Sheridan (New York: Norton, 1977), 6. Future references to this work will appear in the text.
7. Jacques Lacan, "Subversion of the Subject and the Dialectic of Desire in the Freudian Unconscious," *Ecrits: A Selection*. Future references to this work will appear in the text.
8. It is important to remember in this context my earlier comments in chapter 2 regarding existentialism as yet another strategy for management of the Real. Although I wish to be critical of some of the consequences of existentialism's strategies, I do not mean to overlook its importance in postwar Western culture. See also the following note.
9. In this connection, Slavoj Žižek comments on the "existentialism debate" between Sartre and the French Communists after World War II: "The Communists' main reproach to Sartre was as follows: by conceiving the subject as pure negativity, void, emptied of all positive substantial contents, . . . Sartre rejected all bourgeois *content*. What remained, however, was the pure *form* of bourgeois subjectivity . . ." *The Sublime Object of Ideology* (London: Verso, 1989), 217; Žižek's emphasis.

See also Kaja Silverman, *The Acoustic Mirror: The Female Voice in Psychoanalysis and Cinema* (Bloomington: Indiana University Press, 1988), who argues that castration is a metaphor for the experiences of loss that actually precede the recognition of sexual difference. Silverman writes, "The fetish classically functions not so much to conceal woman's castration as to deny man's, and . . . this goal can be achieved only by identifying lack with what is exclusive to woman, i.e., with her anatomy" (20). "Although the phallus is naturalized through its imaginary alignment with the penis," she adds, "it is never more or less than a distillate of the positive values at the center of a historically circumscribed symbolic order" (30). Lacan also says that castration anxiety structures, in a *Nachträglicheit*, the prior experiences of loss: "The fear of castration is like a thread that perforates all the stages of development.

It orientates the relations that are anterior to its actual appearance—weaning, toilet training, etc. It crystallizes each of these moments in a dialectic that has as its centre a bad encounter." *The Four Fundamental Concepts of Psycho-Analysis,* ed. Jacques-Alain Miller, trans. Alan Sheridan (New York: Norton, 1981), 64.

10. Holman comments on Hemingway's style as a manifestation of his theme of loss; what I call "elision," Holman identifies as "Hemingway's ability to make the simplest facts mean two things and imply a whole realm of unexpressed meaning" (143). Holman, that is, sees the style as expressive of an authentic plenitude rather than as the production of an illusion of some lost wholeness.

    Larzer Ziff comments more interestingly on the narrative's style as a reflection of the narrator's passivity: "His uncomplex, chronological presentation of events invites a similar undergoing on the reader's part, a submission to a seemingly unvalued succession of events rather than a participation in them . . . " "The Social Basis of Hemingway's Style," in *Ernest Hemingway: Six Decades of Criticism,* 148. However, Ziff's analysis of style ultimately concludes with a more romantic interpretation, arguing that Jake's repressive mode of writing expresses a belief that "the mere act of articulation falsifies feeling in the receiver and destroys it in the speaker. 'It,' then, must be rendered through the development of a style that evokes feeling without mentioning it . . . " (151).

    See also John Atherton, "The Itinerary and the Postcard: Minimal Strategies in *The Sun Also Rises,*" *ELH* 53 (1986), who argues that "The resistance to metaphor . . . can . . . be seen as a denial of the responsibility for narrating, a desire to shift it elsewhere . . . " (217). Harold Bloom, too, notes generally in regard to Hemingway's style that "parataxis" is "a way of utterance that plays at withdrawal from all affect, while actually investing affect in the constancy of the withdrawal, a willing choice of the void as object, rather than be void of object, in Nietzschean terms." "Introduction," in *Ernest Hemingway's* The Sun Also Rises, ed. Harold Bloom (New York: Chelsea House, 1987), 6.

    I should also note here the similarities of Jake's style to the withholding behavior of Marlow, Kate Croy, and Milly Theale, all of whom identify themselves as bearers of a truth by means of their secrecy.

11. Ernest Hemingway, *A Moveable Feast* (New York: Scribner's, 1964), 75.
12. Ernest Hemingway, *The Sun Also Rises* (New York: Scribner's, 1926), 7. Future references to this work will appear in the text.
13. Mark Spilka, "The Death of Love in *The Sun Also Rises,*" in *Hemingway and His Critics: An International Anthology,* ed. Carlos Baker, American Century Series (New York: Hill and Wang, 1961).
14. Wendy Martin, on the other hand, finds the novel's treatment of the war less deludedly romantic than I have suggested: "In *The Sun Also Rises* Hemingway makes it clear that the postwar sensibility as exemplified by Jake is one of severe loss, emasculation, and impotence. . . . Jake feels tricked by the war congame masterminded by bankers and politicians." "Brett Ashley as New Woman," *New Essays on* The Sun Also Rises, 66. Future references to this work will appear in the text. In my view, however, Jake may well be disillusioned about traditional notions of wartime glamour, but his disillusionment motivates a careful and seductive redemption of his emasculation that makes him complicit with other, more conven-

tional kinds of romanticization of war and violence. In a negative transference, that is, Jake rejects the authority of others to define the meaning of the war and manhood, not to suggest that such truths are delusions but rather to assume such authority to speak the truth for himself.

15. We might remember here Hegel's formulation of stoicism as a moment in the dialectic of self-consciousness: it is the incomplete negation of the master/servant relation in which the subject achieves a limited freedom of self-consciousness. In retreating from the meaninglessness of the world into the self-assurance of individual consciousness, the stoic fails to perform the necessary negation of the determinateness of the world: "This thinking consciousness as determined in the form of abstract freedom is thus only the incomplete negation of otherness. *Withdrawn* from existence only into itself, it has not there achieved its consummation as absolute negation of that existence." *Phenomenology of Spirit*, trans. A. V. Miller (Oxford: Oxford University Press, 1977), 122; Hegel's emphasis. The *incomplete* negation of the master/servant relation thus reproduces it in another form, as I suggested in chapter 1.
16. Michael Harper also analyzes the doubleness or ambivalence of this narrative's political interests, though arriving at conclusions quite different from my own. See "Men without Politics? Hemingway's Social Consciousness," *New Orleans Review* 12 (1985).
17. Sigmund Freud, "Negation," *The Standard Edition of the Complete Psychological Works of Sigmund Freud* (London: Hogarth, 1961), 19:235; Freud's emphasis.
18. For a very different reading of the relation of Brett and Jake, see Martin and O'Sullivan, both of whom argue that Hemingway's representation of this couple constitutes a positive challenge to existing gender distinctions. As my analysis of the bullfight will demonstrate, however, even Jake's and Brett's apparent role reversal is eventually made consistent with conventional gender identities. Hemingway way well *demonstrate* the artificial constructedness of traditional gender identities. If he does so, however, it is not at the level of conscious plotting or character delineation, but rather within an unconscious "scene of writing" inscribed within the representation of the bullfight.
19. Geoffrey Chaucer, *Troilus and Criseyde*, ed. Donald R. Howard and James Dean (New York: Signet, 1976), 651.
20. See Jacques Derrida, "Freud and the Scene of Writing," in *Writing and Difference:* "Translation, a system of translation, is possible only if a permanent code allows a substitution or transformation of signifiers while retaining the same signified, always present, despite the absence of any specific signifier" (210).
21. I am extremely grateful to Donald Schwartz for pointing out to me in conversation the sexual allegory of the bullfight.
22. See Derrida, "Freud and the Scene of Writing," especially 202–3.
23. Jacques Derrida, *Spurs: Nietzsche's Styles*, trans. Barbara Harlow (Chicago: University of Chicago Press, 1978), 53; Derrida's emphasis.
24. Allen Josephs argues, for example, that the bullfight must be seen as the novel's "moral axis," expressive of "archetypal and paradigmatic" themes: "toreo, at its deepest level, . . . recapitulates as spectacle and as rite the oldest myths of the Western world. . . . Hemingway clearly understood, albeit somewhat intuitively,

that toreo was at the still center of sacred time, and that it was still at the center of sacred time, still a part of the eternal present." "Toreo: The Moral Axis of *The Sun Also Rises*, in *Ernest Hemingway's* The Sun Also Rises, ed. Harold Bloom (New York: Chelsea House, 1987), 164–65; Josephs's emphasis. See also Wagner-Martin: "The bullfight became the microcosm of the good world—one with established and sensible rules, honor, bravery, and a higher purpose—just as the matador became a paradigm of a hero" (9).

25. Shoshana Felman, "Rereading Femininity," *Yale French Studies: Feminist Readings: French Texts/American Contexts* 62 (1981): 31. Future references to this work will appear in the text.

Chapter 5

Epigraph from Donald Barthelme, *The Dead Father* (New York: Penguin, 1975), 145.

1. Julia Kristeva, "Women's Time," trans. Alice Jardine and Harry Blake, *The Kristeva Reader*, ed. Toril Moi (New York: Columbia University Press, 1986). Future references to this work will appear in the text.
2. We should remember here from chapter 1 Žižek's account of the totalitarian implications of the drive toward harmony, something I will consider further at the end of this chapter.
3. There are, nevertheless, important differences in the work of these three writers: see in particular Kaja Silverman's critique of Kristeva in *The Acoustic Mirror: The Female Voice in Psychoanalysis and Cinema* (Bloomington: Indiana University Press, 1988), 99–120.
4. Virginia Woolf, *Three Guineas* (San Diego: Harcourt, 1938), 79–80. Future references to this work will appear in the text.
5. Friedrich Nietzsche, *The Birth of Tragedy and the Genealogy of Morals*, trans. Francis Golffing (New York: Doubleday, 1956), 166–68.
6. Marie-Luise Gättens, *Reconstructing Histories: Language, Gender, and Fascism*. (Gainesville: University Press of Florida, forthcoming 1994).
7. Jacques Derrida, "Differance," in *Speech and Phenomena and Other Essays on Husserl's Theory of Signs*, trans. David B. Allison (Evanston, Ill.: Northwestern University Press, 1973), 135.
8. Virginia Woolf, *A Room of One's Own* (New York: Harcourt, Brace, and World, 1929), 102. Future references to this work will appear in the text.
9. Herbert Marder, *Feminism and Art: A Study of Virginia Woolf* (Chicago: University of Chicago Press, 1968), 110. Future references to this work will appear in the text.
10. See for example Elaine Showalter's critique of androgyny as a sign of Woolf's flight from her own femaleness into a myth of transcendence in *A Literature of Their Own: British Women Novelists from Brontë to Lessing* (Princeton: Princeton University Press, 1977), 263–97. There is no need for me to counter Showalter's argument, since Toril Moi and Makiko Minow-Pinkney persuasively demonstrate both the humanist assumptions about the subject in Showalter's reading of Woolf and the limits of those assumptions for a feminist analysis of culture. See Moi, *Sexual/Textual Politics: Feminist Literary Theory* (New York: Methuen, 1985), 2–8; and Minow-Pinkney, *Virginia Woolf and the Problem of the Subject* (New Brunswick, N. J.:

Rutgers University Press, 1987), 12–14. Future references to these works will appear in the text.

11. Nancy Bazin, *Virginia Woolf and the Androgynous Vision* (New Brunswick, N.J.: Rutgers University Press, 1973), 3. Future references to this work will appear in the text.

12. A number of recent analyses, however, diverge from the traditional view of androgyny as a metaphor for unity. Mary Jacobus says androgyny is "a simultaneous enactment of desire and repression by which the split is closed with an essentially Utopian vision of undivided consciousness. The repressive male/female opposition which 'interferes with the unity of the mind' gives way to a mind paradoxically conceived of not as one, but as heterogeneous, open to the play of difference. . . . " *Reading Woman: Essays in Feminist Criticism* (New York: Columbia University Press, 1986), 39. Though I find this definition generally consistent with my own understanding of androgyny, I would argue that there is nothing utopian about the notion if one understands it to describe the "split subject," as I will argue below.

    Minow-Pinkney similarly argues that "androgyny is the rejection of sameness. It aims to cultivate difference on an individual level, in the teeth of a cultural impulse to reduce the two sexes into something which is seemingly neither, but in actuality male" (*Problem* 9). Jane Marcus makes a similar claim that "the idea of the androgynous mind of the artist comes directly after the leaf falls, the ambiguous taxi floats the couple downstream and Woolf expresses her discomfort with notions of sexual opposition and unity. In trying to deal with the maternal imperative, the definition of the feminine as the opposite of the masculine, the imaginary 'cooperation of the sexes,' Woolf hits on a temporary solution in the idea of androgyny . . . " *Virginia Woolf and the Languages of Patriarchy* (Bloomington: Indiana University Press, 1987), 174. However, Marcus also argues, unlike Jacobus or Minow-Pinkney, that "androgyny means erasure of difference. . . . Androgyny, it becomes clear, is a good idea for overly masculine writers to try, though the opposite does not hold true. That is, the arguments [about androgyny] are not logical. She is biased in favor of women" (174). My own view is closer to that of Jacobus and Minow-Pinkney, as I hope will come clear in the following discussion.

13. See Peggy Kamuf, *Signature Pieces: On the Institution of Authorship* (Ithaca: Cornell University Press, 1988). Kamuf's reading of *A Room of One's Own* in conjunction with Foucault's *The History of Sexuality* produces a similar suggestion about the divided subjectivity Woolf's narrative represents. According to Kamuf, informing Woolf's text is "the notion of sexual differentiation as a historical production, which, if it has produced a privileged masculine subject, cannot also be understood as originating in the subject it only produces. To the extent, however, that one accepts to see 'man' at the origin of his own privilege, then, one chooses paradoxically to believe the most manifest lie of 'phallosophy': that of a man giving birth to himself as an origin that transcends any difference from himself" (152). Kamuf further notes that Woolf's text "[turns] away from this historical preoccupation with the subject, closing the book on the 'I'" as it is classically conceived (154). This final claim is one I will elaborate on at a later point.

14. Jacques Lacan, "The Mirror Stage as Formative of the Function of the I," in *Ecrits: A Selection*, trans. Alan Sheridan (New York: Norton, 1977), 1.

Minow-Pinkney also addresses the Lacanian view of the subject (13–14), but perhaps even more interestingly introduces Kristeva's notions of the subject-in-process/on trial to elucidate the dynamic relations of conscious and unconscious material or processes in Woolf's writing. See in particular her discussion of Kristeva's theory of the semiotic (17–20) and her account of how, in Woolf, the term androgyny itself names a dialectic of the semiotic and the symbolic that ideally occurs in writing: "For Woolf, writing should be . . . an androgynous alternation, an impossible dialectic which aims to be 'integrated' at the moment of maximum dispersal. Her ambition is to summon 'silence' into the order of speech, to introduce the repressed into an order made possible only by that exclusion of 'the other' " (159).

15. Anthony Wilden, "Introduction," in *The Language of the Self: The Function of Language in Psychoanalysis,* by Jacques Lacan, trans. Anthony Wilden (New York: Delta, 1968), 160.
16. Other critics of Woolf have commented specifically on narrative strategies of disruption in this text. Kamuf, for example, refers to this "self-raveling text" in which "interruption marks the scene of writing"; she also comments on "zigzagging fault lines in Woolf's speculations about woman's writing" that "can be too easily overlooked when this text is taken as a model authority for a critical practice content to go on making nasty caricatures of Professor von X . . . " (*Signature Pieces* 152). Moi also claims that Woolf "practise[s] a non-essentialist form of writing" (9) and argues that "to remain detached from the narrative strategies of the text is equivalent to not reading it at all. For it is only through an examination of the detailed strategies of the text on all its levels that we will be able to uncover some of the conflicting, contradictory elements that contribute to make it precisely *this* text, with precisely these words and this configuration" (10; Moi's emphasis). However, because of the nature of her own task in this book on feminist literary theory, Moi points to the need for but cannot actually engage in a detailed reading of Woolf's textual practices. See also Alice Fox,"Literary Allusion as Feminist Criticism in *A Room of One's Own," Philological Quarterly* 63 (1984).
17. See also Rachel Blau DuPlessis, *Writing Beyond the Ending: Narrative Strategies of Twentieth-Century Women Writers* (Bloomington: Indiana University Press, 1985), x, 34.
18. I am grateful to Donald Schwartz for pointing this out to me in conversation.
19. See Marcus for a fuller catalogue of the violations of the lecture conventions: *Languages of Patriarchy* 145–46, 148, 165.
20. Perhaps this is a very literal example of what DuPlessis calls "writing beyond the ending" in her book of the same name: "Writing beyond the ending begins when authors, or their close surrogates, discover that they are in fact outside the terms of this novel's script, marginal to it" (6).
21. But see Marcus for a very different account of the relation of speaker to reader in this text: *Languages of Patriarchy* 149, 167; See also Jane Marcus, "Still Practice, A/Wrested Alphabet: Toward a Feminist Aesthetic," *Tulsa Studies in Women's Literature* 3 (1984): 80, 86.
22. See Kamuf for a comparison of the speaker's "I" to Foucault's in *History of Sexuality,* vol. 1 (Kamuf, *Signature Pieces* 155–57). She notes the very different discursive

positions assumed by these speakers and comments on the strategies by which "a discourse like Foucault's can still retain a place in the privileged domain of patriarchal thought, a train of thought which has been trained, precisely, to think without interruption" (156). Kamuf's argument thus strongly contradicts the impression of it given by Marcus in "Still Practice," which claims that Kamuf's essay, among other works on Woolf, "fails to keep faith with its [feminist] subject" because it reads Woolf "through Foucault, Descartes, and *The Odyssey*" (89). Marcus objects to such a reading because, in its attention to works written by men, it makes Woolf "only . . . a writer whose texts are decoded with male tools" and therefore "den[ies] the authority of the female text" (89). However, Kamuf's chapter on Woolf exemplifies both the principles and practices of intertextual reading, the assumption, in Kamuf's words, that "The writing of . . . a text [like Woolf's] is not attributable to any subject, whether singular or collective. On the contrary, it is the subject that is written into the text, and thus into the play of differences with itself" (164). In this sense, Kamuf's method allows Woolf to open up and comment on Foucault as much as it finds Foucault useful for elucidating Woolf's work. But Marcus is of course correct that Kamuf's method denies the "authority of the female text," at least as authority is conventionally understood, since her project (and my own, and, I would argue, Woolf's) is precisely to call into question traditional notions of authority, subjectivity, and control.

23. The negative connotations of harmony in this context should make us wary of unconsciously accepting the term's conventionally positive meanings when we encounter it later on in the discussion of androgyny.

24. In an earlier version of her chapter on Woolf, Kamuf noted something similar: "[the] liberation of some new subject must always be read as possible prelude to a new subjection." "Penelope at Work: Interruptions in *A Room of One's Own*," *Novel* 16 (1982): 11.

25. See Jacques Lacan, "God and the *Jouissance* of The Woman. A Love Letter," *Feminine Sexuality: Jacques Lacan and the école freudienne*, ed. Juliet Mitchell and Jacqueline Rose, trans. Jacqueline Rose (New York: Norton, 1982): "There is no such thing as *The* woman, where the definite article stands for the universal. There is no such thing as *The* woman since of her essence—having already risked the term, why think twice about it?—of her essence, she is not all" (144). Bruce Fink is helpful in glossing these statements. Fink first clarifies that the essence Lacan refers to here is not biological but has to do with the subject's relation to the symbolic, the different ways in which men and women in culture tend to experience alienation in language. Fink further explains the meaning of this "not all" that characterizes the feminine structure: "*not all* of a person who, regardless of anatomy, psychoanalytically speaking falls into the women's camp is defined by the phallic function: not all of a woman falls under the law of the signifier. . ." " 'There's No Such Thing as a Sexual Relationship': Existence and the Formulas of Sexuation," *Newsletter of the Freudian Field* 5 (1991): 73; Fink's emphasis. The reason for woman's partial exceeding of the phallic function derives, I believe, from her relation to castration, inevitably different from man's. For man, symbolic castration occurs as an ostensible *deferral* of the achievement of the object of desire; for woman, symbolic castration *apparently* mirrors her actual castration. Woman, that is, is not permitted to

imagine that the achievement of her desire is merely *delayed;* she must recognize it to be fundamentally *impossible,* or possible only in radically displaced forms. Such a radical loss of the fantasy of satisfaction is a disadvantage in some sense, but also the source of a knowledge, and a *jouissance,* that is not available to men.

26. See Kamuf, *Signature Pieces,* for a discussion of how "*A Room of One's Own* defines a novel position in relation to the locked room of history. That is, since women's history cannot be studied in the library, it will have to be read into the scene of its own exclusion. It has to be invented—both discovered and made up. As it spins around its promise to decide on the place of woman's writing, this text *ravels* the crossed threads of history and fiction. It ravels—which is to say it both *un*tangles, makes something plain or clear, and it *en*tangles or confuses something" (151–52; Kamuf's emphasis).
27. Jacques Derrida, *Of Grammatology,* trans. Gayatri Chakravorty Spivak (Baltimore: Johns Hopkins University Press, 1974), 144–45.
28. Derrida comments on this elusiveness of woman:

    There is no such thing as the essence of woman because woman averts, she is averted of herself. Out of the depths . . . she engulfs and distorts all vestiges of essentiality, of identity, of property. . . . There is no such thing as the truth of woman, but it is because of that abyssal divergence of the truth, because that untruth is "truth." Woman is but one name for that untruth of truth. . . . Because, indeed, if woman *is* truth, *she* at least knows that there is no truth, that truth has no place here and that no one has a place for truth. And she is woman precisely because she herself does not believe in truth itself, because she does not believe in what she is, in what she is believed to be, in what she thus is not. (*Spurs: Nietzsche's Styles,* trans. Barbara Harlow [Chicago: University of Chicago Press, 1978], 51–52; Derrida's emphasis)

Chapter 6

1. Julia Kristeva, "Women's Time," trans. Alice Jardine and Harry Blake, in *The Kristeva Reader,* ed. Toril Moi (New York: Columbia University Press, 1986), 203. Future references will appear in the text.
2. See note 25 in chapter 5.
3. Shoshana Felman, "Rereading Femininity," *Yale French Studies* 62 (1981): 31.
4. I am grateful to Dennis A. Foster for permitting me to borrow this formulation, which he arrived at during a reading-group discussion of Butler's work. See Judith Butler, *Gender Trouble: Feminism and the Subversion of Identity* (New York: Routledge, 1990). Future references to this work will appear in the text.
5. Slavoj Žižek, *The Sublime Object of Ideology* (London: Verso, 1989), 230–31; Žižek's emphasis. Future references to this work will appear in the text.

Works Cited

Achebe, Chinua. "An Image of Africa." *Massachusetts Review* 18 (1977): 782–94.

Allen, Elizabeth. *A Woman's Place in the Novels of Henry James*. New York: St. Martin's, 1984.

Atherton, John. "The Itinerary and the Postcard: Minimal Strategies in *The Sun Also Rises*." *ELH* 53 (1986): 199–218.

Baker, Carlos. *Hemingway: The Writer as Artist*. Princeton: Princeton University Press, 1963.

Barthelme, Donald. *The Dead Father*. New York: Penguin, 1975.

Barthes, Roland. *Image-Music-Text*. Trans. Stephen Heath. New York: Hill and Wang, 1977.

———. *Writing Degree Zero*. Trans. Annette Lavers and Colin Smith. New York: Hill and Wang, 1967.

Baudrillard, Jean. *Simulations*. Trans. Paul Foss, Paul Patton, and Philip Beitchman. New York: Semiotext(e), 1983.

Bazin, Nancy. *Virginia Woolf and the Androgynous Vision*. New Brunswick, N. J.: Rutgers University Press, 1973.

Benjamin, Walter. "The Author as Producer." In *Reflections*. Ed. Peter Demetz. Trans. Edmund Jephcott. New York: Harcourt Brace Jovanovich, 1978.

Benson, Jackson J. *Hemingway: The Writer's Art of Self-Defense*. Minneapolis: University of Minnesota Press, 1969.

Bloom, Harold. *The Anxiety of Influence: A Theory of Poetry*. London: Oxford University Press, 1973.

———. "Introduction." In *Ernest Hemingway's* The Sun Also Rises. Ed. Harold Bloom. New York: Chelsea House, 1987.

Brantlinger, Patrick. "*Heart of Darkness:* Anti-Imperialism, Racism, or Impressionism?" *Criticism* 27 (1985): 363–85.

Butler, Judith. *Gender Trouble: Feminism and the Subversion of Identity*. New York: Routledge, 1990.

Chaucer, Geoffrey. *Troilus and Criseyde*. Ed. Donald R. Howard and James Dean. New York: Signet, 1976.

Comley, Nancy. "Hemingway: The Economics of Survival." *Novel* 12 (1979): 244–53.

Conrad, Joseph. *Heart of Darkness*. Ed. Robert Kimbrough. New York: Norton Critical Edition, 1988.

Cooper, Stephen. *The Politics of Ernest Hemingway*. Ann Arbor: University Microfilms, 1987.

Coward, Rosalind, and John Ellis. *Language and Materialism: Developments in Semiology and the Theory of the Subject*. London: Routledge and Kegan Paul, 1977.

de Man, Paul. "Literary History and Literary Modernity." In *Blindness and Insight: Essays in the Rhetoric of Contemporary Criticism*. New York: Oxford University Press, 1971.

Derrida, Jacques. *Of Grammatology*. Trans. Gayatri Chakravorty Spivak. Baltimore: Johns Hopkins University Press, 1974.

———. "Structure, Sign, and Play in the Discourse of the Human Sciences." In *The Structuralist Controversy: The Languages of Criticism and the Sciences of Man*. Ed. Richard Macksey and Eugenio Donato. Baltimore: Johns Hopkins University Press, 1970.

———. *Speech and Phenomena and Other Essays on Husserl's Theory of Signs*. Trans. David B. Allison. Evanston, Ill.: Northwestern University Press, 1973.

———. *Spurs: Nietzsche's Styles*. Trans. Barbara Harlow. Chicago: University of Chicago Press, 1978.

———. *Writing and Difference*. Trans. Alan Bass. Chicago: University of Chicago Press, 1978.

DuPlessis, Rachel Blau. *Writing Beyond the Ending: Narrative Strategies of Twentieth-Century Women Writers*. Bloomington: Indiana University Press, 1985.

Eagleton, Terry. *Literary Theory: An Introduction*. Minneapolis: University of Minnesota Press, 1983.

Edel, Leon. *The Life of Henry James*. 5 vols. Middlesex, England: Penguin, 1977.

Eysteinsson, Astradur. *The Concept of Modernism*. Ithaca: Cornell University Press, 1990.

Felman, Shoshana. "Rereading Femininity." *Yale French Studies: Feminist Readings: French Texts/American Contexts* 62 (1981): 19–44.

———. *Writing and Madness (Literature/Philosophy/Psychoanalysis)*. Trans. Martha Noel Evans and the author with the assistance of Brian Massumi. Ithaca: Cornell University Press, 1985.

Fink, Bruce. "'There's No Such Thing as a Sexual Relationship': Existence and the Formulas of Sexuation." *Newsletter of the Freudian Field* 5 (1991): 59–85.

Fogel, Daniel Mark. *Henry James and the Structure of the Romantic Imagination*. Baton Rouge: Louisiana State University Press, 1981.

Foster, Dennis A. *Confession and Complicity in Narrative*. London: Cambridge University Press, 1987.

Foucault, Michel. *The History of Sexuality: Volume I: An Introduction*. Trans. Robert Hurley. New York: Vintage, 1980.

Fowler, Virginia. *Henry James's American Girl: The Embroidery on the Canvas*. Madison: University of Wisconsin Press, 1984.

Fox, Alice. "Literary Allusion as Feminist Criticism in *A Room of One's Own*." *Philological Quarterly* 63 (1984): 145–61.

Freud, Sigmund. *The Standard Edition of the Complete Psychological Works of Sigmund Freud*. 24 vols. London: Hogarth, 1957.

Gättens, Marie-Luise. *Reconstructing Histories: Language, Gender, and Fascism*. Gainesville: University Press of Florida, forthcoming 1994.

Harper, Michael. "Men without Politics? Hemingway's Social Consciousness." *New Orleans Review* 12 (1985): 15–26.

Hay, Eloise Knapp. *The Political Novels of Joseph Conrad: A Critical Study*. Chicago: University of Chicago Press, 1963.

Hegel, Georg Wilhelm Friedrich. *Phenomenology of Spirit*. Trans. A. V. Miller. Oxford: Oxford University Press, 1977.

———. *The Philosophy of History*. Trans. J. Sibree. New York: Dover, 1956.

Hemingway, Ernest. *A Moveable Feast*. New York: Scribner's, 1964.

———. *The Sun Also Rises*. New York: Scribner's, 1926.

Holland, Laurence Bedwell. *The Expense of Vision: Essays on the Craft of Henry James*. Princeton: Princeton University Press, 1964.

Holman, C. Hugh. "Hemingway and Vanity Fair." In *Ernest Hemingway: Six Decades of Criticism*. Ed. Linda W. Wagner. East Lansing: Michigan State University Press, 1987.

Ian, Marcia. "The Elaboration of Privacy in *The Wings of the Dove*." *ELH* 51 (1985): 107–36.

Jacobus, Mary. *Reading Woman: Essays in Feminist Criticism*. New York: Columbia University Press, 1986.

James, Henry. *The Art of the Novel: Critical Prefaces*. Ed. R. P. Blackmur. London: Scribner's, 1934.

———. *The Beast in the Jungle*. New York: Signet, 1962.

———. "The Tempest." In *Selected Literary Criticism*. Ed. Morris Shapira. Westport, Conn.: Greenwood Press, 1978.

———. *The Wings of the Dove*. New York: Norton, 1978.

Jameson, Fredric. *The Political Unconscious: Narrative as a Socially Symbolic Act*. Ithaca: Cornell University Press, 1981.

Johnson, Bruce. "Conrad's Impressionism and Watt's 'Delayed Decoding.'" In *Conrad Revisited: Essays for the Eighties*. Ed. Ross C. Murfin. Tuscaloosa: University of Alabama Press, 1985.

Josephs, Allen. "Toreo: The Moral Axis of *The Sun Also Rises*." In *Ernest Hemingway's* The Sun Also Rises. Ed. Harold Bloom. New York: Chelsea House, 1987.

Kamuf, Peggy. "Penelope at Work: Interruptions in *A Room of One's Own*." *Novel* 16 (1982): 5–18.

———. *Signature Pieces: On the Institution of Authorship*. Ithaca: Cornell University Press, 1988.

Krieger, Murray. *The Tragic Vision: Variations on a Theme in Literary Interpretation*. Chicago: University of Chicago Press, 1960.

Kristeva, Julia. "Women's Time." Trans. Alice Jardine and Harry Blake. In *The Kristeva Reader*. Ed. Toril Moi. New York: Columbia University Press, 1986.

Krook, Dorothea. *The Ordeal of Consciousness in Henry James*. London: Cambridge University Press, 1962.

Lacan, Jacques. *Ecrits: A Selection*. Trans. Alan Sheridan. New York: Norton, 1977.

———. *The Four Fundamental Concepts of Psycho-Analysis*. Ed. Jacques-Alain Miller. Trans. Alan Sheridan. New York: Norton, 1981.

———. "God and the *Jouissance* of ~~The~~ Woman." In *Feminine Sexuality: Jacques Lacan and the école freudienne*. Ed. Juliet Mitchell and Jacqueline Rose. Trans. Jacqueline Rose. New York: Norton, 1982.

Laplanche, J., and J.-B. Pontalis. *The Language of Psychoanalysis*. Trans. Donald Nicholson-Smith. New York: Norton, 1973.

Levinson, Michael. "The Value of Facts in the *Heart of Darkness*." *Nineteenth Century Fiction* 40 (1985): 261–80.

London, Bette. *The Appropriated Voice: Narrative Authority in Conrad, Forster, and Woolf*. Ann Arbor: University of Michigan Press, 1990.

Lukács, Georg. "The Ideology of Modernism." In *Marxism and Human Liberation*. Ed. E. San Juan, Jr. Trans. John and Nekke Mander. New York: Delta, 1973.

McFadden, George. "Henry James's Remorse for *The Wings of the Dove*." *Henry James Review* 9 (1988): 114–27.

Marcus, Jane. "Still Practice, A/Wrested Alphabet: Toward a Feminist Aesthetic." *Tulsa Studies in Women's Literature* 3 (1984): 79–97.

———. *Virginia Woolf and the Languages of Patriarchy*. Bloomington: Indiana University Press, 1987.

Marder, Herbert. *Feminism and Art: A Study of Virginia Woolf*. Chicago: University of Chicago Press, 1968.

Martin, Wendy. "Brett Ashley as New Woman." In *New Essays on* The Sun Also Rises. Ed. Linda Wagner-Martin. Cambridge: Cambridge University Press, 1987.

Meisel, Perry. *The Myth of the Modern: A Study in British Literature and Criticism after 1850*. New Haven: Yale University Press, 1987.

Mercer, Caroline G., and Sarah D. Wangensteen. "'Consumption, heart-disease, or whatever': Chlorosis, a Heroine's Illness in *The Wings of the Dove*." *Journal of the History of Medicine and Allied Sciences* 40 (1985): 259–85.

Miller, J. Hillis. *Poets of Reality*. New York: Atheneum, 1974.

Miller, Jacques-Alain. "The Analytic Experience: Means, Ends, and Results." In *Lacan and the Subject of Language*. Ed. Ellie Ragland-Sullivan and Mark Brache. New York: Routledge, 1991.

Milne, Fred L. "Marlow's Lie and the Intended: Civilization as the Lie in *Heart of Darkness*." *Arizona Quarterly* 44 (1988): 106–12.

Minow-Pinkney, Makiko. *Virginia Woolf and the Problem of the Subject*. New Brunswick, N. J.: Rutgers University Press, 1987.

Mizruchi, Susan L. *The Power of Historical Knowledge: Narrating the Past in Hawthorne, James, and Drieser*. Princeton: Princeton University Press, 1988.

Moi, Toril. *Sexual/Textual Politics: Feminist Literary Theory*. New York: Methuen, 1985.

Moon, Michael. "Sexuality and Visual Terrorism in *The Wings of the Dove*." *Criticism* 28 (1986): 427–43.

Morrow, Patrick D. "The Bought Generation: Another Look at Money in *The Sun Also Rises*." *Genre* 13 (1980): 51–69.

Nietzsche, Friedrich. *Beyond Good and Evil: Prelude to a Philosophy of the Future*. Trans. Walter Kaufman. New York: Vintage, 1966.

———. *The Birth of Tragedy and the Genealogy of Morals*. Trans. Francis Golffing. New York: Doubleday, 1956.

O'Sullivan, Sibbie. "Love and Friendship/Man and Woman in *The Sun Also Rises*." *Arizona Quarterly* 44 (1988): 76–97.

Parry, Benita. *Conrad and Imperialism: Ideological Boundaries and Visionary Frontiers*. London: Macmillan, 1983.

Pecora, Vincent P. *Self and Form in Modern Narrative*. Baltimore: Johns Hopkins University Press, 1989.

Robinson, Lillian S., and Lise Vogel. "Modernism and History." *NLH* 3 (1971): 177–99.

Rose, Jacqueline. "Jeffrey Masson and Alice James." *Oxford Literary Review* 8 (1986): 185–92.

Rowe, John Carlos. *Henry Adams and Henry James: The Emergence of a Modern Consciousness*. Ithaca: Cornell University Press, 1976.

Said, Edward W. "Intellectuals in the Post-Colonial World." *Salmagundi* 70–71 (1986): 44–64.

———. *Joseph Conrad and the Fiction of Autobiography*. Cambridge: Harvard University Press, 1966.

———. *Orientalism*. New York: Vintage, 1979.

Sartre, Jean-Paul. *Being and Nothingness: An Essay on Phenomenological Ontology*. Trans. Hazel E. Barnes. New York: Philosophical Library, 1956.

Schwarz, Daniel R. *Conrad:* Almayer's Folly *to* Under Western Eyes. Ithaca: Cornell University Press, 1980.

Sears, Sallie. *The Negative Imagination: Form and Perspective in the Novels of Henry James*. Ithaca: Cornell University Press, 1968.

Sedgwick, Eve Kosofsky. "The Beast in the Closet: James and the Writing of Homosexual Panic." In *Sex, Politics, and Science in the Nineteenth-Century Novel*. Ed. Ruth Bernard Yeazell. Baltimore: Johns Hopkins University Press, 1986.

Seltzer, Leon F. "The Opportunity of Impotence: Count Mippipopolous in *The Sun Also Rises*." *Renascence* 31 (1978): 3–14.

Shakespeare, William. *Hamlet*. *The Riverside Shakespeare*. Boston: Houghton Mifflin, 1974.

Showalter, Elaine. *A Literature of Their Own: British Women Novelists from Brontë to Lessing*. Princeton: Princeton University Press, 1977.

Silverman, Kaja. *The Acoustic Mirror: The Female Voice in Psychoanalysis and Cinema*. Bloomington: Indiana University Press, 1988.

Smith, Johanna M. "'Too Beautiful Altogether': Patriarchal Ideology in *Heart of Darkness*." In *Heart of Darkness*. Ed. Ross C. Murfin. New York: St. Martin's, 1989.

Smith, John H. "U-Topian Hegel: Dialectic and Its Other in Poststructuralism." *German Quarterly* 60 (1987): 237–61.

Spilka, Mark. "The Death of Love in *The Sun Also Rises*." In *Hemingway and His Critics: An International Anthology*. Ed. Carlos Baker. American Century Series. New York: Hill and Wang, 1961.

Sterne, Laurence. *The Life and Opinions of Tristram Shandy, Gentleman*. Ed. James Aiken Work. Indianapolis: Bobbs-Merrill, 1940.

Stewart, Garrett. "Lying as Dying in *Heart of Darkness*. *PMLA* 95 (1980): 319–31.

Strouse, Jean. *Alice James: A Biography*. New York: Bantam, 1982.

Torgovnick, Marianna. *Gone Primitive: Savage Intellects, Modern Lives*. Chicago: University of Chicago Press, 1990.

Wagner-Martin, Linda. "Introduction." In *New Essays on* The Sun Also Rises. Ed. Linda Wagner-Martin. Cambridge: Cambridge University Press, 1987.

Watt, Ian. *Conrad in the Nineteenth Century*. Berkeley: University of California Press, 1979.

Wedin, Warren. "Trout Fishing and Self-Betrayal in *The Sun Also Rises*." *Arizona Quarterly* 37 (1981): 63–74.

Wilden, Anthony. "Introduction." In *The Language of the Self: The Function of Language in Psychoanalysis*. By Jacques Lacan. Trans. Anthony Wilden. New York: Delta, 1968.

Woolf, Virginia. *A Room of One's Own*. New York: Harcourt, Brace, and World, 1929.

———. *Three Guineas*. San Diego: Harcourt Brace Jovanovich, 1938.

Ziff, Larzer. "The Social Basis of Hemingway's Style." In *Ernest Hemingway: Six Decades of Criticism*. Ed. Linda W. Wagner. East Lansing: Michigan State University Press, 1987.

Žižek, Slavoj. *Looking Awry: An Introduction to Jacques Lacan through Popular Culture*. Cambridge: MIT Press, 1991.

———. *The Sublime Object of Ideology*. London: Verso, 1989.

Index